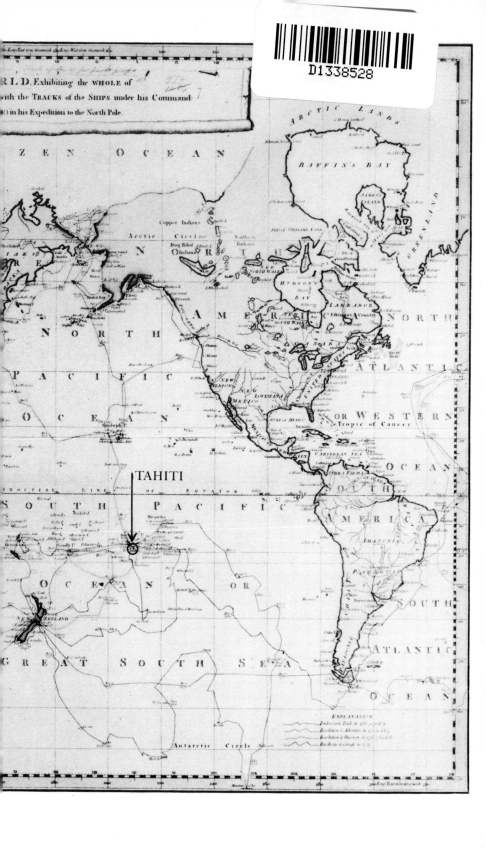

R L D, Exhibiting the WHOLE of
with the TRACKS of the SHIPS under his Command
) in his Expedition to the North Pole.

TAHITI

D1338528

TAHITI

TAHITI

A Paradise Lost

DAVID HOWARTH

HARVILL PRESS
8 Grafton Street, London W1
1983

*Harvill Press Ltd
is distributed by
William Collins Sons & Co Ltd
London · Glasgow · Sydney · Auckland
Toronto · Johannesburg

BRITISH LIBRARY CATALOGUING IN PUBLICATION DATA

Howarth, David, 1912 –
Tahiti.
1. Tahiti—Discovery and exploration
I. Title
919.6'211'04   DU870

ISBN 0–00–262804–X

First published 1983
© David Howarth 1983
Photoset in Baskerville by W & G Baird Ltd
Made and printed in Great Britain by
Robert Hartnoll Ltd Bodmin

CONTENTS

ILLUSTRATIONS

PART I
INNOCENCE
1767-68

••E)(3••

ONE

The Misty Dawn

On 18 June 1767 an unknown island was sighted in mid-Pacific from the British frigate HMS *Dolphin*, Captain Samuel Wallis, on a voyage round the world. She approached it cautiously in the night. Dawn was misty, but as the sun rose the mist rose with it, like a theatrical curtain, to reveal an unexpected scene – the first scene, as it turned out, of a century's drama. The ship was close under the shore of the island, which rose in tier after tier of wooded peaks, and she was surrounded by hundreds of canoes. They were full of tall, brown, conspicuously handsome men, who were gazing at her in amazement and eagerly discussing what they saw. It was the first time Europeans had met Tahitians, and the first time Tahitians had met any strangers at all.

Nobody knows for certain how long these Polynesian people had lived alone on their island. It was probably fifteen hundred years. If so, while Europe was still under Roman rule, Polynesians were putting to sea somewhere on the eastern coast of Asia, and sailing in canoes from island to island, west to east across the Pacific. At all the prolific islands they came to, they dropped off families or clans; but some were always impelled to go further to find what lay beyond. The impulsion may have been a growing population, or perhaps a native restlessness, or perhaps the threat of the warlike Melanesians to the west. No doubt a good many met disaster, and starved or drowned at sea. If it was restlessness that drove them on, it vanished as soon as they came to an island they liked which had nobody to disturb them, and everywhere from Hawaii to New Zealand they settled down to a life that was

9

usually peaceful and always uneventful. Alone through the ages, they forgot how they came to be there, and ceased to imagine a world beyond their neighbouring islands. Their climate hardly changed from season to season, so they never took much account of time. They lived from day to day, with no memory of the distant past and no fear of the future. All through the hectic evolution of northern Europe from the barbaric fringes of the Roman Empire to the brilliant age of the eighteenth-century savants, the Tahitians stayed the same.

So when they saw the frigate in the mist of dawn, it surprised them as much as a flying saucer would surprise us now, or perhaps even more, and they reacted as we would react, with a mixture of fear and fascination. But the explorers, too, were soon amazed, for they found that the Tahitians, far from being the savages they expected, had created in their solitude a human society which seemed to be happier, more kindly, more stable and harmonious than any in Europe.

Such an unexpected discovery needs qualification. The Tahitians did not write, and their society was destroyed by Europeans in the next seventy-five years; so the only descriptions of it are in the writings of voyagers who saw the island and its people in their pristine state. Yet all history has this same defect of being second-hand. It all derives from documents, written at best by eye-witnesses of events; and all the people who wrote the documents had human failings, sometimes an axe to grind, and often a natural inclination to make a good story better. Some historians have been driven to say that no historical fact has reality. But facts, they would probably agree, come closer to reality if they are reported by several diverse and independent witnesses whose idiosyncrasies cancel each other out. Scores of witnesses wrote about what they saw of Tahitian life, and they were certainly diverse. It is true that they were all eighteenth-century Europeans and observed with European eyes – true also that none of them understood the foundations of Tahitian life. But some had experience and education – naval captains, scientists, mathematicians, astronomers and artists – and some had almost no education at all. There were Englishmen, Spaniards, Frenchmen and Russians, a few Swedes and Germans, and Americans from New England. Some, the more prudish or inhibited, were shocked because Tahitian inhibitions were quite different from their own, while others were perceptive and broad-minded; yet when one allows for all their preconceptions they are unanimous in their affection and admiration – even the earlier missionaries, who came with a prejudice of their own. The quality of Tahitian society is therefore as real a fact as most of the rest of history. One has to accept it.

This is the story of that old society: the facts of what it was like, from the many journals of people who saw it, and the facts of what happened to it. It is a difficult bit of history to write, because the sober accounts of the explorers were received with strong prejudice in Europe: some people over-praised the Tahitians, and others reacted by being over-critical. So the facts were obscured by a layer of legend. One has to weed out the prejudice and legend, yet try to see the events with sympathy through the eyes of the late eighteenth and early nineteenth centuries. In the end, of course, one is left with twentieth-century prejudice: one has to recognize that for what it is, and hope that most readers will share it.

It is no use looking for the story in Tahiti now. The island and the people have changed too much. The old society died hard, but it was dead by the 1840s – and so were nineteen out of twenty of the old Tahitians; not on the whole through cruelty, but just because they did not want to go on living in a world that changed. Since then, for 140 years, the remnant has been ruled by France, a rule that began with harshness but became, as time passed, benign. Recently, the island has been well and gently led into the modern world. It has begun a new life, but modern it is. It used to take six months to get there and another six months to get back. Now Tahiti has an international airport, the jets land there from both sides of the Atlantic, and that is a measure of the difference.

The people are somewhat international too. A majority is Polynesian, but few if any pure-blooded Tahitians remain. One in five is a European, and a good many are Chinese. It used to have no town, but it has one now, the very sophisticated seaport of Papeete, and a third of the people live there. Not many of them know about the ancient civilization the island used to have, and probably they would not be pleased if they did. They are happy as they are.

The story therefore scarcely exists in the place where it happened, or in folk-memory, or in human relics. Even today, the splendid scenery of Tahiti is easy to recognize from the explorers' accounts, and places outside Papeete can be recognized too. But most of the buildings and artefacts of the old Tahitians were wooden, and they disappeared long ago, or were purposely destroyed. Some bits of the story are very well-known in English history – Cook's voyages, and the mutiny on the *Bounty*. But in detail, it exists only in the furthest shelves of the biggest libraries.

The *Dolphin*'s crew stayed only a matter of weeks on the island, long enough to grow fond of its people, but not long enough to learn more than the obvious facts about them. But other voyagers followed quickly in the next decade: first, two French ships under Louis de Bougainville in 1768; then James Cook on his first voyage in 1769; two Spanish ships from Peru three times between 1772 and 1775; and Cook on his second and third voyages, in 1773 and 1777. Then the Tahitians were left alone again for eleven years, until the disastrous voyage of William Bligh in the *Bounty* marked the end of the era of exploration and the start of the era of exploitation. Each of these early voyages added a little more knowledge of Tahitian life.

No news of the *Dolphin*'s discovery reached England until she returned, almost a year after the event. She anchored in the Downs on 20 May 1768, and a few days later a letter written on board, a kind of press release, was published in the *London Chronicle* and several other journals: 'We have discovered a large, fertile and extremely populous Island in the South Seas. The *Dolphin* came to an anchor in a safe, spacious and commodious Harbour, where she lay about six Weeks. From the Behaviour of the Inhabitants, we had Reason to believe she was the first and only ship they had ever seen.'

The letter told of misunderstandings, fights, and forgiveness, the usual story of such early encounters. 'The first day they came alongside with a Number of Canoes, in order to take Possession of her; there were two divisions, one filled with Men and the other with Women; these last endeavoured to engage the Attention of our Sailors, by exposing their beauties to their View, while the Men from the Canoes threw great Quantities of Stones, by which several Seamen were hurt; however, as they had no Kind of Weapons, they were soon beat off, and a few Vollies of Small Arms obliged them to retire in Great Confusion.'

The next day, when an armed party had been sent ashore for water, more canoes came for what seemed to be a stronger attack on the ship. To defeat it, the ship fired grapeshot from her guns and a few roundshot at the shore, which knocked down houses and trees and, the letter said, struck the people with awe. 'They immediately shewed the greatest desire of being at Peace with us, and did not seem to resent the killing a Number of their People, as they now appeared to be sensible that we had only made use of those dreadful Engines against them when their Rashness had forced us to it. We took possession of the Island in His Majesty's Name, and called it KING GEORGE'S LAND. During the Remainder of our Stay we continued to trade with the Natives in the most amicable Manner, giving them Nails, Buttons, Beads, and Trinkets in Exchange for fresh Provisions, which we were greatly in Want of.'

The letter was reticent about the people, except to say that they were 'pretty much civilized', generally taller and stronger than the English, swam like fish, and possessed no kind of metal. It was more enthusiastic about the country. ''Tis impossible to describe the beautiful Prospects we beheld in this charming spot; the Verdure is as fine as that of England, there is great Plenty of Live Stock, and it abounds with all the choicest Productions of the Earth. Besides the large Island, there are several lesser ones.'

It was interesting news, but something short of exciting. Wallis, after all, was an ordinary naval captain, and his crew an ordinary crew; nobody among them had been chosen for his powers of observation or description. Moreover, Wallis may have been uncertain of his reception by the Admiralty. Sent to search for a continent, he had come back with only a little island. So he made the *Dolphin*'s alleged defence a victory to boast about, and did not suggest that it had all been easy – that perhaps the Tahitians' stone-throwing was only an expression of bewilderment and fear, and could not possibly have put the ship in danger. As for the women's behaviour, it was certainly not a subtle tactical ruse, as his crew soon discovered: it was a Tahitian welcome. But there was far more to come in the journals of some of his men, and most of all, no doubt, in the stories, now forgotten, that his sailors told in the taverns of dockyard towns.

Not only Wallis but all three of the *Dolphin*'s commissioned officers were sick when they found Tahiti. Wallis himself had what he called a 'bilious cholic', so bad that he could only drag himself out of his cabin when there was a crisis. The first lieutenant, William Clarke, had been sick through most of the voyage and unable to stand his watch; and the second lieutenant, Tobias

Furneaux, was also ill from time to time and confined to his bunk. Thirty of the hundred and twenty lower-deck men were in various stages of scurvy, but nobody had yet died.

Most men who made discoveries at sea were young when they did it, and Wallis, who was thirty-eight, was much older than any of his officers, and probably the oldest man in the frigate. Clarke and Furneaux were both in their twenties, and so were the two senior warrant officers, George Robertson, the ship's master, and George Gore, master's mate. The midshipmen, or 'young gentlemen', of whom there were eight in training, were teenagers, and the average age on the lower deck was normally not much over twenty. Robertson and Gore were both acting officers of the watch, and all the young officers were carrying responsibility beyond their age and rank. Not that they were incapable: Furneaux in particular was a born explorer, who went on to Command the *Adventure* on Cook's second voyage and became the first man to go round the world in both directions; and Gore, the master's mate, who was American born, had already gone round it in the *Dolphin* under Byron, and went round a third time in Cook's *Endeavour*.

But without a captain fit to keep them in order, there were rivalries and smouldering quarrels. Everyone liked Tobias Furneaux, 'a gentle, agreeable, well-behaved, good man', Robertson wrote. But nobody liked the first lieutenant, Clarke, and Robertson especially detested him. He rejoiced when Clarke did something stupid, like trying to anchor in 120 fathoms of water, and in his journal he always called him 'Mr Knowall', or 'Old Groul'. Clarke, for his part, was always trying to humiliate Robertson. It was a disorganized ship that made the first encounter.

Nineteen journals of the voyage still exist, but most of them are brief. The most detailed, observant and amusing is George Robertson's. Clearly, the master was an intelligent man, but his spelling and punctuation were very eccentric, even for that era. 'They padled all round the ship,' he wrote of the canoes in the misty dawn, 'and made signs of friendship to us, by holding up branches of plantain trees, and making a long speech of near fifteen minutes, when the speech was over he that made it throwd the plantain branch into the sea, then they came nearer the ship, and all of them appeared cheerful and talkt a great deal but non of us could understand them, but to pleas them we all seemd merry . . . We made signs to them, to bring of Hogs, Fowls and fruit and showd them coarse cloth Knives sheers Beeds Ribbons etc, and made them understand that we was willing to barter with them, the method we took to make them Understand what we wanted was this, some of the men Grunted and Cryd lyke a Hogg then pointed to the shore – oythers crowd Lyke cocks to make them understand that we wanted fowls, this the natives of the country understood and Grunted and Crowd the same as our people, and pointed to the shore and made signs that they would bring us off some.'

Among the conversation of grunts and crows, that first visit came to a sudden end when one young Tahitian who had ventured on board was butted from behind by a goat, which alarmed him so much that he dived overboard, followed by everyone else. (Perhaps it was the celebrated goat that went twice round the world in the *Dolphin* and earned a Latin epigram from Dr Johnson.) 'One of the fellows', Robertson added, 'was standing closs by one of our young gentlemen who wore a Gold Laced Hatt, this Glaring Hat attracted the fellows fancy and he snatchd it of and Jumpt overboard with it in his hand.'

The encounter had started well. But the *Dolphin* was still at sea, and between themselves and the shore the sailors could see a long coral reef on which the swell was breaking. For the next four days they sailed along the coast from one end of the island to the other, searching for an opening in the reef and a safe anchorage inside it, and admiring all they saw. Robertson wrote (to correct now his tedious spelling): 'The country had the most beautiful appearance it is possible to imagine. From the shore one, two, and three miles back, there is a fine level country that appears to be all laid out in plantations, and the regular built houses seem to be without number; they appeared like long farmers' barns and seemed to be all very neatly thatched, with great numbers of coconut trees and several other trees that we could not know the name of. The interior part of this country is very mountainous, but there are beautiful valleys between the mountains. This appears to be the most populous country I ever saw, the whole shore side was lined with men women and children all the way that we sailed along . . . This ought to be the winter season here if any such there be, but there is not the least appearance of it to be seen, all the tall trees is green to the very top of the mountain.'

Trouble began, however, when boats went in through gaps in

the reef to take soundings. Robertson and Gore took charge of these expeditions, and found themselves surrounded by hundreds of canoes. It was certainly enough to put anyone's nerves on edge: two boats and perhaps two hundred canoes, a couple of dozen Englishmen among a couple of thousand Tahitians, who for all the English knew might be cannibals; no weapons except muskets, which did not awe the Tahitians because they did not know what they were for, and not a single word of communication. To the English it seemed the Tahitians were in two minds. Some, with apparently friendly gestures, were urging them to come ashore; some were trying to drive them away. The canoeists grew bolder, and began to try to ram the boats. At last one succeeded. Three or four men in it were poised to jump on board, and Robertson, thinking to save his own crew, told two Marines to shoot. One Tahitian fell wounded in the sea and another dead.

Next day, though, one boat got so near the shore that its crew could make signs for water, which was the most pressing of their needs. Some of the islanders cheerfully filled calabashes at a river and swam out with them to the boat. To tempt the English ashore, they also lined up a sort of parade of girls, and with lascivious gestures invited them to come and take their pick.

To say this sight surprised the English sailors would be the most ridiculous understatement. It was exactly a year since they had said goodbye to their wives or the prostitutes of Plymouth, or perhaps to both, and they expected another year to pass before they would see them again. Yet here, just half-way round the world, were girls in dozens; and not unattractive savages, but girls of astonishing beauty, very young, some dark brown and others as white as Europeans, all with long, black hair hanging sleekly over their shoulders and decorated with flowers, bare-legged and dressed with provocative simplicity, some naked to the waist. What was more, they were all cheerful, laughing and excited, and giving every sign of being eager to meet the sailors; while their men, far from disapproving, were clearly encouraging them. The sailors could not believe it, but being sailors they were quite determined to put it to the test. When, under orders, they put off in their boat again, the girls, still laughing, but now in derision at their feebleness, pelted them with apples and bananas.

Alongside the ship, the bartering grew busier every day. The canoes came off with pigs, fowls and bundles of fruit, and the English offered the usual trinkets that ships of exploration carried for natives: cheap beads, knives, and looking-glasses. But they found that what the Tahitians wanted most were nails. Nobody knew at first why they wanted nails, and since they had never seen iron before, it is still remarkable how quickly they saw how it could be used: the nails could be made into fish-hooks, which hitherto they had carved, with long labour, from mother-of-pearl. It was the best of good bargains for the *Dolphin*. Nails in those days were known by their price. A five-penny nail, which was 1½ inches long, cost five pence per hundred; a ten-penny nail, 2½ inches long, ten pence per hundred and so on up to a forty-penny nail, 4½ inches long, at forty pence per hundred. A twenty-pound piglet cost the *Dolphin* one ten-penny nail; the *Dolphin* was getting 200 pounds of fresh meat for a penny. But the Tahitians were delighted, so it seemed fair enough.

On the fifth day, Robertson found an excellent anchorage, sheltered behind a low point of land and offering what they needed most – fresh water: a river ran along the back of the beach, only twenty yards from the sea. This was Matavai Bay, which Cook was to make the most famous harbour in the South Pacific. On the way in, the *Dolphin* ran aground on a shoal in the entrance, known ever after as the Dolphin Bank; but on 23 June she was at anchor.

When she was moored close in to the shore, the bartering came to a climax. By eight o'clock next morning, Robertson reckoned five hundred canoes were round her, with four thousand men in them jostling to get close enough to show their wares. He noticed the girls – not boatloads of them, as the first report had put it, but 'a fair young girl in each, who played a great many droll wanton tricks, which drew all our people upon the gunwales to see them . . . The whole traded very fair and honest, and all the men seemed as hearty and merry as the girls.'

One very large canoe, a catamaran, had come out from the beach and was lying apart from the rest, and some of the Englishmen thought it gave a signal. Suddenly the trading and merriment stopped and a hail of stones was thrown at the *Dolphin*. A lot of her men were cut and bruised. Somebody ordered the sentries to shoot, but that had no effect: 'they all gave another shout and poured in the stones amongst us'. The ship opened fire with grape and roundshot from her guns, 'which struck such terror among the poor unhappy crowd that it would require the pen of Milton to describe, therefore too much for mine'. Of course a roundshot that hit a canoe smashed it to pieces, and at point-

The first encounter: HMS *Dolphin* opened fire against the canoes

blank range the gunners could hardly miss the crowd. The grape, three-pounders loaded with seventy musket balls, did awful slaughter. The frantic canoeists tried to paddle away and haul wounded friends from the water, and when they had been scattered far enough the ship ceased fire. But when the story spread that the large canoe had signalled the attack, the English concluded that the king of the island was in it, and they shot at it until it broke in half. Robertson was surprised to see half a dozen small canoes rally round it, rescue its wounded and try to tow its shattered ends away while it was still under fire. That was bravery he had not expected in savages, and it made him wonder 'what these poor ignorant creatures thought of us'.

Even now, when one understands the Tahitians a little better, one can only surmise what they thought when they first saw the frigate. To them, the *Dolphin* was literally supernatural, something that had never existed in their experience of the natural world. It would not be surprising if some of them had tried to fit it into their concept of the spiritual world. But they did not make the mistake – or not for long – that the Californians made with Drake or the Haitians with Cook, of treating the ship's leaders as gods. Robertson thought their opinions were divided, and he was certainly right. One party, led perhaps by their numerous and influential priests, regarded the giant canoe as a threat to be driven away by stones, which was what they did if they were threatened by people like themselves from other islands. The other party saw it as novel and interesting and a source of nails, and they welcomed the strangers with the cheerful, indiscriminate friendliness which proved to be the most notable trait of Tahitians.

Evidently, at least some of the canoeists who came off to the ship on that fatal day came ready for both possibilities: they brought their goods for barter, and their girls to amuse the strangers, but they also brought their stones. What turned it from a fair to a fight remains a mystery. It could not have been a signal: the Tahitians were quite incapable of feigning merriment then abruptly starting a battle when they were told. Perhaps something suddenly frightened them, or perhaps the warlike party started it and it spread in a panic. But anyhow, they provoked a much more terrible retaliation than they had ever dreamed of, and whoever had favoured war was discredited. With one accord, they set about showing they were sorry.

But the English were still very far from understanding the Tahitians' thoughts. They expected them, as savages, to be fierce and cruel. They had no idea as yet that they had come across a simple but ancient civilization, with religious beliefs, moral standards, and social conventions all its own. The stone-throwing had been frightening – not perhaps the stones themselves, because a naval frigate could not conceivably be defeated by throwing stones at it, but the vast numbers of men and their incomprehensible shouts. Perhaps it might have been argued that a quick, decisive show of strength was merciful. But the *Dolphin* went beyond that. The Tahitians never attacked her or threatened her, or indeed any other ship, again, but two days later, when another crowd of canoes came into the bay, the *Dolphin* opened fire again with grape and roundshot, and also fired at people on the shore.

Almost worse was an order that Wallis rose from his sick-bed to give. The canoes were drawn up empty on the beach, and he sent all his boats ashore with men armed with guns and axes. In two or three hours of destruction they chopped eighty canoes in half, some of them forty or fifty feet long. This was a reckless deed, enough to antagonize anyone; for even the English could see that the canoes were beautifully and elaborately built, and each one, indeed, was the product of weeks or months of somebody's crafts-manship. It was useless too, because there were hundreds if not thousands more canoes on the island's shores.

It was the crew of the *Dolphin*, not the officers, who first came to friendly terms with the islanders. For three weeks, Wallis and his first lieutenant were too sick to go ashore, and they remained suspicious and defensive, expecting a counter-attack in revenge for the havoc they had caused. The first official landing was made by Second Lieutenant Furneaux with a well-armed guard of Marines. On the narrow strip of beach between the river and the sea, he formally announced that the place was named King George's Land, and planted a flagstaff with a pennant on it as a symbol of British possession. He tested the river water and found it good, and mixed it with some rum for all aboard to drink a loyal toast. Hundreds of islanders watched the ceremony from the other side of the river. All of them carried green branches as emblems of peace, and a few ventured across with presents of pigs, fruit, bales of home-made cloth, and two of a peculiar kind of edible veg-etarian dogs with their legs tied together. All these they laid on the sand at a respectful distance. Furneaux accepted the offering, but untied the legs of the dogs, which ran a mile, Robertson said, before they looked back at their deliverers. The people seemed to think the pennant was a present for them. They were seen that evening offering boughs and pigs to it, and two old men came off to the ship with two fifty-pound pigs, which they indicated were thanks for the gift. That night they took it away, and two years later Cook saw it again, converted into a ceremonial girdle for their highest chief.

After that, armed parties were landed every day to barter, but, on Wallis's orders, the river became a frontier. The gunner was put in charge of it because no senior officer could be spared, and he was the only man allowed to trade. Sailors were forbidden to cross it, and although there were always crowds of people on the other side with offerings of pigs and fruit, only one bearded old man, with a youth who was thought to be his son, was allowed to wade over, bringing the goods and taking back a nail or two in payment.

Not even naval discipline could take the strain. The beach was narrow and intolerably hot. Beyond the river, the shady groves of palms and breadfruit trees were irresistibly alluring. So, above all, were the girls, openly inviting the sailors with their 'droll wanton tricks', and the men who beckoned the sailors over to enjoy the girls. The Marine guard began to take turns off-duty and sneak across while the gunner pretended not to be looking. Every day, more and more men proposed jobs which would take them across the river – parties for collecting wood, others for cutting grass to make hay for the livestock on board, the coopers to mend the barrels. Finally, the surgeon decided to land his thirty scurvy patients every morning. They were put on an island in the river with a sail to shelter them from the sun, and instantly, the girls invaded. Before long, there was not a man in the crew, or a midshipman, who was not defying the captain's orders, crossing the river and wandering off into the woods, each with a thirty-penny nail, which was the only reward the irrepressibly cheerful girls expected.

It was a sexual orgy, but not only that. The whole land between the sea and the foothills was a well-tended orchard of exotic fruit, and to any sailor who had not been ashore for six months – and then only on the barren rocks of Magellan's Straits – it was delightful simply to stroll around in the shade of the trees among the streams which fell in cool cascades from the mountains. They soon found that people were afraid of them if they carried muskets, so they went unarmed. Nobody molested them; on the contrary, everywhere they went they were welcomed, invited into the houses and fed until they could eat no more, by people who always seemed to be happy and laughing. They played with the children, taught English words to the men and old women, and learned a few Tahitian words in exchange.

This went on for nearly a fortnight before the senior officers found out. The gunner told Robertson that trade was falling off, and prices in nails were rising – and no wonder: there was not much point in parting with a pig for a nail when the girls were getting all the nails they wanted. Robertson had only one moral qualm about it. He consulted Furneaux, who was acting captain, and they both consulted the surgeon. Was there a risk they might be bringing syphilis or gonorrhoea to a people who seemed to have no diseases at all? The surgeon told them were was no venereal disease in the ship. No doubt he believed he was right. But there had been twenty cases when they left England, the last reported cure was in the Strait of Magellan, and no surgeon then could be sure his cures were complete. Moreover, a man under treatment for venereal disease lost part of his pay, so victims had an incentive to hide the symptoms if they could. In fact, one of the very early crews of explorers brought this scourge to Tahiti. Perhaps they all did, but every one blamed the others.

Robertson's only other worry, when he heard what was going on, was where all the nails were coming from. He asked the carpenter, who assured him his stores were safe under lock-and-key. But once alerted the carpenter soon found that all the cleats in the ship, to which the running rigging was made fast, were loose. The nails had been pulled out of them. And the boatswain discovered that two-thirds of the crew were sleeping on the deck, because the nails their hammocks were slung on had gone. This had to stop, before the ship was damaged beyond repair. The officers talked of stopping shore leave, but the surgeon opposed it: the girls, or the change of air, were curing his patients. Not one man of the crew would admit he had taken a nail. At length they agreed to make a scapegoat of one man they all disliked, and several of them accused him. Robertson condemned him to run the gauntlet: to run three times round the deck while every man in the crew took a swipe at him with an unravelled rope-end. But Robertson knew very well that this man was not the only culprit, and let him off when he had gone round twice, threatening worse punishment to anyone caught going ashore with a nail in the future. The sailors then started giving their shirts to the girls.

It was about the time of this farce, when the *Dolphin* had lain three or four weeks at the island, that they first met anyone in authority. This was a woman whom they took to be the queen. Her name seemed to them to be Oberea. They were not quite right; the initial O was a kind of article, and her name was more exactly Purea. But in later years she became a close ally of Captain Cook and, it was suspected, a mistress of Joseph Banks; and as they also called her Oberea it seems pedantic not to do so now.

They were also wrong in thinking she was a queen. Tahiti had no king or queen, but was ruled by nine or ten chiefs, each with his own territory. As later explorers discovered, they had an unusual system of succession. As soon as one of these chiefs had a son, he abdicated in favour of the baby and became its regent. Oberea was the wife of one of the chiefs, and she had a son who was then about five years old. This child was chief of the district which included Matavai Bay, and Oberea, who was a much more forceful character than her husband, had taken it on herself to act as regent. She was away from the district when the *Dolphin* came, but somebody must have gone post-haste to tell her. She came back with a fleet of canoes and, on 11 July, she paid a ceremonial visit to the ship.

Robertson described Oberea as 'a strong, well-made woman about five feet ten inches high'. Wallis said she was 'about five and forty years of age, of a pleasing countenance and majestic deportment . . . She behaved, all the while she was on board, with an easy freedom that always distinguishes conscious superiority and habitual command.' One of Cook's artists, who met her two years later, called her, with less respect, 'a fat, bouncing, good-looking dame'. Joseph Banks, who came to know her better than anyone, said she was tall and lusty and might have been handsome when young. Everyone agreed that the orders she gave to her people were instantly obeyed.

Poor Wallis was in bed again when she came aboard, and could not get up to receive her, but the other officers showed her round the ship and gave her retinue of men dinner and Madeira wine in the gun-room. Oberea refused to eat or drink – Tahitian women never ate with men – but the rest devoured everything they were offered, except rum and brandy punch: one sniff of that was enough for them. It was a jollier and less formal reception than Wallis may have believed. Oberea was not too dignified to enjoy a little horseplay, and she took a great fancy to Robertson, or so he said – especially to his hairy chest. She insisted on seeing and feeling his legs, which she was surprised to find were not tattooed, as all the Tahitians' were. Among all the fun, there was some serious talk of drawing up a document granting possession of the island to King George, although it could not have had any possible meaning for Oberea: but Wallis, who was consulted, had some kind of paralysis in his right hand and could not hold a pen to sign his name, so the idea was dropped. Oberea invited him to come and visit her.

Feeling rather better next morning. Wallis therefore went ashore for the first time, taking Clarke, the first lieutenant, the purser, the surgeon, and a guard of Marines. Oberea met him on the beach with a vast crowd of people. Knowing that he was sick she insisted he should be carried over the river and all the way to her house. (To be carried on men's backs was an honour also accorded to the highest of Tahitian chiefs, whose status was half divine.) The house, which was probably not the place where she lived but a meeting hall, was the same as all the others, a mere thatched roof supported on pillars, but it was huge: somebody must have measured it, for Wallis recorded its exact dimensions, 327 feet long, 42 feet wide, and 30 feet high to the ridge. There Oberea appointed four young girls to undress and massage him, and Clarke and the purser, both of whom had also been ill.

That pleasant process came to a sudden halt in utter consternation. The surgeon, hot from his walk, took off his wig. 'In a moment,' Wallis wrote – the only glimpse of humour in his journal – 'every eye was fixed upon the prodigy, and every operation was suspended: the whole assembly stood some time motionless, in silent astonishment, which could not have been more strongly expressed if they had discovered that our friend's limbs had been screwed on to the trunk. In a short time, however, the young women who were chafing us, resumed their employment, and having continued it for about half an hour, they dressed us again, but in this they were, as may easily be imagined, very awkward: I found great benefit, however, from the chafing, and so did the Lieutenant and Purser.' Oberea then had some bales of native cloth brought in and dressed Wallis in them. He resisted at first, unwilling perhaps to seem ridiculous in the eyes of his crew, but he had to give in. So garbed, and feeling much better for the massage, he insisted on walking back to the beach; still, whenever they came to a puddle or a stream. Oberea picked him up in her arms and carried him over.

After that pleasing experience. Wallis managed to see Oberea – 'my Princess, or rather Queen', as he called her in his journal – almost every day. She never stooped to barter, but they loaded each other with presents: on one day he was given forty-eight hogs. But not many days had passed before he had to move on. All the sick had recovered, except himself and the two lieutenants, and the ship was loaded with more provisions than anyone could eat. One suspects also that under the island's insidious charm the crew was getting out of hand, and discipline was in danger of breaking down: a corporal of Marines was punished twice for insubordination, insulting an officer, and knocking down the master-at-arms. When Wallis told Oberea he was going, she burst into tears, 'threw herself down upon the arm-chest, and wept a long time with an excess of passion that could not be pacified'. She begged him to stay a little longer, but he was adamant. When the morning of departure came the ship was again surrounded by canoes and the decks full of people, men and women, who 'embraced us all', Wallis wrote, 'with such tenderness of affection and grief, as filled both my heart and my eyes'.

So the *Dolphin* had discovered Tahiti; but she discovered almost nothing about the Tahitians, as Wallis admitted – with the explanation that he had been sick all the time. They had not sailed round the island to look at the other side, and only one party, led by the master's mate, John Gore, had explored on land, taking a day's walk into the mountains. Her crew had learned that the islanders were happy, kind, hospitable, and carefree except when they were frightened; and of course the crew had one and all discovered that the girls were beautiful and willing. But they still knew nothing about the way the island was governed, what religion it had, what laws or conventions. All this remained for later explorers to discover. None of the *Dolphin*'s people, so far as one can tell, had even paused to wonder how a human society could exist and prosper without any sexual inhibition. But that was the core of the story they took back to England: Tahiti was the fulfilment of a sailor's dream, a dream as old as the legend of the Sirens. And that was also the beginning of the Tahitians' downfall. The cheerful welcome of their girls, in the course of time, attracted the toughest of sailors to enjoy it, and the strictest of missionaries to suppress it.

TWO

'The Real Youth of the World'

————••❦••————

IT IS EASY ENOUGH to imagine a distant voyage from a European point-of-view: sea convention produced the officers' logs and journals, and all sorts of people with nothing much to do started to keep diaries. It is more difficult to see things from the Tahitian point of view, but one can get some idea of what Tahitians did, and what they thought, before the Europeans came by putting together the observations of scores of people.

In European history, the day the *Dolphin* anchored was the start of an epoch that was not unimportant, but in Tahiti it was much more than that. History implies change, and until that day nothing had changed in Tahiti, certainly nothing in the Tahitians' memory and probably nothing in centuries. So it is no exaggeration to say that Tahitian history began that day.

After the *Dolphin*'s fight there was mutual goodwill and affection, but hardly any mutual understanding. The fact was that nobody on either side could understand the other – even when he had learned a little of the language – unless he was willing and able to discard, for the moment, all his own ethical ideas and start again from the very beginning. That was a feat of mental gymnastics that nobody in the eighteenth century could perform, except the most erudite theorists, and it is not perfectly easy even now. But at least one can do one's best.

Tahiti and some of the other Polynesian islands had a combination of qualities that was unique. They had been left entirely alone since mankind first came to live in them, and they had all the needs of human life and comfort. So the people had an opportunity nobody else had ever had. Unthreatened and untaught, they created a society and a religion on the basis that there was plenty of everything for everyone, and nobody had to be either poor or rich. They were perfectly content with what they had, and never yearned for more.

The islanders made sure that everyone had what he needed by a custom of mutual giving. It was not trade, because they had no money; nor was it barter. A Tahitian would give anything to anyone who needed it, and expected nothing in exchange except the knowledge that if he was ever in need himself, somebody would do the same for him. As a matter of course, they gave food to anyone who was away from his home and hungry, and with equal innocence they gave the pleasure of sex to anyone who was hungry for that. If a man's canoe was wrecked, his house blown down, or his net torn by sharks, his neighbours would give him their own and set to work to help him build another canoe or house or make another net. Nobody thought of himself as the permanent owner of anything. They had never heard of private property, except perhaps family ownership of land. So they were never tempted into the sins of envy, selfishness, or avarice. Nor were they cruel or unkind, either by nature or example.

Therefore, the religion they created did not have to assume that mankind was sinful, as European religions did. Apart from that, it was not entirely unlike them. It had one supreme god, called Te Atua, which simply appears to have meant the godhead, the concept of god. He could not be personified. There were also lesser gods who were known by personal names, and innumerable spirits. These were the spirits of ancestors, who were revered; people called on them for help or protection in special circumstances, much as some Christians pray to saints. Te Atua was the arbiter of life and death, but the only demands he made of mankind were reverence to divinity and kindness to each other. Lack of reverence he might punish by sickness, even mortal sickness. But he threatened no other punishment in life, and none after death. Tahitians conceived a heaven but no hell. Nor did they think of a devil. There were malevolent spirits, who prowled about in the dark in the form of mists and frightened people, but these were not symbols of temptation, like the Devil in Christianity.

Tahitians found it easy to satisfy Te Atua's demands. Reverence was no trouble, nor was kindness to each other, partly because they were made that way and it was the general habit, and partly because they were very much like each other. They were uniformly intelligent, although their only education was gained by copying their elders. Some Tahitians must have had better brains than others, but nobody's intellect had to be trained or stretched above the norm, because society did not evolve, and there was thus no call for innovation or inventiveness. On the contrary, everyone's experience of life was the same, and everyone could perfectly understand the environment and the place of mankind in it. So everyone thought the same. Some of course had special skills, in building canoes, for example, or navigating, but their only reward was in thanks and the pleasure of crafts-manship: their skill did not make them rich. They did not need to be told to love their neighbours: everyone did, and when they met strangers they expected them to be very much like themselves, and instantly lovable. An outsider might think such uniformity was dull, but no outsider yet had ever seen it, and it did not seem dull to the Tahitians, only natural. And dullness was relieved because every man and every woman had a 'best friend', called a *taio* – a word which also meant friendship in general. A man and his *taio* exchanged names and had a uniquely close relationship, and every attractive European was invited by somebody to become his *taio*.

Their laws and system of government were as simple as their religion, and as effective. There was no formal code of law, because they did not write; but there was a very strong tradition of what was right and what was wrong, based, like the religious rules, on whether an act was kind or unkind. Unkindness was *taboo* – one of the Tahitian words that crept into English. This law had the merit, unlike European law, that everyone could under-stand it. The people were loosely governed by their chiefs, some superior chiefs who ruled a number of districts, and some lesser chiefs, each of whom ruled a little district of his own; and some of the reverence due to Te Atua rubbed off on the chiefs and their families, because they were directly descended from gods.

But day-to-day legal decisions belonged to the heads of fam-ilies. A Tahitian family was very large. It was not just a man and his wife and their children, but included all the aunts and uncles, grandparents, cousins, nephews, and nieces, who lived together in a group of houses. The family was so closely united that only one word existed for each generation: the word for 'mother' was also the word for all the aunts; 'father' also covered all the uncles; 'son' and 'daughter' included all the small nephews and nieces, every-one who was not quite grown-up; and bringing up the children was everyone's concern.

Each family chose one patriarch, or a council of patriarchs, to uphold the law. If anyone was decreed to have broken the law, his whole family was responsible, and public opinion, or family opinion, was the strongest possible deterrent. To be arraigned by one's grandfathers, to disgrace and be held in disgrace by all one's relations, and to have to undo one's wrong or know that one's family had to undo it was enough to make crime very rare, and although other more drastic punishments were hinted at (taking a miscreant out to sea and drowning him, for example), no European ever reported that they were used.

The early reports of Tahitian life are often contradictory in detail. Visitors were inclined to think it was more highly organized and more homogeneous than it really was; so when they noticed some peculiarity of custom or behaviour, they reported it as a general rule. In fact, the only thing that was homogeneous throughout the island was religion. Since there was so little central government, and since the rules could never be written down and reduced to a code of law, in practice each chief and each head of a family interpreted the rules as he went along. What visitors observed might sometimes be a general rule, but more often was only the rule of one chiefdom or one family, and might be different on the other side of the hills or in a neighbouring bay.

Most of the early enthusiasts thought Tahitian society was democratic. They wanted it to be, but it was not. The Tahitians were as class-conscious as anyone in Europe, and their system of government was nearer feudalism than democracy. It was rather like the system of Saxon England before the Norman Conquest, which had one supreme head, blessed by God, and under him earls who each ruled part of the country. Every man in the Saxon system owed duties to those above and below him: villeins owed produce and labour to thanes, who were the heads of villages, thanes owed military and other services to earls, earls owed the support of their armies to the king, and the king owed everything to God: and starting at the top, everyone owed protection, justice and help to those below. Two democratic institutions made the Saxon system work: there were moots, or committee meetings, at every level, which everyone had a right to attend and where everyone could speak his mind, or appoint a spokesman to do it for him, and there was always a possibility of rebellion. An earl or even a king who misused his power could be overthrown by the people he ruled.

All this was true of Tahiti. The supreme chiefs, called *arii rahi*

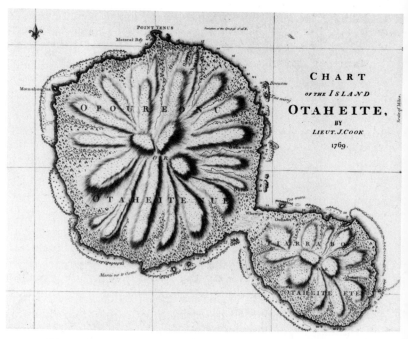

Plan of Tahiti by Lieutenant Cook, surveyed on his boat
trip round the island

(there was always more than one), corresponded to the king in their holy status, although they had less practical power and fewer duties; the lesser chiefs, called *arii*, corresponded to the English earls; and the heads of families were not unlike thanes. Each had autocratic power within the scope of his rank, but each could be thrown out of office if he misused it.

The difference was that Tahiti was so small: mostly covered by mountains, shaped like a figure 8, and only thirty-three miles from end to end. Saxon England had roughly a million and a half people, and six earls: Tahiti had perhaps a tenth of the number of people and twice as many chiefs. So Tahitian government was more personal. A chief could walk all round his chiefdom in a day if he wanted to. He ruled only a few thousand people, and all of them were related to each other, if not to him. He would know almost all of them, and would certainly know every family. Equally certainly, they all knew him well enough to tackle him with any problem and complain if they thought his judgements were unfair.

The chief's own immediate family formed an aristocracy, quite separate from the ordinary people, and also provided him with a council. Their privilege was closely guarded: they could never marry beneath them, and the girls, unlike any others, were firmly expected to be virgins when a husband of equal rank was found for them. Aristocratic boys could do what they liked, but if one of them fathered a baby with an unsuitable mother, the integrity of the family demanded that it should be allowed to die at birth. Some chiefs were obliged to have two or three wives because the family's power depended on them to produce heirs. Since they abdicated as soon as they had one, most of the active chiefs were regents, and most of the nominal chiefs were children. There were also many ex-chiefs, who had retired because their heirs were grown-up, and they were often consulted for their wisdom.

Of course the system was open to abuse, as any autocratic government must be, but the evidence is that in the old days abuse was rare. Tahitian chiefs were more aware of their dignity than their power. They believed, and so did everyone else, that they were descended from gods and they had to live up to it. Their material rewards did not amount to much, only a sort of tax which, since there was no money, was paid in kind. They always had a right to claim food for their families, who often ate too much; but that was no great burden for the community, and nobody minded having to feed the people appointed by gods to rule them. Envy and jealousy were not part of the Tahitian character. Besides, they had never heard of any other means of government. So far as they knew, the whole human race was governed by chiefly families of divine descent. It was the natural state of affairs.

But the chiefs could also impose an extra tax when they wanted to, usually when they had visitors to entertain, and this was sometimes resented. European visits were expensive. Oberea must have levied a special tax in pigs when she gave forty-eight to Captain Wallis – and in later years she suffered the fate of any chief who went too far and became oppressive: she was deposed. Other chiefs also made a special tax when Europeans came, and some of their people said they would not pay it. The response was to outlaw them and their families. Tahitians dreaded being out-lawed. It meant leaving home and going to live in the mountains, where food was scarce and the air was cold, and it shut them out from the cosy and comfortable life of their community. It made them unbearably lonely. Their only way of escape was to ask their friends for the goods the chief had demanded. But Tahitians were so accustomed to giving when anyone was in need that the exile seldom lasted long. Someone always gave them the price of their freedom. Before the Europeans, nobody had ever refused to take part in this general game of giving.

The eighteenth-century explorers reported the end-results of this unusual civilization, but never understood how it worked. They observed that Tahitians were kind and gentle and astonishingly generous, and above all that they were happy – always full of fun, always laughing – unless they were frightened or upset by a glimpse of cruelty, when they burst into tears. They always wept, men and women, when sailors were flogged, and begged the officers to forgive the offenders.

As time went on, the explorers also observed that the Tahitians had a few customs which in the Europeans' eyes were outrageous sins. One was human sacrifice: sometimes, but not often, their gods required a human sacrifice to support a particularly urgent prayer. Another was infanticide – as when a baby was born to a chiefly boy and a lowly mother – which took the place of contraception and abortion. (They sometimes tried abortion, but did not often succeed.) Of course these things were neither sinful nor illegal to Tahitians: they were custom, regrettable perhaps, but necessary. A third thing often judged sinful was their sexual freedom – though most Europeans enjoyed it, sinful or not.

Sex became for Europeans the most astonishing and important thing about Tahiti, and the most discussed, so it needs to be specially mentioned and the Tahitian view of it made plain. Nobody had ever suggested to them that sex was ever sinful, much less a matter for salacity, secrecy, or self-restraint. It was simply a normal hunger, to be satisfied as naturally as eating, and the pleasure it gave was simply one – though perhaps the greatest – of the shared pleasures of life.

Accordingly, from the earliest possible age, Tahitian children were taught its refinements by their elders, and as teenagers they were allowed and encouraged to practise it, in pairs or groups, whenever and wherever they wished. Any chance encounter of boy and girl was likely to lead to sex. As they were mentally so much alike, physical beauty and sexual skill were what they most admired, and these were also sources of pride for their parents. The more lovers young people had, the better their chance of

Tahitian *Girl with a Fan* by Paul Gauguin

making a good choice in the end – and better still if a young girl became pregnant, though that seems to have happened less often than one would expect. It proved she was fertile. When she finally made her choice and married, her husband gladly accepted extra babies, and in the meantime there were plenty of parents, aunts, and uncles all eager to help her.

They all married in the end, after eight or ten years of cheerful promiscuity. Marriage was normally monogamous, except for chiefs who needed an heir, but it was not exclusive or possessive: so although divorce was easy, it seldom happened. It was perfectly proper for a wife to have sexual relationships with her husband's brothers and cousins and best friend – she married the whole family – and likewise for a man; and for both, though more often the wife, sexual hospitality was an accepted obligation, unless there was a suitable teenager to take over. Only two things were banned: one was marriage across the class barrier, and the other was incest.

This curious system worked perfectly well. Sailors who encountered it made an orgy of it, and others who heard of it, imagining themselves in such a world, supposed that the Tahitians lived in a permanent orgy. But they did not. People do not overeat when food is free unless they are afraid it will be rationed tomorrow, and Tahitians, with perpetual plenty in food and sex, lived in perpetual mental and physical health. Captain Cook observed them longer than anyone else and took only a philosophical interest in their sexuality. With his usual wisdom he remarked that 'it can hardly be called a Vice, because neither the State nor Individuals are the least injur'd by it'.

Although the custom of giving was not barter but simple mutual kindness, it passed very easily to barter when the frigates came. The strangers were evidently far from home and hungry, so the Tahitians gave them food. They were delighted when the strangers gave them nails, but at first they did not see it as a direct exchange, or understand that the strangers, in their own minds, had fixed a price in nails for every pig. Indeed fruit, which everyone could afford to offer, remained a free gift all the time. But barter passed equally easily to bargaining. The Tahitians found that the strangers would give two nails where before they had given only one. So they started to ask for two: they were not stupid. And likewise with the girls: the Tahitians assumed the strangers must be hungry for sex, so they offered sex, and gladly offered it for nothing. But when the girls were given nails or shirts, they soon began to ask for nails and shirts, and their happy gift became a sort of prostitution.

Putting all the collected observations together, perhaps one may imagine a Tahitian day, the day a Tahitian man expected when he woke up in the morning. One does not have to say a 'typical' day: almost all days were the same, lived entirely within the family, meeting only a few close neighbours, and very seldom disturbed by any intrusion. At once one comes up against a minor contradiction. Some reports say that men and women slept in separate houses, some that men slept with their wives, some that the men slept for preference with their canoes in houses specially built to shelter canoes, and some that a lot of visiting went on after most people had settled down for the night. This must be one of the many things there were no rules about. Probably everyone slept wherever he happened to be when he fell asleep. It did not need any forethought. One could lie down anywhere on the mats in any house, with or without a covering: the nights were always warm. Women took off the cloth they had been wearing as a skirt and spread it over themsleves as a sheet, and if somebody else crept under it too, nobody worried much.

Everyone began to stir at dawn, and the first thing all of them did was bathe in a river pool or under a waterfall. This does appear to have been a general rule: there are stories of old people dying from the effort of staggering to the river because they could not contemplate a day without two or three baths. The bathing was done with decorum. Women thought no more than men of revealing their upper half, but both men and women were embarrassed to be entirely naked in public. They could not bathe in their clothes because the cloth they dressed in was really a kind of paper, made from the bark of certain trees, and it tended to fall to pieces like paper when it was wet; so they took their clothes off and discreetly slipped into the water, hiding whatever they wanted to hide with a handful of leaves. There must have been a lot of laughter, horse-play, shouting, splashing, and practical jokes. Tahitians always showed their feelings.

Then breakfast. Meals and going to temples were the only times men and women were segregated. Although they bathed together, many accounts agree that women did not eat with men, even their closest relations, and some say men's food was prepared by boys and women's by girls. But all of them ate under trees in the open air unless it was raining, when they had to go under the roofs to keep their clothes intact. The food was laid out on fresh plantain leaves, in calabashes and polished coconut shells. They lived on fruit and vegetables, fish and shellfish when someone had caught some, and pigs and occasionally dogs for feasts. The invaluable breadfruit, which Europeans had never seen, was a basic food. All the food except meat and breadfruit was eaten raw, because the Tahitians had no cooking pots, iron, or earthenware, and the only way they could cook was by baking in underground ovens. These were simply holes in the ground, heated by a layer of hot stones in the bottom. The stones were covered with leaves, then the pig or the breadfruit, also wrapped in leaves, was laid on top, followed by another layer of stones and leaves and a covering of earth. After two or three hours, it was all dug up again. Every European who tried it agreed it was the most delicious way of cooking pork. All in all, the Tahitians had the healthiest possible diet, and it showed in their physique and especially their teeth, which were perfect. They drank only water and the milk of coconuts, and got enough salt by dipping their fingers in shellfulls of sea water and licking them.

Some chiefs had a drink of their own, which was made from the roots of the shrub called *ava*. Only chiefs could afford it, partly because the shrub was rare and partly because a squad of willing servants was needed to prepare it. They chewed the tough roots and spat the proceeds into a bowl. A privileged lady filtered the saliva and mixed it with water, and that was what the chiefs liked to drink. Although it was not alcoholic, it contained a drug which had the same effects as alcohol. Some chiefs were addicted to it, and often seemed to be drunk. European preachers, of course, declared it sinful.

Europeans often said the Tahitians were lazy. So they were, when colonists in later years tried to make them work regular hours for money. But it was not strictly true when they were left to themselves. Even in a perfect climate, self-sufficiency needs effort, and it needed particular effort in Tahiti because the islanders had no beasts of burden and had not invented wheels, so everything that had to be moved had to be carried, dragged or rolled along the ground, or floated down the rivers. They entirely lacked the European idea that hard work was a virtue in itself; though there are no reports of anyone shirking his part in the family chores. Nobody had ever hustled the Tahitians, or told them they ought to work, or what work they ought to do. It was just natural that everyone should do something useful for a short time every day, and everyone did it, in his own time, at his own speed, and according to his own ability. There was always plenty to do.

After breakfast, the teenagers disappeared for their amorous enterprises; nobody expected them to do anything else. The smaller children went out to play; the dangers were negligible, they could swim as soon as they could walk, and there were no prized possessions they could damage, so they looked after themselves. The adults wandered off at a leisurely pace to fish, to tidy the houses and prepare the food, to cut down trees with stone axes for building houses or canoes, to do a little simple gardening, to carve fish-hooks from bones or mother-of-pearl, to make nets and fishing lines from coconut fibre or – the finest sort – from plaited human hair, to make mats or baskets, or climb the more convenient trees and pick the fruit before it fell. They were not hunters, because there were no animals to hunt. There was no need to hurry. The women made cloth, but spent more time making themselves attractive. The old men, in the shade of a meeting house, discussed the affairs of the family, the administration of justice, and even, perhaps, matters of wider philosophy. As the day grew hotter, everyone gave in to a comfortable lethargy. In the afternoon, most of them fell asleep again, and when they woke up they all went to bathe again, and then had their second meal. Somehow, everything important got done, enough to ensure forever that tomorrow would be the same as yesterday.

Intermingled with things that might be called work were things that were purely pleasure. In practice, there was no very clear division between the two. The only object of work was to maintain the pleasures of life; anyone could see they could not enjoy the refinements of sport or dancing or sex unless they had provided food and cleanliness and comfort.

Lazy or not, the Tahitians put plenty of energy into entertaining themselves and each other. When they had caught enough fish (it was no good catching too many because they could not preserve them) the fishing expeditions turned to the pleasures of sailing, which they loved, swimming, especially in the breakers on the reef, and surf-riding, which they invented. Ashore, almost anything could become a competitive game. Picking breadfruit could turn into a kind of football which was both a game and a dance, with rules of its own which no foreigner understood. If somebody got out his bow to shoot a bird, an archery competition began – but not to hit a target, only to shoot the arrow as far as possible and further than anyone else. Damming streams and making irrigation channels was as much fun as it was a necessity. Climbing trees could soon become a race, and so could the least of journeys. The only prizes were prestige and the admiration of the other sex.

Whatever they were doing, there was always time to stop and talk, or sing, or dance, or make love, or listen to someone telling stories or reciting poems. Some were love-stories, but most were a kind of heroic ballad designed to be sung, with verses for soloists and refrains for a chorus. Without any writing, there was no other way of preserving traditions of the past, no other history.

The only welcome interruptions in this placid life, the only days that were different, occurred when the *arioi* came. The *arioi* were a religious sect which, it was believed, had been founded in a distant age by a god named Oro. But they were so unlike any Jewish or Christian sect that visitors often refused to believe they had any religion at all; for they were not only a kind of priesthood but also travelling players, men and women, who gave professional and highly polished entertainments, called *heivas*, of singing, dancing, play-acting, and wrestling, which everyone from miles around attended. Some of their plays were historical, but most were satires and comedies which made fun of the mannerisms of chiefs and later of Europeans. All the dances were more or less erotic; some were performed in the nude and gave demonstrations of special sexual techniques.

Off-stage, too, their behaviour was not what Europeans expected of a priesthood: they did not marry but, among themselves, continued the teenage practice of free indiscriminate love into adult life. When they had babies they let them die: the second example of infanticide. They travelled in parties large and small all over the Society Islands, the group of islands of which Tahiti was part, and there were similar institutions in some other parts of the Polynesian world. Large parties sailed from island to island in fleets of sea-going canoes, festooned with flowers and wearing – if they wore anything – a uniform of yellow girdles of leaves and red cloaks, singing rhythmical choruses and playing flutes and drums. One of Cook's reliable observers saw them in a fleet of seventy canoes which he reckoned carried seven hundred *arioi*. They must have been like a plague of locusts – they all expected to be fed wherever they went – but when they were heard or seen approaching everyone prepared to welcome them, all other work was abandoned, and the day became a gala.

None of the first three frigates to visit the island, English, French, or Spanish, happened to be in Tahiti when the *arioi* were there, and two Spanish padres were the first to see or hear a *heiva*. They were outraged and terrified. Cook was the first European to understand that these festivals were religious. The *arioi*'s creed had a strange superficial likeness to the Christian story: Oro was the son of the supreme god, Te Atua, and he had come down to earth and then returned to heaven. The *arioi*'s gospel had the same historical relationship to established religion as Christianity had to Jewry, and the *arioi* were its apostles. But there the similarity ended. Oro's motive in coming to earth (he came down a rain-bow) was typically Polynesian: he had tired of heavenly wives and had his eye on a beautiful girl on the holy island of Raiatea. The *arioi*'s proselytism was typically Polynesian too. Everyone, pre-sumably, had a subconscious wish to go on behaving like a teenager all his life; so the *arioi* offered that privilege to their members. And everyone enjoyed seeing comic plays and erotic dances, so that was what the *arioi* gave their congregations. However, the *arioi*'s creed and the older traditional beliefs were not mutually exclusive. On the contrary, the *arioi* were revivalists. Their visits were not too frequent, and they gave the people and the traditional priesthood a fresh vitality. Their entertainments always began with prayers, and they preached peace among the islands. Most seafaring visitors, not understanding the language, did not recognize the prayers for what they were; but most admitted, more or less shamefaced, that they liked the perfor-mance.

Anyone could join this strange society; it was the only thing equally open to people of every class. Novices had to be good at dancing and singing and also had to know the society's sacred traditions and songs by heart, and show they were inspired by falling into religious ecstasy. But class played a part in promotion to the higher ranks. The society had seven grades of membership, and strict examinations had to be taken to rise from one to the next. Ordinary people seldom rose beyond the lower grades; the upper ones were filled by the families of chiefs. Only two vows were demanded: to obey superior officers and to kill any children that were born. This second, drastic promise did not worry the men: 'every woman [in the *arioi*] is common to every man', Cook reported in his journal, and so no man could know if he had fathered a baby or not. Perhaps the women made the promise because they were stage-struck and concerned, like other actresses and dancers, with their appearance and agility. They did not want children who would have put a stop to their roving life. But the vows were not expected to be endless, and most members of the *arioi* left it sooner or later to marry and live a family life like anyone else. As retired stars, they kept the prestige and respect they had won in their prime.

Of all the many misunderstandings between Tahitians and Europeans, misunderstanding of sexual morals was the most profound, or at least the most talked about. It was fifty years before the Tahitians began to understand European prohibitions, which were finally made clear to them by English Calvinist missionaries; and even now, many Europeans know of Tahitian sexual freedom but do not understand it. Of course when they first heard of it, and especially if they heard of the *arioi*, some were scandalized and felt it was their duty to put an end to it. Others, a large majority perhaps, imagined what they would do if they were suddenly freed from all restriction, and indulged in fantasies of a perpetual orgy. The few Europeans who had the chance, in particular the English crews, did make an orgy of it while they could. But by making sex as commonplace as dinner, the Tahitians ran a risk of making it as unexciting as cookery. Even the *arioi*, with their exceptional freedom in adult life, must have been limited like anyone else by their physical ability. What the Tahitians achieved was not excess but a healthy balance which was enjoyed by everyone and did no harm to anyone, either social, psychological or physical – unless to the infants allowed to die before they drew breath, who one might say ought not to have been conceived. And trying to put all prejudice aside, one has to say that freedom, unless it does proven harm, is always better than compulsion or prohibition.

The peaceful life and uneventful days passed by in endless summer and prolific natural beauty. The Tahitians made no recorded comment on the beauty of the place they lived in. Of course they had nothing to compare it with; they had no conception of a bleak or barren shore, or the squalor of a slum. But most of mankind is aware of beauty; it is part of the religious instinct. Tahitians certainly recognized it in each other, and they certainly loved flowers, which they wore in their hair and ears and wove into garlands and bracelets; and as deeply religious people they must have felt their gods had been good to them in the shade of the fruit trees, the graceful curve of the palms, the mountains and waterfalls, the unsullied sand of the beaches, and always, glimpsed between the boles of the trees, the placid blue lagoon and the flashing breakers on the reef beyond. Everyone who met them said they were happy.

The early explorers observed Tahitian life, admired its virtues and exploited its customs. But none of them perceived a whole viable system of ethics fundamentally different from their own; or if they did, they lacked the courage to say so.

Tahiti was a small civilization perfectly in balance. But the balance was pathetically easily upset by intrusion. In spite of their good intentions, Europeans fatally upset it merely by their presence, and especially by the introduction of their diseases and two of their ineradicable concepts: the concept of private property and the concept of sin.

THREE

The French in Arcady

————— ••E)(3•• —————

IT WAS PURE CHANCE that no European had seen Tahiti before
1767. Two hundred and fifty years had passed since the Spanish
soldier Balboa marched across the isthmus of Panama and found
the Pacific Ocean and claimed it all for his king; and only eight
years after that discovery, in 1521, Ferdinand Magellan had
entered the ocean by the straits that bear his name and sailed,
with unimaginable hardship, right across it to the known islands
of the East Indies. Since then, probably a score of captains had
sailed across, most notably the Spaniards Mendaña and Quiros,
the Dutchmen Schouten and Le Maire and later Roggeveen, the
Englishmen Drake and Cavendish, and several buccaneers of
dubious nationality. For the past thirty years, indeed, a Spanish
ship known as the Manilla Galleon had made a more or less regular
double crossing there and back, starting from Acapulco in
Mexico, taking millions of dollas in Peruvian silver and bringing
back the goods of the east to the Spanish American colonies.
Among the most recent crossings were the British naval expeditions of Anson in 1740, who captured the Galleon, and Byron in
1760, who used the same frigate as Wallis, HMS *Dolphin*, the first
ship to go twice round the world.

From a modern map of the Pacific, one would think it unlikely
that a ship could sail across without seeing plenty of islands. But
the early Europeans found few. One reason, of course, was that
the islands were far less conspicuous in the ocean than they are on
a map. Charles Darwin crossed in 1835 and observed: 'It is
necessary to sail over this great ocean to comprehend its
immensity . . . Accustomed to look at maps drawn on a smaller
scale, where dots, shading and names are crowded together, we do
not rightly judge how infinitely small the proportion of dry land is
to the water of this vast expanse.'

Another reason why early explorers found so little was that
they never knew where they were themselves. With astrolabe and

cross-staff they could observe the elevation of the sun and work out their latitude within, say, a degree, or sixty miles; but until the middle of the eighteenth century they had no way of observing longitude, and sometimes their guesses were two thousand miles wrong. To avoid getting utterly lost, they sailed up to the known latitude of some place on the far side, usually in the Moluccas or the Philippines, and then stuck to it. Consequently most of them tended to follow roughly the same track, and it was a track which did not have many islands.

When they sighted an island, they could not record its position to enable later voyagers to find it again. The Solomon Islands, for example, were discovered by Mendaña in 1568, and named in the far-fetched belief that they were the land of Ophir, the source of King Solomon's gold; but nobody saw them again for two hundred years. And since all explorers gave new names to new islands, nobody could be sure if an island he found had ever been found before.

The object of these explorations, in any case, was not to discover islands: it was either to find a feasible westerly route to the East Indies, the Spice Islands, whose trade was already making fortunes, or else to discover the great southern continent, Terra Australis Incognita, which had been thought to exist since Ptolemy drew his maps in the second century AD. Yet they had to hope that they would find islands. Without landing, the vast breadth of the Pacific was beyond the strength of the crews. To cross it took Magellan almost a year, and Byron, two hundred and fifty years later, almost eight months. All that time, their progress within the circle of a blank horizon was imperceptible. They had only a rough idea of how far they had come, and no idea at all of how far they still had to go. They had only the faith, expressed by the Elizabethan Frobisher crossing the North Atlantic, that 'the sea at length must needs have an ending'. After the first month or two they were all haunted by fear of death from starvation or thirst, or, most of all, from scurvy.

Nobody knew the cause of this awful affliction, its swollen gums and legs, its internal bleeding, mental depression, and lassitude, which led to death. But they knew they could cure it by putting men ashore and giving them fresh meat, fruit, and vegetables. They longed for land. Yet the islands they saw most often were coral atolls, verdant and tempting but with no anchorage and a surf which stopped them sending boats ashore. When at last they did find an island with a harbour, most of them were at their last gasp and desperate to get their hands on its produce.

The captains all started out with good intentions, and most with orders that if they met natives they should treat them well. The Spaniards in particular longed to convert them to Christianity. But it never worked out as they hoped. Both races, when they met, were at their worst. Both were frightened, the natives by the sudden apparition of mysterious ships and men like mythical monsters, and the Europeans by the threat of death they lived with; and both, of course, misunderstood the other because they had no mutual language. Usually, therefore, the first encounters were short and murderous. Both sides as a rule began with gestures of friendship, but if anyone made a false move, the natives were apt to throw stones with slings and brandish spears, and the Europeans to shoot them down with muskets. Then, surprisingly soon, there would be signs of regret, followed by cheerful forgiveness, until the same thing happened again.

The Marquesas Islands, for example, north east of Tahiti, were discovered by Mendaña and Quiros in 1585. They were islands of great beauty, like Tahiti, and their people were peaceful, like the Tahitians. Both commanders were pious, well-intentioned men. But they could not control their crews, who were crazed with impatience for fresh food – some of whom, indeed, said frankly they enjoyed shooting natives and needed no reason for doing it: it was fun. They got their food partly by force, and partly by bargaining with beads and looking-glasses in moments of peace; but in a stay of a fortnight they reckoned they killed two hundred people – 'evil deeds', Quiros wrote in remorse, 'not to be praised or allowed, or let pass without punishment if it were possible'. As for converting people, they taught only one man to say 'Jesu Maria' and make the sign of the cross – without, of course, the least idea what it meant.

Many of these explorers passed close to Tahiti, some to the north and some to the south. In 1595, 1616, and 1722, ships were within a hair's breadth of sighting it. In 1765, Byron passed it on the northern side and saw birds flying off southward in the evenings, usually taken as a certain sign of land. But he was a man without the exploring instinct, his crew were already sick with scurvy, and he was intent on pressing on to the west. So he did not turn aside.

In 1767, however, when the *Dolphin* lay off the island, some things were changing. People were learning not how to prevent scurvy, but how to delay its attack. The *Dolphin* was better equipped than she had been under Byron. She had stores of food that were thought to be anti-scorbutic, and she had a still for making fresh water from the sea. Her crew were given diluted lemon juice every day. So they could make the long crossing in rather less desperate fear of death. When they came to Tahiti the scurvy had begun, but so far nobody had died. They could still afford to be patient in bartering for the food they needed.

Navigation had also suddenly improved. The sextant had been invented, a much more accurate instrument than the cross-staff or astrolabe, so that latitude could be observed more truly. The chronometer, which solved the problem of longitude, had been invented too. But chronometers were still very rare and expensive, and Wallis did not have one (nor did Captain Cook until his second voyage). Meantime, however, another method, called lunars, had been devised for finding longitude. Astronomers had calculated tables relating Greenwich time to the angles between the moon and certain stars. These angles could be measured with a sextant; so, by observing the sun at its zenith, could local time. Thus both local and Greenwich time could be found in a ship at sea, and the difference between them gave a measure of longitude. It was a difficult, new-fangled calculation, beyond the scope of many sea-captains, but Wallis could do it. When he sighted Tahiti, he had the means and the skill to observe and report its position. Any explorer after that could find it again – and when Wallis brought home his report of its charm, it was certain that somebody would. So the encounter in that misty dawn became the first permanent contact between Europeans and Polynesians.

However, while Wallis was still on his way home, in April 1768, Tahiti was found, again accidentally, by two French ships, the frigate *Boudeuse* and the store ship *Etoile*, commanded by Louis de Bougainville.

Bougainville was a more distinguished man than Wallis, a man with the breadth of interest typical of an eighteenth-century gentleman. Among other things, he was a classicist, a mathematician, and a diplomat. When he was twenty-five he wrote a thesis on the integral calculus which earned him membership of the Royal Society in England. In that century of frequent wars, he was drawn into the army, and through his elegant manners became aide-de-camp to the Marquis de Montcalm in Canada. He fought against the English in the siege of Quebec, and rose to become a colonel. Then he moved to the navy, and volunteered to found a colony in the Falkland Islands at his own expense. He survived the French Revolution, and ended his life as an admiral, a senator, and a member of the Legion of Honour. His name survives today in the climbing shrub Bougainvillea, which he found in South America and brought back to adorn the houses of the Mediterranean. He was the first explorer to fall in love with Tahiti.

It was the Falklands expedition that took him to the Pacific and round the world, although his colony was something of a farce. The islands had been known for a long time – they were first seen by the Englishman John Davis in 1592 – and although they were barren and uninviting, everyone coveted them as a resting place for ships before they rounded Cape Horn. Bougainville set up his colony in 1764, but Byron, sent on the same mission, set up another in 1765 in a different part of the islands. Neither of them knew the other was there, although to their astonishment they sighted each other's ships in the Strait of Magellan. Two years later, Bougainville was ordered by his government to sell his colony to Spain. Spain and England then threatened each other with a war to decide who owned the islands, but Spain gave in and ceded them to Britain. Two hundred years after that, the argument did come to war between Britain and Argentina.

After handing over the colony, Bougainville had to go back to Rio to fetch his store ship, and while he was there Wallis passed him. So they both set off to cross the Pacific, both using the same old route that so many ships had used before; but neither knew the other was there, and Bougainville was ten months behind Wallis.

He approached Tahiti a little further north, and so came to anchor on the opposite side of it. Probably none of the people he met had seen the *Dolphin*, but they had certainly heard of her, and they welcomed a visitor of their own with joy. While he was still at sea, searching for a way in through the coral reef, and admiring the enchanting prospect of the waterfalls, the tree-covered mountains, and the houses under the fruit trees, the canoeists came out to him with green boughs as tokens of friendship, and presents of bananas and coconuts, fowls and pigeons. He gave them nails and ear-rings. He had difficulty warping in through the reef among the crowds of canoes and swimmers and the noise of people shouting

46

'*taio*'. Closer inshore, the canoes were full of girls, who in beauty, he said, might vie with any in Europe. Most of them were naked: the men with them, he believed, had made them take off their clothes.

In fact they had probably only lowered their upper garments to their waists, which was a sign of respectful greeting among Tahitians, men or women – like a European man taking off his hat. But far from suspecting a trap, like Wallis, Bougainville accepted the scene with Gallic humour: 'The glances which they gave us seemed to discover some degree of uneasiness, notwithstanding the innocent manner in which they were given; perhaps because nature has everywhere embellished their sex with a natural timidity or because even in those countries, where the ease of the golden age is still in use, women seem least to desire what they most wish for. The men soon explained their meaning very clearly. They pressed us to choose a woman and come on shore with her; and their gestures, which were not ambiguous, denoted in what manner we should form an acquaintance with her.' It was very difficult, amidst such a sight, to keep at their work some hundreds of young French sailors who had seen no women for six months. Bougainville tried to keep the women out of the ships, which still had to come to anchor, but one managed to get on board and posed at an open hatch below which the men were working the capstan. 'The girl carelessly dropt a cloth, which covered her, and appeared to the eyes of all beholders as Venus showed herself to the Egyptian shepherd, having, indeed, the celestial form of that goddess. The capstan was never hove with more alacrity. At last our cares succeeded in keeping these bewitched fellows in order, though it was no less difficult to keep the command of ourselves.'

Only one girl had got on board, and only one sailor, against orders, got ashore. He was Bougainville's cook, who had already chosen his girl. As soon as he was on the beach, a crowd surrounded him and undressed him from head to foot. They meant him no harm: they only wanted to find out if he was an ordinary man like themselves underneath his clothes, and when they found he was they gave him back his clothes and brought him his girl, inviting him there and then to 'content his desires'. But the poor cook was overcome by embarrassment and had to be taken back on board, where Bougainville was told 'that I might reprimand him as much as I pleased, but that I could never frighten him so much as he had just now been frightened on shore'.

The Tahitians were still puzzled when Bougainville and some officers went ashore that afternoon. A huge crowd of men and women surrounded them, showing every sign of joy. 'The boldest among them came to touch us; they even pushed aside our clothes with their hands, in order to see whether we were made exactly like them.' Indeed, it must have been hard to imagine that eighteenth-century officers, in their cocked hats and wigs, breeches, stockings and buckled shoes, their frogged and embroidered coats with ruffles of lace at the throats and wrists, had ordinary bodies underneath. Once satisfied, the local chief, whose name the French wrote down as Ereti, invited the visitors to his house and fed them on fish and fruit. While they were eating, a lieutenant missed his pistol, which had been very neatly stolen out of his pocket. Bougainville contrived to tell the chief, presumably in mime, that a pistol was dangerous and the thief might kill himself: the next day the chief came on board the ship, bringing a present of a pig and some fowls, and the missing pistol.

So on their very first day, the French discovered the three most obvious qualities of the Tahitians: their inborn friendliness, sexual freedom, and inclination to steal. But Bougainville was more able than Wallis to be philosophical about these things, and to look below the surface – and so was his surgeon-botanist, Dr Philibert Commerçon.

Theft was a perpetual nuisance to explorers, not only in Tahiti but anywhere they met simple races of people. The Spaniards called one group of islands in the western Pacific the Ladrones, the Islands of Thieves, and the name is still on the map today. The Elizabethans Davis and Frobisher, searching for the North-West Passage, had just the same trouble with Eskimos. Some took awful reprisals, but most felt an exasperated admiration for the natives' sleight of hand. The skill of Tahitians, Bougainville wrote, was worthy of the best – or worst – of Parisian pickpockets.

He came near to understanding it. The Tahitians, he noticed, never stole from each other. Whether they were at home or not, their houses were always open. Their furniture, such as it was – not much more than baskets and sleeping mats – lay around unguarded. So did their clothes and ornaments, their simple home-made tools, and even their canoes. But nobody took these things. Everyone helped himself to fruit from any tree, and knew he would be fed in any house he entered. Necessities belonged to everyone, and nothing more than necessities existed.

Dr Commerçon was even more philosophical. 'What is theft?' he wrote in a letter. 'It is taking a thing that is somebody else's property. To complain justly of having been robbed, one must claim that an object has been taken to which one's right of property had been established and recognized. But does this right of property exist in nature? No, it is pure convention. A convention is not binding unless it is known and recognized. The Tahitian, who owns nothing, but offers and gives generously whatever one desires, knows nothing of this exclusive right.' Tahitians who gave pigs and other gifts to the visitors, he thought, were not giving their own property but the joint property of their families or of the whole community; and by the same token, those who stole things that caught their fancy had no thought of making them their personal property, but took them for the pleasure of sharing them or giving them to somebody else. It seemed that the idea of theft as a crime or a sin had not existed in the island before the Europeans brought it.

Over the next few years, when the Tahitians' reputation as thieves began to spread in Europe, most of the early explorers jumped to their defence. One such came up with a different explanation. This was John Marra, a seaman who tried to desert from Cook's crew in Tahiti, but failed. 'Perhaps that propensity to theft,' he wrote, 'for which the inhabitants of all the isles in the South Seas are so lavishly stigmatized by Europeans, may yet be found, upon examination, to be less criminal in them than it is generally esteemed. Is it not very natural, when a people see a company of strangers come among them, and without ceremony cut down their trees, gather their fruits, seize their animals, and, in short, take whatever they want, that such a people should use as little ceremony with the strangers as the strangers do with them; if so, against whom is the criminality to be charged, the Christian or the savage? He that sets the example or he that follows it? . . . Why then upbraid the savage with thievery? Is it because in other respects he shames the Christian by the innocence of his life? or that, having one crime in common with the Christian, all his other virtues are to be cancelled?'

Marra's story was evidently written for him. No doubt the thoughts were his own, but the language is the anonymous ghost-writer's. He might have added that all the early visitors, English, French, and Spanish, claimed possession of the entire island for their own kings. Wallis had hoisted a flag; Bougainville inscribed his claim on an oak plank and buried a sealed bottle containing the names of his officers as witnesses; the Spanish set up a cross and inscribed their claim on that. This was theft, or intended theft, on a grand scale, but they did not tell the Tahitians what these ceremonies meant.

Bougainville tried to discover how the island was governed, and observed that it was divided into many small districts, each with its own chief. 'Yet there does not seem to be any civil war,' he added with an air of surprise, 'or any private hatred in the isle. It is probable that the people deal amongst each other with unquestioned sincerity.' They always did what Ereti told them to do, except in stealing. Ereti disapproved of stealing, or at least knew that the Europeans disapproved of it, and when they pointed out a thief he chased him, usually caught him, set about him with a stick, and made him give back whatever he had taken. But he could not stop them doing it.

Commerçon came nearer to the point. The people, he said, were not governed by a king but by the fathers of their families, who kept them in order just as any old-fashioned father kept his children in order. The French would have understood better how it worked if they had come across the Tahitian word *taboo*. It simply meant forbidden. Some *taboo*s were Te Atua's: it was *taboo* to desecrate holy places. Some were empirical: a chief could make fishing *taboo* while the fish were spawning, or picking breadfruit *taboo* before it was ripe; or he could make his own servants *taboo*, which protected them when they had to run errands to other districts. But the great majority of *taboo*s were simply the age-old matter of custom, things that everyone recognized were 'not right'. Stealing amongst themselves was a *taboo* so ancient and well established that nobody thought of it; if you needed something, you only had to ask. But the arrival of the Europeans, with their concept of private property and their own *taboo*s about it, upset the delicate balance of behaviour. It was something entirely new, probably the first novelty in Tahitian morals for centuries, and there was no established custom to meet the problem. Did the old *taboo* extend to the visitors' goods? Evidently some people thought it did not. It was in the power of the chiefs to extend the *taboo* or create a new one, but they seem to have hesitated to do so, perhaps because it needed consultation with other chiefs, or perhaps because they feared it would be defied, and they had no power to enforce it.

The Tahitians' sexual behaviour also collided head-on with a European *taboo*, but this collision the explorers were happy to accept. Some of them wrote about it with salacious chuckles, some with classical rhapsody, and some with clinical analysis. Bougainville, on the whole, was one of the chucklers. 'Our people were daily walking in the isle without arms, either quite alone or in little companies. They were invited to enter the houses, where the people gave them to eat; nor did the civility of their landlords stop at a slight collation; they offered them young girls; the hut was immediately filled with a curious crowd of men and women, who made a circle round the guest, and the young victim of hospitality. The ground was spread with leaves and flowers, and their musicians sung an hymeneal song to the tune of their flutes. Here Venus is the goddess of hospitality, her worship does not admit of any mysteries, and every tribute paid to her is a feast for the whole nation. They were surprised at the confusion which our people appeared to be in, as our customs do not admit of these public proceedings. However, I would not answer for it, that every one of our men had found it impossible to conquer his repugnance and conform to the customs of the country.'

It could even happen to captains. Bougainville was visited by a neighbouring chief whose name was Toutaa. 'We were obliged to repay this visit at his house, where we were very well received, and where the good-natured Toutaa offered me one of his wives, who was very young and pretty handsome. The assembly was very numerous, and the musicians had already begun the hymenean. Such is their manner of receiving visits of ceremony.'

Dr Commerçon, on the other hand, was a rhapsodist. 'They know no other god than love,' he wrote. 'Every day is consecrated to him, the whole island is his temple, all the women are the idols and the men the worshippers. And what women! The rivals of the Georgians in beauty, and the sisters of the unveiled graces. Here, modesty and prudery lose their tyranny. The act of procreation is an act of religion; its preludes are encouraged by the voices and songs of the assembled people, and its end is greeted by universal applause.'

This was all nonsense. The Tahitians did not take sex so seriously, and it had nothing to do with religion. They simply enjoyed it, men and women, in perfect innocence, as one of the many pleasures of their lives, like eating or sleeping, dancing or singing; and it had never occurred to them that anyone might do otherwise. Nor was it normally a public performance. Nobody ever minded if there was anybody looking or not, and the girls laughed when English sailors wanted to hide in the bushes. The crowds of spectators the French reported were probably only inquisitive to see if the strangers had brought any novel ideas.

But Commerçon was more nearly right when he added: 'Perhaps austere censors will see this as merely a debauchment of morals, a horrible prostitution, a bare-faced cynicism; but is it not really the state of natural man, born essentially good, free from all prejudice, and following without guilt the gentle prompting of an instinct that is always sure, because it has not yet been corrupted by reason?' Both these men observed that it was only the young boys and girls who were totally promiscuous. But even among older people in monogamous marriage, sexual jealousy was an unknown passion, and the husband commonly persuaded his wife to 'yield to another'.

The French stayed only a very short time at the island, but it was long enough for them to taste the nature of Tahitian society and to write of it afterwards as an idyll. Strolling among the little streams and houses in the shade of the trees, Bougainville thought he was 'transported into the garden of Eden . . . Everywhere we found hospitality, ease, innocent joy and every appearance of happiness.' And again: 'Accustomed to live continously in pleasure, the people of Tahiti have acquired a witty and humorous temper, which is the offspring of ease and joy.' He seems not to have seen that this contentment, so stable while it was left alone, was also pathetically fragile and might be shattered like crystal by intrusion. Only one doubt entered his mind on his journey home: some of his men had caught syphilis.[1] He rightly thought it could not have existed on the island before the Europeans came. He blamed the previous English visit for bringing it there, and later English visitors blamed him. Almost certainly, both of them had left this awful legacy in their Eden.

Explorers under sail could never relax, and Bougainville's visit was cut short by a storm after only seven days. The anchorage he had found was not so secure as Wallis's; an on-shore wind

---

[1] The early explorers may have meant gonorrhea: in English, they usually called it the 'venereal distemper'. There is a suggestion the Polynesians were more or less immune to syphilis because they had yaws (their only apparent infection), which is allied to syphilis but not venereal.

raised a heavy sea and drove it over the surrounding coral reef and through the gap the ships had come in by. Nor was it good holding ground. When they sounded, the lead had brought up mud, which is good for anchoring, but the mud had coral boulders scattered in it, and as soon as the ships began to pitch in the sea the coral began to chafe the anchor cables. During the next three days, eight cables parted. Both ships were helpless within the confines of the reef; there was no room to make sail or get underway. Both were sometimes only yards from grounding and could only be saved by rowing more anchors off to windward.

In the midst of these dangers a message was brought from the shore that three Tahitians had been killed with bayonets and all the islanders had vanished. Bougainville thought they might be assembling to attack in revenge, and he sent a lieutenant and a few men out to find them and try to make peace. He found a great crowd of them a couple of miles away with Ereti – who, far from planning revenge, was 'all in tears, and fell at his feet and kissed his hands, repeating over and over, "*Taio, maté*", you are our friends and you kill us. By his caresses and demonstrations of friendship, he at last succeeded in regaining their confidence. The good islanders applauded the reunion, and in a short time the usual crowd and the thieves returned to our quarters, which looked like a fair. This day and the following, they brought more refreshments than ever.'

At length a boat sent out to prospect found another passage through the reef, to leeward. The store ship *Etoile* escaped by it, followed next day by the frigate *Boudeuse*. As the *Boudeuse* came out, they had the worst moment of all. In the narrow passage, the wind dropped suddenly to a calm. The swell began to carry her down on the reef, where it was breaking violently. 'The worst consequences of shipwreck, with which we had hitherto been threatened, would have been to pass the remainder of our days on an isle adorned with all the gifts of nature, and to exchange the sweets of the mother country for the peaceable life, exempted from cares. But now shipwreck appeared with a more cruel aspect; the ship being rapidly carried on the rocks, could not have resisted the violence of the sea two minutes, and the best swimmers could hardly have saved their lives . . . A westerly breeze, springing up, brought hope along with it; it freshened by degrees; and at nine o'clock in the morning we were quite clear of all dangers.'

When Ereti saw them setting sail, he jumped into a canoe

alone and came on board, where he hugged all the officers with tears running down his face. Soon after, his largest canoe came alongside laden with gifts and his weeping wives, and bringing also a man called Aotourou who had decided he wanted to go with the Frenchmen. On the spur of the moment, Bougainville agreed. In the canoe also was a young and handsome girl, whom Aotourou went to embrace. 'He gave her three pearls which he had in his ears, kissed her once more; and notwithstanding the tears of this young wife or mistress, he tore himself from her and came aboard the ship. Thus we quitted this good people; and I was no less surprised at the sorrow they showed on our departure, than at their affectionate confidence on our arrival.' He named the island Nouveau Cythère, after the island in Greece where the goddess Venus first emerged from the sea.

It is remarkable how much Bougainville learned in his few days on the island. The visit was no more than the equivalent of a modern week's package holiday in a country with an unknown tongue; yet he came away with some idea of the islanders' government, customs and character. He also learned more from Aotourou in the eleven-month voyage back to France.

He was criticized afterwards for taking a Tahitian away from his home; but it was a thing explorers had often done, some much more callously. Eskimos and North American Indians had been abducted and taken as exhibits to England, where all of them quickly died, and Spaniards had taken thousands of Caribbean people with them as slaves. Bougainville at least befriended Aotourou, who of course had not the least conception of what he was in for: but he turned out to be a rather unsatisfactory example of a Tahitian. Most people thought he was stupid. He survived the journey and lived a year in Paris, but he never learned more than ten words of French. It was thought he had an impediment in his speech, and he was taken to a learned teacher of the deaf and dumb, who had no success with him. However, with his help Bougainville made and published a Tahitian dictionary of two or three hundred words, and found that the language had almost no syntax and was very short of consonants. It seemed to have no *b*, *d*, *f*, *g*, *k*, or *s*, so a Tahitian had to learn to make these sounds before he could begin to speak a European language.

Aotourou also had the difficulty common to all people who try to learn the language of a totally different culture: many words represented concepts quite outside his experience, so that he had to learn not only a new word but a new concept. All this was too much for him. For a while he was an object of interest in learned circles, but everyone soon grew bored with him.

So Aotourou led a lonely life in Paris, unable to communicate with anyone. He gave signs of gratitude when people were kind, and he found his way round the city alone, but he discovered only one pleasure: taking himself to the cheapest gallery at the opera, from which he could peer at the stage through windows in the backs of the boxes. He seemed to love the dancing. Perhaps it was the only thing that reminded him of home.

In the end, Bougainville paid the equivalent of £1500, which he said was a third of his fortune, to a shipowner who said he would try to take the stranger home. The ship was bound first for Mauritius in the Indian Ocean, which was then a French possession. But that was a very long way from Tahiti, and nobody except the original Polynesians had ever reached the island from that direction. Somewhere on the way Aotourou disappeared, and was never heard of again. One report said he died of smallpox.

PART II

TRESPASS
1769-89

————•◦❊◦•————

FOUR

Endeavour

THE PURPOSE OF the most famous of all the early visits had nothing to do with Tahiti or the Tahitians. It was to measure the distance of the sun from the earth. This distance, if it could be discovered, would be a base-line for all the other measurements of astronomy. In theory, it could have been found by triangulation, the ordinary method of surveying on earth, but no terrestrial base-line was long enough. It would have meant measuring angles to a three-millionth part of a degree, and no instrument then was anything like so accurate. There was a better chance of working out the distance when a planet was in the direct line between earth and sun, but that needed simultaneous observations from widely-separated places on the earth.

Venus had been in that position, in transit with the sun, in 1639, and had been observed by the prodigy Jeremiah Horrocks, a highly-respected astronomer who died when he was twenty-one. Horrocks was also a curate in Lancashire, and had calculated that the transit would take place on a Sunday, when he would have to be in church. But he did his duty and observed the transit too. At the end of the service he dashed out of church just in time to see Venus against the sun before it set.

In 1716 the astronomer Edmund Halley predicted that Venus would be in transit with the sun again on 6 June 1761 and 3 June 1769, and never again until 1870 and 1882, then 2004 and 2012. In 1761 a great international effort was made to observe the event from scores of places all over the world, but it was not a success: when the results were collated and the possible errors allowed for, the result was almost as vague as before, somewhere about ninety million miles.

The Royal Society, founded a century before, might have claimed to be the most prestigious scientific club in the world by the 1760s, and it decided to try the observation again, on its own, at the next opportunity in 1769. The French and Germans, not to mention the Danes and Swedes, were also talking of doing it again; rather than international co-operation, it looked like becoming a national competition. The Royal Society wanted three observatories, one at the North Cape in Norway, one at Fort Churchill in Hudson's Bay, and the third in the south Pacific. But it could not afford the cost itself.

Early in 1768, therefore, it petitioned the King for funds, and also for a naval ship to carry the southern expedition. The King granted £4000 and two ships, one for the South Seas and one for the North Cape. But there was no island whose position was certain in the right part of the Pacific. No British ship had sighted one. Some people thought the Marquesas Islands would do, but when the Spaniard Mendaña had discovered them he had only the vaguest idea of where he was, so before they could be used they would have to be 'discovered' all over again. The Royal Society accepted that it would have to start with a voyage of exploration, but time was getting short if it had first to find an island, and then be ready to observe the transit in June the following year. It wanted to send out a ship at once, in March; but by March a ship had not even been chosen. Then, in April, Wallis came home with the *Dolphin*, and the first part of the problem was solved: he had found an island in a suitable position, and had observed, using lunars, exactly where it was. There were no second thoughts: King George's Land was to be the place.

But there was the question of a captain. The Royal Society had assumed all along that a man called Alexander Dalrymple would command the expedition. Dalrymple was an eccentric, who believed and repeatedly said that he was a scientist, an astronomer, a navigator, an explorer, and a ship's captain. Strictly speaking he was none of these things. He had worked for the East India Company and had travelled quite a lot in the Indies, but never as a captain and never more than twenty miles from land. The rest was a dream: he was passionately excited by exploration, but all he knew about it was second-hand, from the journals of real explorers; and as for astronomy and navigation, anyone could have learned what he knew from books. However, he was an expert salesman, and persuaded the pundits of the Royal Society, very clever but perhaps unworldly men, that he was everything he said he was.

Not so the Admiralty. One thing he could not pretend to be was a naval officer, and the Admiralty was adamant: it was happy to provide a ship and crew, but only a naval officer could possibly be allowed to command it. It merely informed the Royal Society that it had bought a ship into the navy for the voyage, and asked what instructions the Society wished it to give its commander. When Dalrymple was told of this, he refused to go on the expedition at all.

Yet the Admiralty's choice has surprised historians ever since. There were many captains and lieutenants on half pay who would have been happy to go, but the man it chose was not a commissioned officer at all. Mr Cook was a master, which was the highest rank of warrant officer, and normally a dead end with no hope of further promotion. A master's usual job was the practical and technical work of sailing a ship wherever her captain decided she should sail, and Mr Cook had done this too: but his main job had been surveying, and his only command had been a surveyor's schooner. He had made a name for himself in the highest naval circles by the meticulous accuracy of his charts of the River St Lawrence and the coast of Newfoundland, but it needed a stroke of brilliance in the Admiralty to detect his latent genius: the genius for always going further than anyone else would have gone, for commanding utterly isolated ships on voyages years long, for keeping men healthy and contented, and for understanding people of distant races. It is the last of these qualities that most concerns us here. Cook was the ideal observer of Tahitians: shrewd, dispassionate, tolerant (except of stealing), thoughtful and sympathetic, but never sentimental; and the prose he used to describe them was like himself: plain, unostentatious, wise, and perfectly lucid.

Many people have thought Cook chose the ship for his voyage; she came from the Yorkshire port of Whitby, and so did he. But the ship was chosen by the Navy Board, which was in charge of all naval ships, and Cook was appointed three or four weeks later – and it was later still before he learned the sort of voyage he was expected to make. No doubt she was the kind of ship he would have chosen if he had had the choice – she was the kind he did

choose for his later voyages. But the first time, it was coincidence –
unless perhaps the Navy Board was consciously looking for the
same qualities in the ship that the Board of Admiralty was looking
for in the commander: a rugged reliability.

She was a cat-built vessel, or cat, under four years old, called
the *Earl of Pembroke*, which happened to be lying idle in the
Thames. Cats were built for carrying cargo, mostly coal, up and
down the east coast of England; they were the ships, and this was
the trade, in which Cook had learned his seamanship before he
joined the navy. Cats were slow, strong, broad in the beam and
almost flat in the bottom – built that way so that if they ran
aground on a North Sea sandbank, which was apt to happen with
the best of pilots, they could sit there undamaged and nearly
upright until the tide took them off again. It was expected to be a
useful build for exploration. For her size, a cat could stow far more
stores than a naval ship, she could be beached for repairs, and if
she ran aground by mistake she had a good chance of surviving.
The Admiralty bought the *Earl of Pembroke* for £2800, changed her
name to *Endeavour* and listed her as a bark.

This famous ship was small: 104 feet in length overall (the
Dolphin frigate was 130), just under 98 feet on her upper deck, 29
feet 3 inches in beam, and in tonnage 369. In trade, she would
have been sailed with a crew of less than twenty, and at first the
Admiralty planned to give her thirty-five for her long projected
voyage. But all through the weeks of preparation more and more
men were added, and in the end ninety were crammed on board,
with everything they needed for two years all alone. A crew of that
size could not be commanded by a mere warrant officer, but
rather than change their minds, the Admiralty commissioned
Cook as lieutenant. It was unusual to commission a warrant
officer, and it did not always work. Sailors were snobbish: they felt
they had a right to be commanded by gentlemen, and warrant
officers were not defined as gentlemen; sailors felt degraded if
their captain was what they called a 'tarpaulin'. But it worked
very well with Cook. He would never have claimed to be a
gentleman, but he had a natural authority that nobody defied.
Before she sailed, second and third lieutenants were appointed to
serve under him.

Among the last additions to her company was Mr Joseph
Banks, who brought with him a 'suite' of eight people. Banks was
twenty-five years old: when he was eighteen, he had inherited a

large estate in Lincolnshire and a very large income to go with it. He had been to school at both Harrow and Eton, and had then read botany at Oxford. His home and Cook's were not very far apart, but they could not have been further apart in background: Cook the self-made man, the son of a farm labourer, and Banks the spoilt child of landed gentry. It was astonishing that they survived three years of claustrophobic confinement together, and were still friends at the end of it. It might have been a disaster, but it was saved by Cook's patience and tolerance and Banks's boyish, exuberant charm.

Banks might easily have been a playboy; most men who were so rich so young would have gone that way. But he had a passionate hobby: botany. The great Linnaeus, who began the classification of plants, was still alive and active in Sweden, and Banks regarded himself as one of his many disciples. He was perfectly willing to spend his vast income on two things: social life in London, where he bought a house and made friends of most of the leading scientists of the day; and collecting new species of plants from the remotest places he could reach. He expected that this voyage would help him in both activities, and it did: it made him a social lion, and also a respected figure in the world of science.

One begins by feeling suspicious of Joseph Banks, as Cook must have felt when he met him. Nobody deserves to be so rich. But he certainly became an asset, and so did his 'suite'. This was an age when no firm boundaries separated the sciences, and an inquisitive man could comprehend them all. Banks's botany could easily be stretched to all kinds of biology and zoology, and even to facts that finally found a place in ethnology, sociology, or psychology. He collected not only plants but animals, insects, birds and fishes, pickled them all and brought them home. With the same impulse, he tried to collect a man and bring him home alive. Cook did not like that idea, and it failed; the man died on the way, and so did a boy he brought with him as servant. But Banks extended his energy to studying Tahitians, and got to know them better than most.

The senior member of his 'suite' was Dr Daniel Solander, a Swedish botanist and pupil of Linnaeus, who had a dull but respectable job at the British Museum. His knowledge was much more deep and solid than Banks's, but narrower. Purely a botanist, he was the man who, with endless patience and energy, catalogued and preserved the specimens Banks and he collected.

61

What was more important, perhaps, he was a man that everyone liked, cheerful, modest, and friendly. Then there were two artists, Alexander Buchan, a painter of portraits and landscapes, who had the misfortune to be epileptic and died in a fit soon after he reached Tahiti; and Sydney Parkinson, a serious-minded young Quaker with an astonishing talent for drawing plants and flowers in watercolour. Banks's secretary was another Swede, Herman Spöring, who, among other things, had been a student of surgery and a watchmaker. He also brought four servants with him – two Lincolnshire men from his estate and two black men, both of whom died of cold on an expedition ashore in Tierra del Fuego – and two greyhounds.

The baggage of these people took up an enormous amount of space: not only their clothes for every occasion and climate, but also a library of natural history, all kinds of 'machines' for catching insects and fish, cases of bottles for specimens and boxes for seeds, chemicals and waxes, and 'even a curious contrivance of a telescope, by which, put into water, you can see the bottom at a great depth, where it is clear'. To accommodate all the people and all their activities, the cabins – not for the first time – had to be rearranged and all the officers, including Cook, moved into tighter quarters.

Banks, Solander, Buchan, Parkinson, Spöring, and Cook himself: these were not all the learned men on board. There was William Monkhouse, the surgeon, William Perry, the surgeon's mate, and Charles Green, another Yorkshire farmer's son, who had been assistant to several astronomers royal and was appointed by the Royal Society to help Cook with the observation of Venus and also the endless mathematical labour of navigating by lunars. There were several experienced explorers too, men who had sailed with Byron or Wallis – among them John Gore, the American master's mate, now promoted lieutenant, who had joined the *Endeavour* from the *Dolphin* after only two or three weeks in England. All these men, one way or another, were trained in scientific thought and observations.

From March to August 1768, the history of Tahiti had passed from the island, where nothing unusual was happening, to the august headquarters of the Royal Navy in Whitehall and the Royal Society in the City of London, and many of the finest brains of Britain had been applied to it. Not that the island or its people were their prime concerns: those were, first, the transit of Venus and then, as ever, the discovery of the great southern continent. But they recognized that their bevy of scientists could not visit Tahiti without observing Tahitians, and among the voluminous instructions the *Endeavour* carried was one that applied to the people they would meet. It was written by the Earl of Morton, who was president of the Royal Society, under the modest heading 'Hints offered to the consideration of Captain Cooke, Mr Banks, Doctor Solander, and the other Gentlemen who go upon the Expedition.' It reminded the gentlemen to observe the utmost patience and forbearance with the natives, to check the petulance of the sailors, and restrain the wanton use of firearms. Shedding the blood of such people would be a crime of the highest nature. 'They are the natural, and in the strictest sense of the word, the legal possessors of the several Regions they inhabit . . . They may naturally and justly attempt to repell intruders, whom they may apprehend are come to disturb them in the quiet possession of their country.' If violence could not be avoided, then 'the Natives when brought under should be treated with distinguished humanity, and made sensible that the Crew still considers them as Lords of the Country'. The gentleness was the same that most rulers recommended to most explorers, but there were two remarkable omissions: the *Endeavour* carried no instructions to claim possession of the island – on the contrary; and although Lord Morton hoped the captain, having no chaplain, would lead the crew in prayers, there was no suggestion whatever of preaching Christianity to the natives.

With these good intentions, the *Endeavour* came to anchor in Matavai Bay on 13 April 1769 after a voyage of eight months, two years after the *Dolphin* had left the same place amidst Oberea's tearful farewells. Many people have described the sight of that bay from the sea, but the most eloquent description was not written until the twentieth century. It is in one of the many biographies of Cook, the one all scholars think the best, by Dr J. C. Beaglehole. 'It is a superb Bay,' he wrote, 'its long line of black volcanic sand backed by the tall innumerable pillars of coconut trees with their wild crowns, immobile and sculptured in a hot still noon or a moon-charmed night, stirring like vast bunches of pennants on a rising wind; given sobriety by the deep green of the sand-haunting casuarinas, drooping and myriad-fingered; absorbing into a general pattern the splay-limbed untidy pandanus; backed with the splendid breadfruit and ancient-buttressed *mape* or chestnut, their arms extended in benedictions of plenty . . . One sees a perfect curve, beyond and above it the cleft uneven lines of the nearer ridges – "uneven as a piece of crumpled paper", as Sydney Parkinson said; beyond them again, the great form of the mountain, its shoulders and steep flanks falling away still hung with green, the peak of Orofena . . . The warm air remains, in bright day or soft night; the green of spontaneous growth, the smell of earth and blossom; enough remains to show why the eighteenth-century sailor should think himself imparadised.' (Dr J. C. Beaglehole, *The Life of Cook* (The Hakluyt Society and A & C Black, London.)

Imparadised: the word does not often escape from the dictionary, but it was apt; and if paradise could be improved, it was improved by the contrast with ship-board life. For eight months, the survivors of those ninety men (five had died on the way: four by accident, one by suicide, none by sickness) had never been further than arm's-length from their shipmates, and most of the time much closer, pressed into a mass of humanity with never a second of solitude. Even asleep, they were bumped and nudged by the bodies of men in the swinging hammocks around them. Perhaps they longed above all for women, but they also longed for earth under their feet, green trees above, fresh running water, room to move about, and quietness. As soon as the anchors were down, Tahitians came off in canoes bringing coconuts and the branches of peace – among them the old man who had carried the *Dolphin*'s goods across the river, whose name now appeared to be Owhaa. Without waiting a moment, Cook went ashore with Banks and the other gentlemen, Owhaa, and a boatload of men under arms.

One can only imagine his feelings – he did not describe them – as the boat grounded, and he jumped ashore on that beautiful alien beach, treading on yielding sand instead of wood or the green baize carpet of his cabin, then waded across the river, which was only thirty feet wide, and plunged into the paradisiacal shade. Banks and Solander, one can be sure, were in ecstasy — they were always ecstatic when they went for a walk; there were always plants to be found and Latin names suggested for any that Linnaeus had not classified. Cook was perhaps less jubilant, but perfectly confident. He was confident that having found the place, he would make the observation of Venus, and confident that nobody could stop him. But he wanted more than that. He wanted to make friends of the islanders, and to do his work without offending them. There were not many around that afternoon. He supposed that most had run away when they saw the ship. But nobody tried to stop him landing, and those he met 'came to us with all imaginable Marks of Friendship and Submission'. Friendship was what he hoped for, but he expected submission; he expected, like any European captain, to be in charge on the island as he was on his ship. So did Banks. 'It was the truest picture of an Arcadia', he wrote, 'of which we were going to be kings.'

FIVE

The Transit of Venus

————— ••€)(3•• —————

COOK KNEW remarkably little about Tahiti; only what he had learned from the *Dolphin*'s people, who had not learned very much themselves. He had never seen anywhere like it, never landed on a tropical shore, never met a simple race of men except the dismal Patagonian giants and perhaps some North American Indians.

Before Cook landed, he issued a set of five rules, derived from the *Dolphin*'s experience and Lord Morton's 'Hints'. The first was 'to endeavour by every fair means to Cultivate a Friendship with the Natives, and to treat them with all imaginable humanity'. The others ordered that only one appointed person would be allowed to trade (in practice Banks took on most of this job); everyone was to be responsible for looking after his own arms and tools on pain of having to pay for them if they were neglected; penalties were threatened for embezzling or offering ship's stores (no doubt he had nails in mind); and nothing made of iron or cloth was to be given for anything but provisions. On the face of it, that posed a problem: what could the sailors offer to the girls when nails or shirts were banned? But they soon discovered that they welcomed cut-glass beads, and the ship had plenty of those.

It goes without saying that the Tahitians knew even less about the Europeans than the Europeans knew about them. They knew that they disguised their bodies with outlandish clothes, and that they had ordinary sexual appetites but no women – a regrettable state of affairs in Tahitian eyes. Up to a point, they could understand their ships, how they were built and rigged and sailed; there was nothing entirely mysterious in that. They could understand their apparently simple social system, with its one supreme chief – the captain – and its lesser chiefs, whom everyone else obeyed. Perhaps they supposed the officers were descended from gods. But where they came from, and why, and where they were going, and, above all, their behaviour, especially their *taboos*, remained a puzzle. Obviously they were immensely rich, but they did not share their riches, unlike even the meanest of chiefs in Tahitian society. Sometimes they were surprisingly generous, and gave away beautiful nails and very valuable hatchets and rather useless clothes; but most of the time they were miserly and made an inexplicable fuss if anyone helped himself to things he needed, even although they had plenty. They had very little sense of decorum, bad manners, and no respect for religion. They were apt to fall into rages for no reason that anyone could understand, and they punished their own people brutally; yet in many ways they seemed to mean to be kind, and occasionally they showed a sense of humour. It was a pity they were so dirty.

It is remarkable how quickly the Tahitians began to make allowances for all this strange behaviour, and to imagine a totally different country, a different race of men with different standards and beliefs – although they had such limited experience and such a simple language, which depended on gestures, not only words, to express its shades of meaning.

It is also remarkable how carefully Cook did his best not to give offence, and how the officers, and Banks and his gentlemen, followed his lead. They were always aware that they were treading in a forest of susceptibilities, etiquette, and customs which they could not foresee, and they knew they sometimes put a foot down clumsily. The paradise was full of moral pitfalls. When the surgeon, Dr Monkhouse, picked a flower from a tree he was surprised by the islanders' violent resentment – until he understood it was a sacred tree, growing on a *marae*, and that what he had done was like robbing the altar of a village church. On the other hand, when Banks lost his temper and shouted to get his own way, as rich men did in Europe, nobody seemed to be surprised or hurt.

When Cook met a dozen or so of the chiefs and their relations, he was baffled to know what signs of respect he should pay to each of them. In fact, Cook never did sort out the Tahitian hierarchy on his first voyage. He needed to build a temporary fort to protect the astronomical instruments, and he wanted to find somebody in supreme authority to give him permission to do it. He conceived that somewhere there must be a king, but he could not find him, and Oberea, who Wallis had thought was the queen, had disappeared. He had to make do with people who seemed to be subordinate chiefs. He began building his fort and waited to see if anyone objected.

The second day was even more enjoyable than the first. The weather was perfect. Crowds of people came off in canoes and climbed on board ('they climb like munkeys'). It was hard to stop them stealing anything they could reach (they were 'Prodigious Expert' at that), but they were so friendly that at first it seemed only amusing. Two of them appeared to be chiefs, and Cook gave them hatchets; then, with those two and all the gentlemen, he went by boat to another bay, where they met a great crowd of friendly people and two superior chiefs, whom Banks insisted on giving classical nicknames, 'Hurcules' (as Cook spelled it) and 'Lycurgus'. Lycurgus provided a feast of fish and coconuts, and warned the visitors to take care of their pockets; nevertheless, Solander lost his spy-glass and Monkhouse his snuff-box. Banks made a scene about it, and Lycurgus dispersed the crowd: 'the method he made use of was to lay hold of the first thing that came in his way and throw it at them, and happy was he or she who could first get out of his way'. Lycurgus offered the visitors everything in his house in recompense, but they demanded their property back, and he soon retrieved it.

Next day, however, things went wrong. Cook marked out the ground he wanted for the fort, and put up a tent on it. He tried to explain with sign language what he was doing, and nobody seemed to mind. Then he and the gentlemen went for a walk, leaving their armed guard at the tent. Banks, who had some kind of shotgun, brought down three ducks with a single shot, which so surprised the Tahitians that they all fell down as if they had been shot themselves. Probably Banks was also rather surprised. But more shots were heard from the direction of the tent. They hurried back and found that a Tahitian had snatched a musket from a sentry: the rest of the guard had shot him dead, but another islander had run away with the musket. Everyone was horrified. 'What a pity', young Sydney Parkinson wrote, 'that such brutality should be exercised by civilized people upon unarmed ignorant Indians! They fled into the woods like frightened fawns.' It was just the sort of thing Cook hoped would never happen. He resolved it should not happen again, and while he was in Tahiti it never did; but he punished no one, neither the men who had fired the shots nor the officer in charge, who was a midshipman and may have been only a little boy. Cook must have admitted to himself the contradiction in his 'Rules'. He had told his men to treat the natives with humanity, yet to look after their weapons: what then

James Cook by Nathaniel Dance, 1776

were they to do if the natives stole the weapons? He spent the rest of the day pacifying and reassuring the few islanders he could find, but it had been a near thing. Next day, not a single canoe came off to the ship. It was not until he went ashore again, with the gentlemen but without a guard, that a crowd of thirty or forty islanders gathered round and seemed as friendly as ever. The day after that, Cook spent the night ashore in a tent with Charles Green to observe the eclipse of a satellite of Jupiter. He was always willing to take risks for his principles.

The *Dolphin* men were puzzled to find far fewer people on the shores of Matavai Bay than they had seen two years before; puzzled also that pigs were scarce and cost a hatchet instead of a nail, and that Oberea had vanished. She turned up after a fortnight and took a vigorous fancy to Banks, but it was obvious that she had lost her authority. In fact, between the *Dolphin*'s and the *Endeavour*'s visit there had been a Tahitian war, which the *Dolphin* may unwittingly have caused.

The Europeans never did understand that their very presence, however well they tried to behave, upset the stability of Tahitian society; but it was so. It redistributed wealth, aroused jealousy and ambition, and created new desires. Oberea, as mother of the boy-chief of the district and self-appointed regent, had probably always been too ambitious for her son. The presence of the *Dolphin* had made her worse; it enhanced her importance, at least in her own eyes, and made her richer and prouder. She began to misuse her authority and oppress her people beyond the limits a chief was allowed. In particular, she made them build an immense *marae*, or temple, in honour of her son. Cook and Banks saw it and measured it towards the end of their stay, when they made a surveying trip round the island by boat. It was a solid pyramid, mainly faced with squared and polished stones, 267 feet long, rising in 11 steps, each about 4 feet high. It stood on a plot of land 360 feet square, enclosed by a stone wall. The other chiefs could not put up with such ostentation, the toil it caused, and the disruption of ordinary life it represented; so they ganged up to humble her. The war was fought, and Oberea was beaten. Cook and Banks saw the relics of it: fourteen human jaw-bones hung up on a board, and other bones scattered on a beach. Neither Oberea nor her son were injured or punished – that was not the object – but they lost their chiefly power and privilege; and by the time Cook arrived, there were at least two men, and probably more, who were recognized as supreme chiefs, *arii rahi*: Vehiatua in the smaller south-easterly part of the island, and Tu in the larger part (both these names were titles rather than personal names). Cook met Vehiatua, an old man, white-bearded and white-haired, but he did not understand his rank; he did not meet Tu until his later visits, because he was a timid young man who was controlled and kept out of the way by Lycurgus, whose real name was, approximately, Tuteha. Cook never succeeded in sorting out the relationships of all these people – they were in fact all related, but Tahitian family trees were always difficult to disentangle.

Cook knew very well when he had to be reticent in his journal: a journal written for the Admiralty was not the place for revelations. On things he did not understand he often made no more than a wryly humorous comment, often wise. On religion, for example: some of the gentlemen saw the body of the man who had been shot near the tent exposed, according to Tahitian custom, on a raised bier inside a small hut that was built for the purpose, and left there with offerings of food until it had rotted away. The offerings made him conclude that Tahitians had a supreme god and believed in an after-life. 'It is most likely', he wrote, 'that we shall see more of this before we leave the Island but if it is a religious ceremony we may not be able to understand it, for the Misteries of most Religions are very Dark and not easily understood, even by those who profess them.'

He wrote almost nothing at all about the sexual escapades of his crew, although they were going on all the time. His journal was sure to be widely read, even perhaps by the men's wives. In fact Cook was thought to be the only man in the ship who resisted the girls' allures; they were said to have laughed at him as old and good for nothing. If they did, he did not seem to care: it was anyway quite untrue – he was only forty, and his wife bore him six or seven children. He was either a faithful husband or else had too much on his mind, or both. After he reached home and was preparing his journal for publication, he wrote in a letter that he wished it to be 'unexceptionable to the nicest readers', with nothing indecent in it.

He had only one interest in the morality of what his crew were doing: the 'venereal distemper'. Whether that meant syphilis or gonorrhoea, something like half his men were soon infected. But that was not his worry: sailors always caught it in harbour, but seldom badly enough to stop them working. His worry was that so far as he knew, the same thing had not happened to the *Dolphin*. Therefore, somebody must have brought the infection to the island, which he rightly felt was a crime, and he feared it was his own men – in spite of the tests his surgeon had given them. He was vastly relieved when the islanders told him the *Endeavour* had not begun it: it had been brought by two ships that had come in since the *Dolphin*, commanded by a man named Tootteraso. Cook showed the islanders flags, and they picked out the Spanish one. It was not until he reached Batavia, long afterwards, that he learned the ships were French, not Spanish, and that Tootteraso was a Tahitian version of Bougainville. The Tahitians always got names wrong, but seldom so wrong as that. Cook was known to them as Tooté, for a good reason: there was no *k* sound in their language, and words always ended with a vowel. Nor was there any *b*, so Banks was Tapané, which may have had a meaning of its own.

As for what the Tahitians did amongst themselves, Cook was perfectly tolerant: it was their own affair. He had a curious theory that the early 'amours' of the middle-class girls made them physically smaller than girls of the chiefly class.

The fort was built, and named Fort Venus (after the planet, not the Goddess of Love), and everything was ready for the observation of the transit. For a day, it seemed it was going to come to nothing, because a Tahitian got into the fort at night, in spite of barricades, eight guns, and forty-five men with muskets, and took away the astronomical quadrant, a heavy, complicated, and essential piece of equipment.

Thievery was a problem Cook never solved in Polynesia: indeed, it led to his death years later in Hawaii. 'Their behaviour to strangers and to each other,' he wrote, 'is open, affable and Courteous, and from all I could see, free from treachery, only that they are thieves to a man.' He was not unforgiving: 'One ought not to be too severe on these people when they do commit theft since we can hardly charge them with any other Vice.' Yet he always regarded it as a vice, both a sin and a crime. He never went so far as the Frenchmen in seeing the European sense of property as sacred. It puzzled him because they never stole from each other, and annoyed him because it seemed so foolish of the Tahitians to steal things they could not possibly use, like muskets without any powder or shot, or the doctor's snuff box when they did not know what to do with the snuff, or his own stockings when they never wore stockings or shoes. But sometimes they were things he could not do without. The famous quadrant was typical. No Tahitian could have imagined what it was for, or invented any possible use for it; but without it Cook could not make the observation of Venus, and unless it was found and returned the main purpose of the voyage would be missed.

The only means he invented of getting things back were either to impound canoes (but not to smash them up as Wallis had done), or else to take chiefs and keep them in custody. Those were his first thoughts when the quadrant vanished, but Banks and Green dashed off into the woods with the chief they had called Lycurgus, hot on the trail. Cook followed a little later with a small party of men, and met them four or five miles away on their way back, exhausted but triumphant, with the quadrant. By then it was in several separate pieces, which Green said could be put together again. Meanwhile, Cook's orders had been misunderstood and the chief Tuteha had been interned in the fort. He was waiting there gloomily, expecting to be killed. When Lycurgus came back and found him there, the scene, Cook said, was 'really moving. They wept over each other for some time.' The whole episode ended, as such things usually did, with tears, embraces, and gifts all round.

It may be presumptuous now to suggest a reason for the thievery when Cook did not think of one; but such strange behaviour demands to be explained, and a reasonable explanation does exist. Some of his people seem to have thought of it. It was this: that the Europeans' idea of private property and the care they took to defend it appealed to some Tahitians as a challenge to their ingenuity and courage. Meeting the challenge was not a moral matter, and not malicious: it was quite simply a game of skill.

One learns not to generalize about Tahitian customs, and this could not explain every petty unpremeditated theft, but it does make sense of the more spectacular ones. Obviously, to snatch a musket from a member of a squad of armed Marines was very dangerous indeed. Nobody in his senses would have done it for the sake of the musket, but he might have done it to prove to himself and his friends that he had the cunning to plan a way of doing it and the courage to try. To pick somebody's pocket and vanish into the crowd was another demonstration of skill: or to see some cumbersome bit of ironwork on board the ship, and choose a moment to prise it loose, and hide it, and then come back in the dark, creep on board again and lower it into a canoe in spite of the sentries. As soon as they had succeeded, they lost all interest in the thing they had taken. They did not want to possess it. The game was over by then, and it only remained to hand the thing back to avoid reprisals, which they usually did by giving it to a chief.

Seen as a game, taking the quadrant was a masterpiece. Whoever did it did not want the thing or intend to keep it; but it was surrounded by all the protection the Europeans could devise, the fort, the guns, the armed guard, scores of people. Also, it was large and heavy. To get it away was irresistibly dangerous and difficult; it needed the most ingenious plan and plenty of courage, and it was a triumphant success. It stirred up a most satisfactory hornet's nest and an exciting chase. Of course, having taken it miles away they could easily have hidden it where nobody would ever find it, but they did not. The fun was over, they had dared and won and no doubt they were proud of themselves, and they gave it back as soon as they safely could – unluckily, not quite soon enough to save Tuteha from indignity. Cook never tried to find out who had done it. Not even the chiefs would have told him, although they certainly knew not only who had done it, but also why.

As the day of the transit approached, Cook's officers grew tense and nervous. After all, this was the moment they had laboured towards for a year, the object of all those months of voyaging and of at least an equal number of months to get home again. For several days before there were clouds and showers of rain, and on one day a heavy thunderstorm. In case there were clouds on the day, Cook sent out two separate parties of observers, one far down the coast and the other to a neighbouring island. If those parties could make the observation unprotected, was all the elaboration of Fort Venus really necessary? Probably not, but it had seemed it might be in the early days.

Saturday 3 June dawned cloudless, perfectly clear and very hot. The observations were made, and they failed – not through any fault of Cook or the other nine men who had telescopes, but for a reason no astronomer had foreseen. Viewed through the telescopes against the light of the sun, the planet had no sharp edges but was surrounded by a dark ring which looked like an atmosphere, about an eighth of the radius of the disc itself. Cook saw it distinctly, and so did Charles Green and Dr Solander, who had the most powerful telescope of all. It was impossible to record the exact time when the disc of the planet touched the disc of the sun, or when it left it again. 'We differ'd from one another in Observing the time of the Contact much more than could be expected,' Cook wrote in his journal; and that was all he did write at the time, going straight on: 'Sunday 4th – Punished Archd. Wolf with two dozen lashes for theft, having broken into one of the Storerooms and stol'n from thence a large quantity of Spike Nails.' It was as if the disappointment was almost too much to think about, as if they had all been sent on a colossal fool's errand. Cook seems to have had some vague hope that when he brought the results of the observations home the great astronomers would be able to make something of them. But in the back of his mind he must have known they were useless and that all their labour had been wasted; and it would have been no comfort to foretell that the same method would fail again a century later, as it did in the transits of 1870 and 1882.

After the transit was done, Cook stayed a month more in Tahiti. His boat voyage round the island took nearly a week, and there was work for all hands in repairing the ship, careening her, stocking her with water and firewood, demolishing the fort, and getting back on board all the guns and equipment. Anyway, he had time to spare. It was still the southern winter, and he could afford to wait until spring before beginning on the second part of his orders, which was to sail far south and either discover the great southern continent, or prove it did not exist.

On the whole it was a happy month, with Tahitian concerts, which Cook privately thought were rather boring, and British and Tahitian feasts. Banks managed to get himself invited to a funeral, which meant stripping to a loin-cloth and blacking himself all over and dashing around in the woods like a bogey frightening everyone. He and Cook and Solander enjoyed sleeping ashore in natives' houses, though they soon learned that they had to keep a careful eye on their clothes. It was on one such occasion that Cook lost his stockings, which were taken from under his head even though he was sure he had not been asleep; and Banks, who spent the night with Oberea, seems to have woken up with nothing to put on at all. For Cook the month was marred by what he always regarded as stealing, and not only of clothes. He seems to have lost his patience entirely when a Tahitian used great ingenuity to steal an oven rake, of all things, from the fort. To get it back, Cook seized all the canoes he could lay his hands on, twenty-two of them, and impounded them in the river behind the fort. The oven rake was soon returned, and the fishermen he had ousted from the canoes demanded them back. But Cook then threatened to burn the canoes unless all the other things that had been taken were returned, too. The list of things still missing was really negligible compared with all the things Cook had given away: one musket, a pair of pistols that belonged to Banks, a petty officer's sword and a water cask, and 'some other Articles not worth mentioning'. But he really had no intention of burning canoes, and the threat was no use: the Tahitians simply could not see the difference between the things they were given and the things they took. Some said Tuteha had these objects, and Tuteha's friends said Oberea had them. Nobody would admit that he knew where they were, and the canoes, which were full of fish, were beginning to stink the fort out. Cook had to surrender.

Perhaps there was some sort of justice in that, but there was none in an episode when the ship was at last ready to sail. Two young Marines named Clement Webb and Samuel Gibson disappeared, and Cook was told they had each got a wife and had run away to the mountains.

Of course the ship could perfectly well have sailed without them: two Marines were not a serious loss. But to let them get away with it would have been a dangerous precedent. Long afterwards, it was said that a great many people had thought of deserting – that Banks's gentlemen, among others, had discussed the idea and had only given it up when they heard the crew was discussing it too. This was probably true. Banks's suite had no tie of loyalty except to him, as the man who paid their wages, and he himself had no loyalty to anybody. To a man like Solander, or even to Banks himself, it must have been tempting to spend a year or so in Tahiti, finish their researches and go home when another ship came in, to earn undying fame as the first people to live on a South Sea island and learn all there was to learn about it. But they would not have wanted to be part of a mass desertion. As for the crew, life in Tahiti had obvious charm compared with life in a naval ship or an English dockyard town. Besides, many of them, like Webb and Gibson, had fallen in love.

Cook must have known very well there was a risk of a general desertion, so he collected five chiefs and imprisoned them first in the fort and then aboard the ship, and said he would not let them go until their people brought back the two Marines. Perhaps this was expedient – it was the only thing he could do – but it certainly was not fair. The Tahitians were not to blame: the two young men had not been abducted; they had gone in pursuit of love, and their love was no less real for being inconvenient. Cook's treatment worked in the end: the Tahitians found the men and brought them back. But all the Tahitians were bitterly hurt – for the moment – at having their revered and holy chiefs so badly treated.

One cannot help feeling that Cook was never at his best and greatest in Tahiti. There is no doubt whatever that he loved the place and its people: he went back there whenever he could, wrote of it all with affection, and always sought for and found excuses for everything the people did. Yet perhaps it was rather too soft for him, too languorous and easy-going – in fact, too paradisiacal. He was at his best in adversity and hardship, in the Antarctic ice. in gales at sea, on dangerous shores or in the endless fight against scurvy. He was equally patient and gentle, or more so, with people much less conspicuously attractive than the Tahitians: the Alaskans, for example, or the Australian Aborigines. It must have been hard to care so much about those other peoples: the Alaskans' life, for instance, seemed so dismal that nothing civilization could do to them would make it very much worse. It was the Tahitians' happiness that made them so vulnerable, and Cook cared desperately about what civilization was going to do to them.

Perhaps the transit was a bad beginning in Tahiti. It was an alien job, not a job for an explorer, and it put Cook in a position he would never have chosen: he had to send almost all his men ashore every day to build and then demolish the fort, and about half of them every night to man it. He could not control them when they were ashore as he could when they were on board, whatever rules he made; he could not know how they were treating the Tahitians, or what impression they were leaving on their minds. To trespass in paradise was a grave responsibility; he did not need Lord Morton's hints to make him feel it keenly. But sailors could not be expected to feel the same. No doubt there were kind, gentle, and even sensitive men among them, but most, one cannot deny, were ignorant, tough, drunken, and probably sadistic, and only cared for the most they could get for a cut-glass bead or a stolen nail.

Yet it was the sailors who were giving the Tahitians their introduction to civilization.

Banks, too, may have been sensitive, but he was selfish; he had got his own way all his life, and was not inclined to change. Cook could cope with him aboard the ship, but ashore it was certainly harder. Everywhere Cook went, Banks went too, usually bringing Solander. His youth, good looks and self-confidence made him as much at home in a Tahitian hut as he was in a London drawing-room. He made himself very useful, but he behaved as he liked: he made his own friends, did not care if he made enemies, and had no hesitation in charming any woman into his bed, sometimes two or three at a time – nor, to get his own way again, did he hesitate to treat Tahitian chiefs like under-gardeners in Lincolnshire. This must have put Cook under a strain, and perhaps caused him a twinge of either envy or disapproval. He never let it show, but it cannot have been easy.

Nor was Cook the least bit satisfied with his own behaviour. The shooting, the venereal infection, the internment of chiefs – all these he felt he should have avoided, without knowing how he could have done it. 'We are likely to leave these people in disgust at our behaviour,' he wrote, two days before he raised his anchors. But this remorseful comment was too gloomy. Tahitians were always forgiving, and in spite of everything they still liked the Europeans, and wept sincerely when they saw them go.

There is a very brief glimpse of Cook a few days after he had left the island, and it shows him relaxed and happy again, his true self and the pure explorer, as if he had shaken off his regret for Tahiti. He still had a short time to spare before he had to head south, and he decided to have a look at the neighbouring islands. One of these was Huahine, about a hundred miles west of Tahiti.

Banks had insisted on bringing an addition to his suite, a man he wanted to take back to England as a specimen. 'Thank heaven I have a sufficiency', he wrote in his journal, 'and I do not know why I may not keep him as a curiosity, as well as some of my neighbours do lions and tygers at a larger expense than he would probably ever put me to.' The man was called Tupia. Cook did not like the idea of taking anyone away from an island when he could not be sure of ever getting him back, but Banks talked him into it. The crew did not like Tupia, who expected to be treated as a gentleman. However, a small boy he brought with him as servant, called Taiata, became 'the darling of the ship's company'; and Tupia himself was useful at Huahine, because he had been a high priest (as well as a navigator and one of Oberea's lovers), and was able to perform the proper religious ceremonies expected of visitors.

At Huahine Cook struck up an immediate, genuine and uninhibited friendship with the supreme chief, an elderly man called Ori. 'He had not been long on board,' he wrote, 'before he and I exchanged Names, and we afterwards address'd each other accordingly.' The chief, in other words, called him Ori, and he called the chief either Cook or Tooté. Cook had never done this with anyone in Tahiti, but he knew its significance: it promised the friendship would be life-long, and so it was. He gave the old gentleman a pewter plate, inscribed 'His Britannic Maj. Ship Endeavour, Lieut Cook commander, 16 July 1760 Huahine.' Ori promised never to part with it, and he never did. On that voyage Cook only stayed long enough to survey the island. When he went back on his second voyage, four years later, the 'brave old chief', as he called him, fell on Cook's neck and embraced him while tears of joy 'trinckled' down his cheeks. In his journal, Cook confessed he regarded this old man as a father, and Ori received him 'more like a son than a friend'. Ori feared they might never meet again – in another four years they might both be dead – but Cook, he said, should send his sons, who would always be well received in Huahine.

This was the most open private affection Cook expressed for anyone in his voyages; and here, one feels, he was being himself, and treating a native chief as he had hoped to treat the leaders of Tahiti, as equal and honoured friends.

Of course the *Endeavour* still had far to go – the southern ocean, New Zealand, Australia, New Guinea, and then the disaster of Batavia. That Dutch port was notorious for tropical disease. Seven men had died so far, out of ninety. After Batavia, thirty-one more died, mainly of malaria or dysentery – the 'bloody flux' – among them Tupia and his boy servant, the first lieutenant, Hicks, the surgeon, Monkhouse, the master, Molineux, the astronomer, Green, Banks's secretary Spöring, and the young artist Parkinson. On 12 July 1771, the *Endeavour* came home, preceded by most of Cook's journal, which he forwarded from the Cape, and by a spate of rumours. At that moment, she was the most famous ship in the world, but the Admiralty sold her and she went back to her trade, hauling coal up and down the North Sea.

SIX

Sailors Imparadised

Just a year after he was home, Cook sailed again for the Pacific with two more ships, *Resolution* and *Adventure*, and in August 1773 he sighted Tahiti for the second time.

Banks and his suite were not with him. What had happened is a well-known story, and really nothing to do with Tahiti. But briefly, after he returned, Cook was content to disappear for weeks, living with his wife and family at home in the unfashionable quarter of Mile End. Newspapers were full of the voyage, but always as the voyage of the celebrated Mr Banks, or of Mr Banks and Dr Solander. It was these two who were summoned to St James's Palace to report their discoveries to the King; summoned again to a conference at Richmond with the King and the president of the Royal Society; summoned to Oxford for honorary doctorates. It was they, not Cook, who won fame for it, and all the praise had made Banks, who had never been modest, an impossibly conceited young man. When he heard that two ships had been chosen for a second voyage, the same kind of ships as the *Endeavour*, he took it for granted that he would be in command, and told the Admiralty the ships were unsuitable and too small. This time, he wanted to take a suite of sixteen people, with more baggage than before, and he insisted that the *Resolution* should have an additional deck and poop for his accommodation. She was altered to suit his wishes. The new upper works made her so top-heavy she could not safely be sailed out of the Thames, and they had to be taken off again. Banks fell into a rage, and said that without a proper ship he would not go. It was silly of him to lecture the Admiralty on the choice of a ship, and he got what he should have expected: letters from the First Lord, Lord Sandwich, and from the Comptroller of the Navy, Sir Hugh Palliser, each of which was a model of how to be crushingly rude in the very politest language. 'It may further be observed,' Sir Hugh concluded, 'that to embark a great Number of Passengers, claiming great Distinctions and spacious Accommodations with vast quantities of Baggage, is incompatible with the Idea of a Scheme of Discovery in the Antipodes: If such Passengers do go, they must be content with the Kind of Ship that is fittest.' In his anger, Banks was very rude to Cook, but Cook refused to quarrel and, in a distant way, the two remained friends.

The second voyage was therefore a purely naval affair. The complement of the two ships together was 193 officers and men, double what the *Endeavour* had carried. But there were no passengers, everyone was firmly under Cook's command, and he had chosen most of the officers and some of the seamen himself. In command of the smaller ship, the *Adventure*, was Tobias Furneaux, who had been second lieutenant of the *Dolphin* and in effective command of her when Wallis and the first lieutenant were sick – and the first foreigner to set foot on Tahiti. A dozen men had come from the *Endeavour*, among them Samuel Gibson, one of the two Marines who had tried to desert in Tahiti. He had become a devoted follower of Cook, and incidentally had learned Tahitian so well that he was used as interpreter. There were two astronomers, William Wales and William Bayly, one on each ship. Neither of them was a naval man, but both had been observers of the transit of Venus, one in Hudson's Bay and the other at North Cape; and now they were both under naval orders. There was also another artist, William Hodges, appointed by the Admiralty. In short, there were two good professional naval crews; and useful though Banks had been, Cook must have been glad to be rid of undisciplined *dilettanti*, privileged, albeit in a friendly way, to argue with him and disregard his orders.

The only fly in Cook's ointment was the Reverend Dr John Reinhold Forster, a Prussian of doubtful qualifications whom the Admiralty had rashly chosen as the expedition's natural historian. Dr Forster was an unbelievably pompous and humourless bore, whose only asset was his son George, who came too. George turned out to be a likeable boy of seventeen who seemed to know more natural history than his father. Everyone was disposed to be kind to George, just because he had the bad luck to be lumbered with such an impossible parent. In Cape Town, Forster insisted on recruiting another foreign doctor as his assistant, a Swede called Anders Sparrman, who also had moments of pomposity but was easier to tolerate.

Tahiti was not the prime objective of this voyage. The objective was to search for the southern continent. Cook's plan, which the Admiralty had accepted, was to go round the world in the direction opposite to earlier voyages in the highest latitude he could, rounding the Cape of Good Hope, passing south of Australia and calling at New Zealand, and only to use Tahiti and other tropical islands for supplies and as refuges in the southern winters. On this voyage, therefore, both his visits to Tahiti were short, and both were uneventful.

Thus it was thirteen months after leaving Plymouth before the ships came almost casually in sight of the island. Cook had only one man sick in the *Resolution*, and that one did not have scurvy. Furneaux in the *Adventure* had a good many scurvy cases. The difference must have been due to Cook's personal care. Both ships had the same food, prescribed by the Admiralty doctors, but it was Cook who took endless trouble to force or persuade the reluctant sailors to eat it, who sent them ashore with orders to gather greenstuff wherever he could, who insisted they should wash, and who kept his decks aired with charcoal stoves. To get the *Adventure*'s sick men ashore quickly, he put in to the nearest harbour in Tahiti, which he had noticed on his boat journey the time before. It was on the south-east corner of the island, a long way from Matavai Bay. So it was in the district ruled by Vehiatua.

This time Cook was prepared for both the pleasures of Tahiti and the awful dilemmas of coping with 'thievery'. He was embarrassed to remember how he had offended the chiefs' dignity; but the welcome was just as endearing and friendly as it had always been. After a few days he met Vehiatua – not the old gentleman he had seen on his boat journey, but his son. He thought him a very pleasant young man. Vehiatua spent a day with Cook, walking round arm in arm and sharing the stool which was his chiefly throne. Vehiatua asked after Banks and other people he had seen and remembered, and told Cook some Spaniards had been in the islands. He said he hoped Cook would be able to stay a long time.

However, one thing had changed in Tahiti: provisions were now short. There was plenty of fruit to be had and some vegetables, and the *Adventure*'s sick were soon better; but pigs were hard to find, and people who had any said they could not barter them because they belonged to the chief. After a week or so, Cook moved on to Matavai Bay in the hope of finding more. There at last he met Tu, the man he believed was the king, or at least the 'reigning prince' of the island; and there he learned that there had been another war.

It is hard to know what to make of these wars. War was the Europeans' word for them, but it was certainly wrong in its connotations of wholesale slaughter and vast armies on the march. Most of the Tahitians' wars were squabbles between the chiefs, sometimes caused by ambition and jealousy and sometimes by rightful disapproval of a chief's behaviour. Tuteha, whom Cook knew as Lycurgus, had combined with old Vehiatua to overthrow Oberea. Then the two of them had fallen out and fought each other. Old Vehiatua had died, but Tuteha had lost the war and either died or been killed. Tu, whom Tuteha had always concealed from Cook, had survived by running away to the mountains, and had then become very friendly with the new, young Vehiatua. To visitors, it was all extremely confusing, and a century later they might have compared it to Tweedledum and Tweedledee.

At first sight, Cook was not much impressed by Tu. He was tall and dignified – six feet three – and was still under twenty years old; but he was always said to be timid. Timidity was not a quality the eighteenth century admired, and Cook and his men may perhaps have been too quick to look down on him. To try to do him justice, it may only have been that as a young man he was shy, and carried the gentleness of a Tahitian to an extreme. He recoiled in fear when Cook gave him a sword, and could hardly be persuaded to wear it; he disliked the noise of guns, and he often described himself, and was described by his people, as *matau*, which meant frightened. He was not ashamed of it, and his people did not seem to be critical; after all, they were often *matau* themselves, and ran away in flocks when they were threatened, or thought they might be threatened. It was a Tahitian characteristic, and Cook often found it useful. When an entire population suddenly disappeared, chiefs and all, he knew that somebody had stolen something and everyone was in fear of retribution; and sometimes the fright was so great that the stolen object would be returned before he knew he had lost it.

Matavai Bay, though, was still its beautiful dream-like self, both for those who had been there before and the great majority who were seeing it for the first time; and the girls, in most people's eyes, were still charming, still brimming with cheerful laughter, and still astonishingly willing. But in some of the journals of this

The Resolution *and the* Adventure *at Anchor in Matavai Bay* by William Hodges

voyage are the first signs of a reaction against the ecstatic reports of the earliest visitors: the journal of William Wales the astronomer, for example.

Wales enjoyed his visit, like everyone else. He set up his astronomical instruments on the site where Fort Venus had stood. The site was now protected by only four sentries and a rope, so loosely suspended from stakes that parts of it lay on the ground. Four or five hundred Tahitians of all ranks and ages, men and women, stood outside this token barrier to watch him make his observations, and 'none of us received the least insult or incivility from any of them . . . I scarce ever in my life passed four more agreeable Days than those were.'

While Cook was formally entertaining and being entertained by Tu, Wales made a particular friend of Ereti, the chief whom Bougainville met; a good-natured man, Wales said, sensible and intelligent, who 'readily comprehended our meanings, and enabled us to understand his own'. Ereti often came to breakfast and dinner at the astronomer's camp. He sat at the table, liked tea and biscuits and butter, and even took a glass of port to drink to the health of King George: 'It is true he made strange faces at the first, and some wryish ones even at the 3^d & 4th Glasse; but before we parted, Ereti could drink it with almost as good a grace as ourselves.' It never occurred to Wales, or to anyone else so far as one knows, that it might be wrong to give a Tahitian a taste for alcohol.

One gets the impression that Wales was a good man, perhaps rather too good and solemn, although he wrote with humour; and also that he might have suffered from having his leg pulled by fellow astronomers when they heard he was going to Tahiti. For whatever reason, he was plainly determined not to be ecstatic. Bougainville, he said, had made Tahiti seem 'a Mahomet's Paradise'. He had to admit it was beautiful; but so was any island after a long voyage, and England was just as good. The 'Personal Beauties of the Tahitian Ladies' had also been exaggerated: their stature was small, their features, though regular, had a masculine turn, their noses were flat and their mouths were wide, and their eyes were 'exceeding black and lively', but 'rather too prominent for my liking'. He did not need imagination, he wrote, to describe every part of them down to their very toes; there were plenty who took no care to hide their beauties.

On the other hand, while he tried to deny their attraction, he also felt he had to defend their characters. Those who were willing to 'grant the last favour', he believed, were a distinct class of prostitutes, like those in London. No married woman would do it unless she was made to by a mean husband, and nor would most of the unmarried women. Tahitian ladies had been given a false reputation: one might as well judge all English ladies from the ones who boarded the ships at Plymouth. In fact Wales, like many people after him, had missed the point. In trying to defend Tahitian girls and prove they were not wicked, he had claimed they were guided by the same moral standards as English girls, which was manifestly untrue.

But there was one grain of truth in what he said. By the time he arrived there, the original free and spontaneous welcome of the Tahitian girls had begun to degenerate. This was the sailors' doing. A Tahitian lover might have given a flower to his girl, but he had nothing more to give. The sailors, accustomed to paying prostitutes, gave more, and gave it not as a token of love but as a fee; and the girls had begun to expect it, and even in the end to demand it. Possibly Tu had something to do with this. The sailors disliked him because they said he charged a toll on the teenage girls who flocked ashore from the ships every morning, or out of the tents. If he did, it does seem excessively mean, although as their supreme chief, their *arii rahi*, he had a right to take whatever he wanted. It also, rather vaguely, seems to make an immoral act of what had been innocent, and thus to have been another step on the downward path from the loving sharing of pleasure the Tahitians had enjoyed, towards the dismal traffic of Plymouth or Wapping. Possibly it was also the cause, or one of the causes, of a new tendency Cook noticed at this time. When the sailors had run out of shirts to use as payment, the girls began to ask for dresses of native cloth. They went ashore in the morning wearing their new finery, and came aboard the same evening dressed again in rags, hoping to be fitted out anew.

Cook, however, had no interest in the girls, not even when there were more girls then men in his ships. His interest was in pigs, and Tu's country was as short of pigs as Vehiatua's. Nobody explained exactly why. Cook guessed that either his own ships and others had already taken too many, or else, more probably, that the war had disrupted pig-keeping or even killed off the pigs: winners in wars had been known to destroy the houses and goods of the losers. Whatever had started the shortage, the supreme chiefs had evidently put a *taboo* or embargo on pigs to build up the stocks again – and when people tried to explain that, it was not surprising the English understood them to mean that the pigs belonged to either Vehiatua or Tu. In a sense, they did. But the ships were in urgent need of meat, and after a fortnight Cook left Tahiti, in the usual scene of grief, to try the neighbouring islands, where he had much more success. In four days on Huahine, his friend Ori supplied so many pigs – three or four hundred – that it became a problem not to feed the crews, but to find enough fodder to feed the pigs.

That was in early September 1773. In April Cook was back again, having spent the southern summer exploring the Tonga group, revisiting New Zealand, and edging perilously round the Antarctic ice. He had also been to Easter Island and the Marquesas, which had not been seen for many generations. So he and his people had widened their knowledge and could now make comparisons. The Tongans, he thought, were even friendlier than the Tahitians (he named the group the Friendly Islands), and the Marquesans even more beautiful. But Tahiti remained, so to speak, the heart of Polynesia.

Cook was seriously ill that summer, with something that sounds like an infection of the gall bladder. But when the ship came to anchor again in Matavai Bay, not a single man on board was sick and there was no need, for once, to set up the surgeon's tents ashore.

Cook had intended to stay in Tahiti only a few days, and he chose the bay again only because Wales needed a place whose longitude was exactly known to check the chronometers which Cook was using for the first time for navigation. But Tahiti had changed again, this time for the better. Everywhere were new houses, new canoes, all the signs of returned prosperity: above all, innumerable pigs. What was more, Cook found a new way of bartering. In Tonga, by chance, he and a lot of other people had collected red parrot feathers as souvenirs, and he found that Tahitians wanted red feathers more than anything else – much more than nails or shirts, or the usual beads and 'trinkets'. Red was a holy colour, and red feathers a powerful talisman or religious symbol. For a very small bunch of them the Tahitians would sell almost anything. 'Not more feathers than might be got from a Tom tit', Cook observed, 'would purchase a hog of 40 or 50 pound weight.' Dr Forster reported sourly that the wife of a senior chief, in the hope of earning feathers, 'offered herself to Captain Cook and appeared as a ready victim . . . My spirits were dampened by this unexpected scene of immorality.' He need not have been dampened, for Cook, as ever, declined the offer. So presumably did Forster; but very few others.

Tu, less timid now, came on board with his family and retinue and stayed to dinner; and the next day, to return that call, Cook went three miles along the coast by boat, to the neighbouring bay where Tu had his home. There Cook was astonished to find about three hundred canoes drawn up on the beach, half of them the large catamarans the Tahitians used for war and ocean voyages, and on the shore an enormous crowd of men. By then, Cook had no fear for himself in a Tahitian crowd, however big it was, and he jumped ashore. The crowd divided into two, one group armed and the other not, one shouting 'Taio no Towha' and the other 'Taio no Tu', 'Friend of Towha' and 'Friend of Tu'. Towha turned out to be the man in charge of the fleet. He grabbed one of Cook's hands and an emissary of Tu grabbed the other: 'I was draged along as it were between two parties, both declaring themselves our friends . . . I was like to have been torn to pieces.' Tu was not to be seen; he had vanished inland, *matau* again, because somebody had stolen some of Cook's clothes from the man who was washing them, and he thought Cook would be angry.

It took a long time to discover what was going on, and Cook never sorted it out entirely. Still thinking Tu was king, he offended Towha by regarding him as 'Tu's Admiral'. He was, in fact, another chief, and regarded himself as Tu's equal. Each man, within the next few days, said he was not a friend of the other; yet both of them said they were allies and were going to fight Vehiatua and hoped that Cook would help them. At other times, they said they were going to fight a chief on the nearby smaller island of Eimeo or Morea, who was a vassal of Tu and in revolt, and that Vehiatua was going to fight on their side. It seemed to be true that two chiefs of Eimeo were having a quarrel, and that one of them was Tu's brother-in-law. But Tu had no wish to go and fight for him. Towha, at that moment, was the warlike leader; it was his men who were armed.

All this was probably typical of Tahitian wars. They happened for no reason except that a chief was feeling warlike – in this case Towha. It was almost a matter of chance whom they chose to make war against, or whom they dragged in as their allies. War

satisfied an intermittent instinct, and its political gains or losses were minimal. The dynastic wars of Europe, if one could see them from outside, might look just the same, equally illogical and aimless. But Tahitian wars had one advantage: they did much less harm.

However, this muddled affair gave Cook a chance to see the most impressive display of seamanship and organization Tahiti could manage, and Hodges a chance (at the Tahitians' suggestion) to do the drawings which he worked up later to a series of paintings that are still well known. The double war canoes or catamarans were very big, with enormous sloping stem-posts, some curving and some straight, some plain and some decorated with carving. All of them were rigged with flags and streamers. Cook measured one that was still being built, and it was 104 feet long – as long as the *Endeavour*. He gave Tu a grapnel and cable for it, and an English flag and pennant, and Tu named it *Britannee*.

In war, these big canoes were not sailed, but paddled by thirty or forty rowers. Men who Cook supposed were chiefs or generals stood on platforms, 'drist in their War habits, that is in a vast quantity of Cloth Turbands, breast Plates and Hellmets, some of the latter are of such a length as to greatly encumber the wearer,

Canoes, from a painting by William Hodges

indeed their whole dress seem'd ill calculated for the day of Battle and seems to be design'd more for shew than for use.' The fighting men were on another platform in the bows, armed with clubs, pikes and stones, eight or ten of them in each canoe, but there was only room on the platform for one or two to fight, and Cook surmised they took it in turns.

Among the big canoes was a roughly equal number of smaller ones with masts and sails, each with a little house on it: these he guessed were transports or supply ships. He also saw a few small double canoes 'having on their fore part of kind of double bed place laid over with green leaves each just sufficient to contain one Man, these they told us was to lay their Slain upon, their Chiefs I suppose they meant, otherways their Slain must be very few.' His second guess was the right one: in Tahitian wars, the slain were indeed very few.

At his first sight, Cook was most surprised by the quantity of unsuitable clothes the people were wearing, especially the chiefs or officers. He tried to explain to them that 'when we fought in our ships we took off our Clothes (taking off my clothes at the same time) but they paid little attention to what I either did or said'. From the pictures of their garb drawn by Hodges, however, especially the monstrous headdresses, the men he took for officers were probably *arioi*, who took no practical part in fighting but encouraged the others with prayers or incantations. He hit on the truth when he said their clothes were more for show than for use, and he might have observed that officers in European armies did the same, entering battle in garish, unpractical uniforms. In that era especially, dressing up for war had a psychological purpose. Indeed, not only the clothes but everything about the fleet was a psychological weapon, more for show than war. Its real destructive power was meagre, but approaching an enemy shore it could look intimidating – enough, perhaps, to discourage the enemy and make him surrender without any fighting at all.

As a captain, Cook wondered what battle tactics a fleet like this would use, and probably all his officers discussed it. The general feeling was that it would have to charge an enemy fleet in line abreast, and fight hand to hand like a medieval European fleet or a fleet of Mediterranean galleys. They imagined something like the ghastly carnage of Turks and Christians in the Battle of Lepanto. But Cook discovered later that Tahitians did not really expect to fight at sea. Nobody else in reach had a fleet that was anything like a match for this one. The great assembly was a landing force, designed to put men ashore on a hostile beach; and battle was not expected to begin until the ships were aground and men could jump out and fight waist-deep in the water.

It could not have been only by chance that this formidable force had grown up around Matavai Bay. It was an accidental product of the liking Cook had for that bay; and so was the impending war. He had always known it was foolish to give the Tahitians weapons, especially guns, and he had never done it. But he had bartered or given away huge quantities of axes, hatchets and chisels, not to mention thousands of nails that could be made into tools. The Tahitians were still building the same kind of canoes they had always built – though perhaps bigger – but now that they used iron tools instead of stones and bones and seashells, they could build them quicker. So they had outstripped all their neighbours in the size of the force they could put to sea. By giving them tools, Cook had begun to give them power, a power over their neighbours that no Polynesian chiefs had ever had before. Most of that power, by chance, was going to Tu; and this was the beginning of the process which in the end made Tu what

Cook had mistakenly thought he was, the king of Tahiti – and in doing so, upset the whole system of Tahitian government, from top to bottom.

During this visit, the usual loving friendship was interrupted by the usual fearsome rows about trivial thefts. When somebody stole a water cask and was caught, Cook's revenge was more violent than before. He had the man tied to a post and given two dozen lashes of the cat-of-nine-tails in the presence of Tu, Towha, and some hundreds of Tahitians, who were horrified. Tu did nothing, but Towha made a long speech in which, so far as Cook could understand him, he explained the unfairness and folly of stealing things from the visitors after all the benefits they had brought. Cook thought he had made his point, but a few nights later a sentry fell asleep at his post and somebody took his musket. This time, Tu and everyone else were *matau* and ran away to the hills. But three unknown men came back with the musket, and Cook once more set about the tedious task of pacifying everybody, this time with presents for Tu and – at his request – the firing of twelve guns from the ship 'which he viewed seemingly with more pain than pleasure. In the Evening we entertained him with fire-works, which gave him great satisfaction, thus ended the day and all our differences.' It was the Tahitians' first experience of the alarming joy of fireworks.

Obviously Cook had been pondering for months, if not for years, on his relationship with the islanders, and after the firework show he wrote a long philosophical piece in his journal. Thefts were the only disagreement. He had never thought of them as the Tahitians' idea of a sport, and he never did. Whenever anything important was stolen, everyone took alarm and disappeared, and trading came to an end, which was awkward. Almost always, the chiefs found the stolen things and sent them back; but unless the thieves were caught in the act, the chiefs protected them from him, and would not say who they were. It was in his power to destroy all their property, but he had never done so: if he had, he wrote, 'I was sure to be the looser by it in the end, and all I could expect after distroying some part of their property was the empty honour of obligeing them to make the first overturn towards an accommodation . . . Three things made them our fast friends,' he concluded, 'Their own good Natured and benevolent disposition, gentle treatment on our part, and the dread of our fire Arms; by our ceaseing to observe the Second the first would have wore of[f] of Course, and the too frequent use of the latter would have excited a spirit of revenge and perhaps have taught them that fire Arms were not such terrible things as they had imagined.' It remained, and always would remain, a delicate balance.

Yet without any question, there was a strong affinity between the English and the islanders: and probably the French or anyone else (except perhaps the Spaniards, who were stricter and more experienced colonists) would have felt the same. It was not only the girls: there was affection and admiration also for the men, and many individual friendships. This affinity was most conspicuous when Tahitians took passage in the ships. Before they left England, Banks had requested Furneaux to bring him a Tahitian to replace Tupia, who had died on the *Endeavour*. One wonders why he did not ask Cook, which would have been correct: perhaps it was at a time when Banks was angry with Cook and glad to insult him, or perhaps he remembered that Cook was unwilling to take an islander away from his home when he could not be reasonably sure of taking him back again. But plenty of young Tahitians wanted to go, and on the first visit of this voyage Cook had agreed to take one, because he expected to make a second visit before he went back to England. He had made no strong objection when Furneaux took another. Cook's Tahitian was called Hiti-hiti and Furneaux's Mae, but the English, still putting the super-fluous *o* before names, called them Odiddy and Omai.

It must have taken exceptional charm and personality to join such utterly foreign ships and win the affection and approval both of officers and men. Tupia had not quite succeeded: the officers found him highly intelligent and useful, but the crew disliked him because he expected to be treated as a gentleman – to be Banks's protégé was perhaps an added strain. Tupia's servant Taiata, the 'darling' of the *Endeavour*, succeeded without really trying, and was mourned as sincerely as anyone when died. Odiddy was also a success. He went to New Zealand and the Antarctic ice in the *Resolution*, and though not especially clever he was always good-natured, sweet-tempered, kind and eager to please, and everyone loved him, from Cook to the least of the sailors. 'A youth of good parts,' Cook summed him up, 'and like most of his countrymen of a Docile, Gentle and humane disposition.' Omai was rather more of a problem in the *Discovery*. He also did his best, and never offended anybody, but praise sometimes went to his head and made him vain and foolish. He had pestered Furneaux to take him to England, and Furneaux had promised he would. From the very beginning, that fed Omai's conceit. To be the first Tahitian to go to England made him expect to be famous – and famous he was in the end, but it did him no good. Cook referred to him once in his journal as 'dark, ugly and a downright blackguard', but he crossed the words out before the journal was published, and he only said it, perhaps, because he felt strongly that Odiddy would have been a better representative of his race.

The two ships had been separated in New Zealand, and so Odiddy was the first Tahitian to come back from a long ocean voyage, and Cook had to face the problem of what to do with him. He had been clever enough to learn more English than Cook had learned Tahitian, and Cook relied on him as an interpreter and a messenger he could trust. Tu was greatly impressed by Odiddy's stories of storms, strange lands, and ice, and begged him to stay in Tahiti. On the other hand, scores of his shipmates begged him to stay with them and go to England. Dr Forster, aping Banks, wanted to take a man of his own and have him taught carpentry. Cook said he would certainly not take more than one, and if he took one it would be Odiddy; and the doctor went off in a huff.

Nowhere can one more clearly see Cook in a personal dilemma. It is obvious he was fond of the lad and wanted to take him. Yet he knew Odiddy would be his private responsibility, and it might be life-long. What if Odiddy was miserable in England, and he was unable to bring him or send him back home? He left it to Odiddy to decide. After going to see Tu, 'this youth I found was desirous of remaining at this isle and therefore told him he was at liberty to remain here or at Ulietea [which was where he came from] and Frankly told him that if he went to England it was highly probable he would never return, but if after all he choosed to go I would take him and he must look upon me as his Father, he threw his arms about me and wept . . . He was very well beloved in the Ship for which reason every one was persuading him to go with us, telling what great things he would see and return with immense riches, according to his Idea of riches, but I thought it proper to undeceive him, thinking it an Act of the highest injustice to take away a person from these isles against his own free inclination under any promise whatever much more that of bringing them back again, what Man on board can make such a promise as this.' In the end, to put off the

95

decision, they compromised, and Cook agreed to take Odiddy to the island of Ulietea.

At the same time, there was a reciprocal problem. John Marra, the Irish gunner's mate, decided to stay in Tahiti, and while the ship was sailing out of the harbour he slipped overboard and swam for the shore. He was seen, picked up by a boat and brought back. Desertion from the navy was, at least in theory, a capital offence, but Cook only confined him until they were out of swimming distance and did not punish him at all. His opinion had changed since the two Marines had tried it on the earlier voyage, and now his view, for a naval officer, was most unusual. He had picked up Marra in Batavia, he wrote, and the man had been with him ever since. 'I never learned that he had either friends or connection to confine him to any particular part of the world, all Nations were alike to him, where then can Such a Man spend his days better than at one of these isles where he can injoy all the necessaries and some of the luxuries of life in ease and Plenty . . . I know not if he might not have obtained my consent if he had applied for it in the proper time.'

In Ulietea, where Cook was to leave Odiddy, there was a trivial but pathetic event. Odiddy invited Cook to what he called his *fenua*, which meant estate. There, he said, he could give him an abundance of pigs and fruit. Cook went with him by boat, taking also Dr Forster and his son, with the chief of the island and his wife, son, and daughter. It was a pretty place with a cluster of houses like a village; but when Odiddy arrived with his very distinguished guests he found his brother had taken it over in his absence. Odiddy could not provide any of the gifts he had promised, and the brother made only a formal and minimal presentation of two pigs. No dinner was offered, and to relieve Odiddy's unbearable embarrassment Cook ordered one of the pigs to be killed and cooked at once – and watched and later described the whole process. By the time they went back, 'poor Odiddy', Cook wrote, 'had drank a little too freely either of the juice of peper or our Grog or both and was brought into the boat dead drunk.'

Just before the ship sailed, Odiddy asked Cook to *tattoo* some words for him – to write him a testimonial – and Cook very gladly did so, 'to recommend him to the Notice of those who might come to these isles after me'. But it is not recorded that Odiddy ever showed it to anyone who could read it. He stayed on board until the *Resolution* was almost out of the harbour, and had the final pleasure of firing some guns, as a salute to the island and to mark King George's birthday.

Several of the many journals mentioned that parting moment. 'At ten,' the first lieutenant wrote, 'Weigh'd and sail'd out of the Harbour, at which time our friend O Diddy left us, universally beloved by us all.' John Elliott, who was an able seaman and himself only fifteen years old, called him 'our Young friend and companion, sensible and well-disposed', who had been 'very happy with us, for seven months.' And Cook: 'Our faithfull Companion Odiddy left us with great regret, and nothing but the fear of never returning would have torn him from us . . . I have not words to describe the anguish which appeared in this young man's breast when he went away, he looked up at the ship, burst into Tears and then sunk down into the canoe.'

Perhaps Odiddy's story was not important, but it illustrated something very important: the depth of friendship that could grow between Tahitian men and Englishmen. 'I directed my Course to the West,' Cook concluded his entry for that day, Saturday, 4 June 1774, 'and took our final leave of these happy islands and the good People in them.'

SEVEN

'Noble Savages'

———••❦❦❦••———

THE IDEA OF the 'Noble. Savage' is connected mainly with the French philosopher Jean-Jacques Rousseau, who was still alive, though old and scarcely sane, when the first news came from Tahiti. But the central idea – that simple mankind was essentially good and not essentially evil – is much more ancient. The English phrase itself, with its strangely chosen adjective, seems to have started with Dryden a century before:

> I am as free as Nature first made man,
> Ere the base laws of servitude began,
> When wild in woods the noble savage ran.

The word noble may, in fact, have been applied to savages only to give scansion to those lines. A savage, by definition, could not be noble: to be noble he must be more complex than a savage, a barbarian at least. But the idea goes back much further still, to the ancient concept of the Golden Age, or indeed to the story of Eden.

The thought that men and women might somewhere still exist in a state of primal innocence, like Eden before the fall, clung on through the Middle Ages in the legends of the Islands of the Blest, Atlantis, Lyonesse or Hy Brasil – all islands to the west. Those legends were given a kind of reality when Columbus discovered the islands of the West Indies and the Caribs who lived in them – people he greatly admired but, with his successors, cruelly destroyed. For a while the concept of the Noble Savage was transferred to the Aztecs and Incas, until they also were destroyed by Spain. Then it passed to the North American Indians, and English travellers added to it: Drake in the west and Raleigh in the east, for example. By 1770 those savages too were fighting for their lands and lives against the European invaders.

The pure romance of islands also had a long run in English literature, sometimes as simple story-telling in prose, verse, or plays, and sometimes with a satiric or philosophical intent. It had a peak in the 1720s with *Robinson Crusoe* and *Gulliver's Travels* which, each in their own way, were satirical: Man Friday was a Noble Savage, and so were the Houyhnhnms, in spite of looking like horses. In the next few decades there were many more such stories, popular at the time but forgotten now. People's minds were well attuned to islands.

Rousseau had given the Noble Savage a new dimension. He did it in three published 'Discourses', the first in 1750 and the last in 1762. In France he pointed the way which led to the Revolution, but in England he was not deeply or widely understood. Broadly speaking, he believed that man in his earliest stages had no instinct beyond survival and reproduction: all he needed or enjoyed was food, sleep and a woman – any woman. He had little to fear, because nobody envied him; he was not jealous, because one woman was as good as another; he was not unhappy, because he had no ambition; and he had no vice, because he had not been taught what evil was.

But he was blessed or cursed by learning to feel compassion. Its first expression was in family love; but that led him later to vanity, shame and envy – and to industriousness and property. 'The first man who enclosed a piece of land, thought of saying "This is mine", and found enough people to believe him, was the real founder of civil society.' This stage of man's evolution, he thought, with compassion but little else, was the happiest and most stable era, the least subject to revolutions and altogether the very best that man could experience; there was a balance then between the indolence of primitive man and the 'petulant activity of our own egoism'. Most savage races, he said, had been in this state when they were discovered, which 'seems to prove that men were meant to remain in it, that it is the real youth of the world, and that all subsequent advances, apparently steps towards the perfection of the individual, are in reality only steps towards the decay of the species.'

It made fascinating conversation, not only among philosophers who understood what Rousseau was talking about, but also in fashionable parlours, where people only half understood, but were free to express whatever hypothesis entered their heads, or to quote, if they could, some of Rousseau's provocative remarks: 'It was iron and corn which first civilized man, and ruined humanity.' If they said, as many in England did, that Rousseau wanted man to go back to the woods and resume the life of savages, they were wrong. He admitted the process of learning could not be reversed: once the complexities of civilization were adopted, they could never be discarded, whatever vice and misery came in their train. But the general impression, at least on the minds of the English, was quite entrancing: that man in his natural state was both happy and good; that evil was not due to sin, but to the unnatural bonds of civilized society.

Into this receptive philosophic mood, the news from Tahiti rolled like a tidal wave over a low-lying shore, flowing into every cranny.

The savages discovered before had never exactly fitted Rousseau's concept. Africans were regarded only as fodder for slavery; Caribs had the misfortune to be cannibals; Aztecs and Incas were not savages but (in European eyes) barbarians, and North American Indians were a little too warlike in their own defence. But Tahitians seemed to fit perfectly: beautiful, compassionate people, living in simplicity and peace on a beautiful island. This did appear to be, in Rousseau's phrase, the real youth of the world: mankind in the state he had predicated, the happiest and best of all experience, a race preserved by isolation, encapsulated in the innocence of creation.

In France, Bougainville's journal was published in 1771, just before the last of Rousseau's 'Discourses', and was received with the ecstasy he had felt when he wrote it. It seemed to clothe Rousseau's theories with reality, and it enhanced his reputation in revolutionary circles both as philosopher and politician – so that one comes to the unexpected conclusion that the discovery of Tahiti may have hastened the French Revolution. In England the first brief news had been given in Wallis's message to the press; but that said little about the Tahitians except that they were 'pretty much civilized'. The first solid information came in Dr John Hawkesworth's compilation from the journals of Byron, Wallis, Cook, and Banks, in 1773. But Hawkesworth was a journalist, not an explorer or a seaman. He was writing for a public he knew, or thought he knew, and he gave them what he thought they wanted. Many observations in his massive book were entirely his own, and it was put together in such a way that a reader could not tell what was Hawkesworth and what was Wallis, Cook, or Banks. This was the first of many misleading accounts of Tahiti. One has to suppose the explorers themselves told the truth as they saw it: they corroborated each other well.

But other writers, and general gossips too, were inclined to give the island the qualities they wanted it to have.

Of course it was through gossip, at dinner parties or in clubs or pubs or cafés, that the news first spread, before any official reports came off the press. This was particularly so in England after Cook's first voyage, because that voyage had its rich and influential passenger, Banks. Banks displayed his collections and curiosities at his house in New Burlington Street and invited the nobility and gentry to see them; he presented plants to the Dowager Princess of Wales. He became the greatest lion a society hostess could hope for. Everywhere he went he was the centre of conversation, and Tahiti was its subject; and without much doubt he painted its joys in more or less lurid colours to suit his audience. So the idea of Tahiti was launched in England.

Quite separately, it was also launched at the other very distant end of the eighteenth-century social scale: for the aristocratic society and intellectual brilliance of the age were founded on abject poverty. As the sailors' stories spread, beginning in dockyard towns, Tahiti became the centre of them. One might say that Tahiti's Noble Savage was the first philosophical concept other than the teachings of the church to be eagerly discussed by labourers and the people of the slums; and it was the hopeless poor who had most reason to rejoice that somewhere in the world there was a place which had no poverty, no hunger or oppression, where a man (they believed) could live and make love and bring up his family in honest peace, free from the fear of justice or injustice. This was one distinction between England and France. In England, the novel idea made poor men dream of escaping from the over-civilized world: in France, it made them want to destroy that world and build it anew.

When everyone put his own interpretation on what he was told and believed what he wanted to believe, a reaction was bound to set in. Some rich people, though few at first, perceived the new idea – or rather, the sudden revival of an old idea – as the germ of a threat to stability and so to their own position. The churches, though again very slowly, began to see it as a criticism of Christianity; and some intellectuals simply refused to be stampeded into seeming enthusiastic. One of the latter was Dr Johnson. Boswell, as one might expect, was quite carried away by his own naïve enthusiasm. He had sat next to Cook at a dinner, and when their host apologized for the quality of the food he had made what he called a 'tolerable pun': 'I have had a good dinner, for I have had a good Cook' – a man of good steady moral principles, he thought, who did not try to make theories out of what he had seen. He had also been to France and had actually met Rousseau and said how much he admired him, had met Banks and Solander and even, like many other people, imagined himself on a voyage round the world.

But whenever he mentioned Tahiti to the doctor, he was snubbed. The doctor despised books of exploration: 'There is little entertainment in such books; one set of savages is like another.' So far as one can discover, he remained obstinately ignorant of what was being reported; but ignorance did not stop him using his celebrated wit to demolish opponents. Once a 'gentleman' – it may have been Boswell – quoted a traveller: 'Here am I, free and unrestrained, amidst the rude magnificence of Nature, with this Indian woman by my side, and this gun with which I can procure food when I want it. What more can be desired for human happiness?' *Johnson*: 'Do not allow yourself, Sir, to be imposed upon by such gross absurdity. It is sad stuff; it is brutish. If a bull could speak, he might as well exclaim, "Here am I with this cow and this grass; what being could enjoy greater felicity?"' Or in another conversation: *Boswell*: 'I do not think the people of Otaheite can be reckoned savages.' *Johnson*: 'Don't cant in defense of savages.' *Boswell*: 'They have the art of navigation.' *Johnson*: 'A dog or a cat can swim.' *Boswell*: 'They carve very ingeniously.' *Johnson*: 'A cat can scratch, and a child with a nail can scratch.' Or a final example: *Boswell*: 'I am well assured that the people of Otaheite, who have the bread tree, the fruit of which serves them for bread, laughed heartily when they were informed of the tedious process necessary with us to have bread.' *Johnson*: 'Why, Sir, all ignorant savages will laugh when they are told of the advantage of civilized life. Were you to tell men who live without houses, how we pile brick upon brick, and rafter upon rafter . . . they would laugh heartily at our folly in building; but it does not follow that men are better without houses. No, Sir, (holding up a slice of a good loaf) this is better than the bread tree.'

In this last exchange, they were both in the wrong. Boswell had told a typical story of the Noble Savage school, but it was quite untrue of Tahitians. They had never been guilty, as Johnson was, of laughing at things they did not understand – though they did laugh at some Spanish padres a little later; and Johnson, on the other hand, had never tasted or even seen a breadfruit and did not know what he was talking about. He must have felt in the back of his mind that Rousseau and Tahiti bore a threat to the only kind of life he valued, the kind that acknowledged him as the seer of the age. He did not want to know about them, and would not listen.

One reluctantly has to believe that these were among the more intelligent conversations that were going on. Both sides in the great discussion were content to argue without regard for the facts, and both argued themselves into untenable corners: one over-praised Tahitian life, the other attacked it for the wrong reasons. One side put emphasis on the Tahitians' gentleness and kindness: the other replied with their human sacrifices and infanticide. Nobody who had not been to Tahiti, and few who had, seemed to discern that Tahitians lived, and lived successfully, under totally different moral rules – that to understand or discuss them one had to think oneself out of the fundamental tenets of Christian or Jewish morality and make an entirely fresh start.

One can still see their misapprehensions in the work of artists who had never seen Tahiti. Brought up in a classical tradition, they painted their own conceptions of Arcadia. Tahitian girls became woodland nymphs with vaguely Roman draperies, Caucasian features, ample hips, and negligible bosoms. They danced with classic elegance and decorum, among picturesque ruins and European trees. Even the work of the artists who had been there and seen for themselves was modified by the engravers (and engravings were what most people saw) to suit their own preconceptions and sometimes to support an argument.

So far, nobody in England except the explorers had seen a Tahitian. Some Frenchmen had; but poor Aotourou, whom Bougainville brought home with him, had cut very little ice in Paris because he could not talk to anyone. The ten words of French he learned did not get him far (one wonders what they were), and the ten days or so the French had spent in Tahiti had not taught them much Tahitian. Bougainville took lessons from Aotourou on the voyage home; but Bougainville, like Cook in England, had his own job to attend to. So Aotourou was left to take himself to the opera alone.

Into this vacuum came Omai. Omai was quite different from Aotourou. He learned enough English to be endearingly comic ('How do, King Tosh,' he was said to have said when he was

Omai and Tu (above), Odiddy
(below), from drawings by William
Hodges

presented to King George – and Tosh was not a bad attempt at George); but also, much more importantly, he was taken in hand at once by Banks and Solander. He arrived at the critical moment when interest was beginning to flag in insects, pressed flowers, stone axes, and Sydney Parkinson's botanical drawings, and he became the most prized exhibit in Banks's collection. He first stayed in Banks's house in New Burlington Street, in the smartest part of town, where the rest of the collection was on show, and later he was given a household of his own in Warwick Street, just on the other side of Regent Street. Banks and Solander took him everywhere they went, and they could make up for his shortage of English by displaying their own command of Tahitian. So Omai dined with lords and ladies, went to stay in great country houses (including Hinchinbrooke, the home of Lord Sandwich, First Lord of the Admiralty), visited the House of Lords and the Royal Society Club, and made his bow at St James's Palace in a velvet suit. The King gave him an allowance and a sword, and he learned to wear it and make threatening thrusts. Even his occasional social gaffes were excusable, as when he borrowed a sporting gun at a country shoot and blazed away with equal joy at the pheasants and the barnyard hens.

Nobody ever thought Omai was intelligent, but he did not need intellect to succeed in society; good manners mattered more, and many people remarked on his polished manners. Fanny Burney, the diarist, who was still a teenager, found him enchanting: 'Indeed,' she wrote in a letter, 'he seems to shame Education, for his manners are so extremely graceful, and he is so polite, attentive, and easy, that you would have thought he came from some foreign court.' Even Dr Johnson, who deigned to meet him, was struck with the elegance of his behaviour, though he refused to believe it showed a native grace: 'Sir, he had passed all his time, while in England, only in the best of company; so that all that he had acquired of our manners was genteel.' And Cook was beginning to change his mind – a thing he was always willing to do and to admit he had done. 'He had a natural good behaviour,' he wrote in his most schoolmasterish style, 'which rendered him acceptable to the best company, and a proper degree of pride, which taught him to avoid the society of persons of inferior rank. He has passions of the same kind as other young men, but has judgement enough not to indulge them in an improper excess.'

Cook, with his humble origin, was remarkably unsnobbish,

but here even he had drifted into the outrageous snobbery of his age. It seems to have occurred to nobody, not even to him, that Omai might have been happier, and gleaned more useful information, among 'persons of inferior rank'. The despised Dr Forster came nearest to it: he thought he should have been trained as a carpenter or blacksmith. Travelling round the country as he did, Omai could not have avoided seeing the gnawing poverty English society was founded on, but he saw it through the eyes of his companions, who were of Banks's class, and learned like them to disregard it and make use of it for his comfort and convenience: he learned to look down on the poor. Rousseau himself, who scorned the veneer of manners, would have been saddened to know that Omai was taught nothing else; but Rousseau had been forced into exile by the French establishment and was living in obscurity in England and Geneva, and he wrote nothing more after 1772. As for Omai's youthful passions, it was generally thought that plenty of society ladies happily succumbed to the novelty of being seized by a genuine savage.

In the end, the King and Lord Sandwich told Omai it was time to go home. Probably they were reflecting a general feeling – he was growing too conspicuous in London; perhaps Banks was getting bored with him; or possibly, with more perspicacity, they all understood that if he stayed too long, it would get harder for him ever to go back. Anyhow, these two men had the power to send him back; they, of course, handed the problem to Cook.

Omai was a dead loss as an ambassador, either from Tahiti to England or England to Tahiti. Cook had known all along that he was a second-rate example of a Tahitian, apart from his amiable manners; and Furneaux had only chosen him because he pushed himself forward. It was no good regretting Tupia, the man that Banks had chosen, but there were many other cleverer Tahitians who might have learned better English and might have gone far to explain Tahiti in England – to explain, for example, how they navigated, how they governed themselves, why they fought wars and killed their children, or even the deeper mysteries of their religious dogma and their moral ideals. Such explanations, at that early stage of the contact, could have been immensely beneficial and moderated much of the tragedy that was to come. Best of all would have been a committee or deputation, half a dozen wise Tahitians who could have discussed what they saw in England amongst themselves.

Without any such understanding, a reaction against the idea of the Noble Savage began to grow among the intellectuals of England. It was possibly part of a trend from the laxity of Georgian England towards the primness of the following century. Dr Forster, who was more like a Victorian and ahead of his time, took an intelligent part in the debate, which might have surprised his naval shipmates. Rousseau's idea, he pointed out, could not be universally true. The character of primitive men depended, for one thing, on the climate they lived in. He distinguished between 'hard primitives' and 'soft primitives'. 'Hard primitives' were people like the Patagonians or Alaskans, who always had to contend with a hard climate and developed 'hard' characters and 'hard' virtues. It could be argued, and was, that 'hard primitives' needed and showed more virtue in learning to live in their grim, uncongenial surroundings. The Tahitians were 'soft primitives', who had nothing to contend with.

Hard virtues, in those later decades of the eighteenth century, were beginning to appeal more strongly than soft among the English, who were mobilizing opinion for the great war against France. The kindness and gentleness people had praised in Tahitians were not the qualities needed to win a war, or rebuild the British Empire after it. The hardness of military virtues seemed to be what humanity needed for success. This became, so to speak, the official view, the view of philosophers, pseudo-philosophers and statesmen; and it won the support of the growing Evangelical movement and of the men becoming the leaders of industrial revolution.

This was not supported by the poor, except those trained in the military virtues: the very poor, the down-trodden and under-privileged, the men and women and their children doomed to become the victims of war or industry, continued to be enchanted by the thought of Tahiti as the only place they had heard of that was free from oppression and poverty. While some people's fantasies of Tahiti remained simply lustful, a worthier wish survived in the slums of England: a wish for a world of loving kindness.

EIGHT

Spanish Observers

————••✠)(✠••————

WITHIN A FEW MONTHS of that day in June 1774 when Cook said farewell to the islands so sadly, the Spaniards landed a major expedition on the other end of Tahiti. In fact, they had been there once before, in 1772, but their first visit was brief and unimportant; the second was far more consequential. All in all, in the eight years from 1769 to 1777, Cook and the Spaniards each made three voyages which included visits to the island; but they were never there at exactly the same time or in exactly the same place, and neither ever heard what the other was doing except from vague stories the Tahitians told them. The Spaniards were purposely secretive, and while Cook's expeditions won immediate fame, the Spaniards' remained obscurely hidden in their archives.

The Spanish Empire was already nearing its end. The kings of Spain still laid claim to the whole Pacific and all its islands, but it was a hollow claim: they had neither wealth nor power to support a fraction of it. Ever since Drake's first foray in 1578, the colonists in Chile and Peru had lived in apprehension that either the French or the English would appear in their ocean and defeat them.

There was a particular scare in the 1760s, when a rumour spread that the English had made a secret settlement somewhere on the Pacific side of Cape Horn. The Spanish Viceroy in Peru, whose name was Don Manuel de Amat, was ordered by his King to search for and put an end to it; and search he did, sending boats to inspect every creek and island along the tortuous coast of Patagonia. All they found were the rival French and English settlements in the Falkland Islands – not on the Pacific side, but the Atlantic.

Wallis's return to England revived the scare. The Spanish Ambassador in London copied the first announcement in the papers and sent it to Madrid. He then got hold of a renegade seaman who told a more detailed story, which included the correct latitude and longitude of the island Wallis had discovered and named King George's Land. But the Spaniards thought Quiros and others had sailed through that position long before, and no island was marked on their charts. The only island they knew of anywhere near the reported latitude was Easter Island, many hundreds of miles further east. It had been named (in Dutch) by Roggeveen, who sighted it on Easter Day in 1722, but the Spaniards called it David's Island, misreading the name of the English buccaneer Edward Davis, who had reported it, rather questionably, in 1686.

The Spaniards were so suspicious of the British that they argued themselves into a set of false conclusions. First they thought the Falkland Islands so useless in themselves that the settlement there could only be a staging post for supplying a new colony in the Pacific. They did not believe for a moment that the British or the French were only interested in exploration for its own sake: they must have strategic and economic plans which defied the Spanish claim to own the ocean. Next, they were so accustomed to longitudes being wrong that they did not believe the reported longitude, which in fact was right. Then they got in a muddle over the name. In their reports it appeared as either George's or St George's Island, not King George's Land, and that made them suspect that the British were colonizing two islands and keeping their longitudes secret. One of them might possibly be David's or Easter Island. The other might be the island reported by Bougainville and named New Cythera.

Their discussions and speculations went on for years, because they were conducted between the Ambassador in London, the King and his Secretary of State for the Indies, who were in Spain, the Viceroy in Peru and the Governor in Buenos Aires; and it usually took at least eight months to send a letter from Spain to Peru and get an answer back. The final upshot was an order from the King to the Viceroy, in October 1771, to mount an expedition to Easter Island, to search for the other island along its reported latitude, and to inspect them both to discover if there was a foreign settlement there. It still took the Viceroy a long time to organize the voyage, because he had only one suitable naval frigate, which needed a refit, and because he had to borrow money from commercial magnates to pay for it. But at length, in September 1772, the frigate *Aguila* left Peruvian waters, commanded by Don Domingo de Boenechea and accompanied by a chartered store-

ship called the *Jupiter*, under her owner-skipper Don José de
Andia y Varela.

The Spaniards had and still have a terrible reputation as
colonists because of the unspeakable cruelty and destruction of
their conquests in America. But in the South Sea islands they
generally behaved as well as anyone, and when they found Tahiti,
six weeks' sailing from Peru, their behaviour was strictly correct
and not intolerant. The initial credit for this should go to the
Viceroy, who gave them immensely long and detailed orders, in
thirty-six paragraphs, and was held in such awe – a more formidable figure than the distant King himself – that every instruction
he gave was carried out to the letter. The captain was ordered to
warn the crew and soldiery 'to use the most kindly and inoffensive
treatment within the limits of Christian modesty towards natives'.
No men must go ashore except in organized parties, which should
always march in a body and keep their formation; none were to
stray alone or enter the natives' houses; no women must come
aboard. The objects of the voyage were to discover any foreign
settlements, to persuade the inhabitants that the King of Spain
had the sole right to possess their islands, and – no less important
– 'to rescue the natives from their wretched idolatry and to win
them over by discreet and gentle means to a knowledge of the true
God and the profession of our Catholic religion.' So the Spaniards
had little contact with the islanders, except those who came on
board to barter: nothing remotely like the cheerful freedom the
British and French had enjoyed. Even the numbers who came on
board began to dwindle towards the end of the visit because the
islanders had an epidemic of sore throats and feverish headaches –
influenza, perhaps – and some were said to have died of it. They
believed the Spaniards had brought it with them, and no doubt
they were right.

The Spanish ships lay at anchor for a month at the southern
end of the island, as far, by chance, as they could have been from
the places Wallis and Bougainville knew. Their achievements
were mainly negative. Boenechea sent a boat right round the
island, and proved there was no foreign settlement there; though
the boat's crew learned, through sign language, that a ship had
been there and gone away again, and that it was British: several
people recognized the British flag when it was shown to them, and
one of them performed a British song. The official report of the
voyage was as serious, formal and dull as its intentions.

Boenechea sent the Viceroy a list of the island's produce, but not a word about its beauty, and of the people he only remarked that they were 'tractable, very rational and sagacious, friends to their own interests, very astute, but likewise indolent and prone to thievishness, voracious in regard to food and wanton in sexual licence'. He brought four of them, three men and a small boy, back to Peru and presented them to the Viceroy, who looked after them as best he could in his palace: and to flatter that august person Boenechea gave the island yet another name. King George's Land, or New Cythera, was now to be known as Amat's Island. But none of these new names stuck. Boenechea, like Bougainville, had heard the native name, which sounded to them both like Otaheite, and this name crept into reports of all three nations, spelt in every way one can imagine. It was an admission, half-conscious, that the island had a character of its own, not easily to be changed by European pride or the whims of passing travellers. A little later, people learned that the initial *o* was only a prefix, a kind of definite article, as it was in the name of Oberea, who Wallis had thought was the queen. So they left it out and the name became Taiti, Taete, or Tahiti.

In due course, Boenechea's report was sent to the King, who ordered the Viceroy to send the ships again and persevere in founding a Christian settlement.

The second voyage began just after Cook had left in 1774. It had the same ships and commanders but was a much more interesting affair. It revealed five memorable characters. One was Don José de Andia y Varela, the captain of the store-ship, who wrote the first factual, though unofficial, report of Tahitian customs. Two more were priests, who were left on the island to begin converting the people to the Catholic faith, and who failed ignominiously. The fourth was a young private of Marines called Maximo Rodriguez, who was the first European to learn to speak fluent Tahitian and was left there to help the priests: and the fifth was the chief of the area, Vehiatua.

Nothing is known about Don José de Andia, as his colleagues called him, except that he was born and bred a colonist in Peru, and was rather despised by the naval officers, who were often inclined to look down on merchant captains. Boenechea kept him very firmly under command, and did not invite him to attend his councils. But unlike the naval people, who were only there to do their duty, de Andia was fascinated by the island life and was remarkably observant. Of course his long essay about Tahitians was nothing like complete, but it was nearly all confirmed by later explorers, even though he often confessed he might be wrong. He gave the first glimpse of what life in Tahiti was like before the foreigners came. His book was published in Spain in two editions, with a fifty-year gap between them, but like the rest of the Spanish story it was not translated in other countries until the twentieth century. He gave hardly any explanation of how he discovered so much, only that he had done his best to learn the language, and had been helped by Maximo Rodriguez and by his own seventeen-year-old son, who both spoke Tahitian better than he did. But there it all is: everything from the way the Tahitians made their fish-hooks to the way they worshipped their gods, from the way they cooked to the way they navigated, illuminated here and there by a flight of fancy, as when he wrote, of the white sandy beaches of an atoll, that 'it seemed as if Nature, having gone astray in her design to form an island, had woven a green carpet instead, adorned with rich fringes of silver'.

Of the people he remarked like everyone else that they were generally taller and stronger than Europeans, and added that they varied in colour like the mixed offspring of Spaniards and Indians in his home country of Peru. There were a few who were very fair and had blue eyes. 'They possess good features for the most part,' he wrote, 'and would look still better if they were not generally snub-nosed: but this short-coming, accompanied as it is by the natural vivacity with which God has endowed them, makes them very appealing. They are very light-hearted, agile and lusty. The women are few in number compared with the men; but most of them are tall, with handsome figures, and in beauty need not envy those of other nations. They are very endearing, and possess great charm; and although there are some dissolute hussies amongst them, as in every place, those who do not belong to that class show modesty in their dress, their mien and their behaviour.' (The Spaniards, by all their own accounts, rejected the advances of the hussies, which astonished everyone.)

The houses, he observed, were not grouped together in villages but were scattered haphazardly among the coconut and breadfruit trees. Elsewhere, after all, villages began for mutual protection against wild animals or human enemies, and Tahiti had neither. The only four-footed animals were domestic pigs,

View of Tahiti: watercolour by William Hodges

rats, and vegetarian dogs – 'particularly funny dogs,' de Andia wrote, 'because they absolutely do not bark, or at any rate nobody heard them barking.' All these were cherished by the islanders – even the rats, which they fed on fruit, though they put low fences round their gardens to keep the pigs out, and hung their own food in baskets from the rafters where the rats could not get it. They ate the pigs and sometimes the dogs (Captain Cook tried baked dog and liked it). The only dangerous animal was a poisonous centipede, which terrified the islanders.

The roofs of the houses were gabled, efficiently thatched with palm fronds, and the framework bound together with cords of coconut fibre. They had no walls. The breezes blew through them, and only if a strong wind blew the rain in did the people hang up mats to keep it out. These they took down again as soon as the storm had passed. There was no furniture, because the people needed none, except carved wooden headrests as pillows. The floors were covered with dry grass, frequently changed, with mats on top of it; they ate, sat, and slept on the floor, undefended and without any thought that they might ever need defence.

They were always together in families and crowds, and almost always friendly and happy. Their kindness was only disturbed by occasional outbursts of anger, which quickly passed, like children's; and their happiness faded only when the Europeans did something that upset them, like the custom of punishing sailors by flogging.

Sleeping was a prime occupation: the Tahitians slept all night from dusk to dawn, and slept again in the heat of the day. When they woke up they talked and sang, and spent much of their time in competitive sports and games – archery, dancing, a sort of football that the women played, swimming, sailing and surf-riding, mock battles, and wrestling. They saw no virtue in work and no difference between work and play, and the only time-consuming chores were fishing for the men, which had an element of sport, and cloth-making for the women.

The latter was rather laborious. The women peeled the inner bark from certain trees, mainly a kind of mulberry, and alternately soaked it in rivers and beat it with serrated mallets until it was as thin and pliable as they wanted. Since it lost its strength when it was wet, it could not be properly washed; so as soon as their clothes were dirty, they threw them away. Nor could it be stitched, so the clothes were very simple: a loin-cloth, and sometimes, for the upper part of the body, a sheet with a hole in the middle for the head, like a South American poncho. They were more proud of their tattoos than of their clothes. All of them, both sexes, were elegantly tattooed, mainly on their legs and hips. It was the Europeans' first encounter with tattoos (it is a Tahitian word), and it spread among sailors from Tahiti all over the world. The girls wore clothes as much for provocation as for warmth and concealment, just as they anointed their bodies with scented coconut oil and wore garlands, and flowers in their ears and their long black hair.

For all their supposed laziness, they were fastidiously clean. All of them, men and women, swam in the sea and bathed three times a day in the rivers, washed their hands and mouths before

Tahiti Revisited by William Hodges

and after they ate, and washed their feet before they entered a house to avoid putting dirt on the grass and mats. De Andia noticed that if anyone wanted to spit indoors, he cleared away the grass, spat on the floor and covered it up again, and that if a house had a bad smell in it, they were apt to abandon it entirely. Such cleanliness makes it seem strange that the girls liked sailors, who seldom, if ever, washed while at sea and must have stunk abominably. (Captain Cook was the first to insist on regular washing, and Wallis had made his people bathe in the sea and wash their clothes in the straits of Magellan – but that was in February, and they did not reach Tahiti until June.)

The houses were easy to build, a communal effort with all the neighbours to lend a hand. If enough people could be gathered together, they could even be moved bodily from one site to another. A much more wonderful artefact was the Polynesian canoe. Europeans marvelled that such boats could be built with nothing but stone tools and shark-skin as sandpaper. The basis was a log hollowed out by fire and chiselling, but sides of planking were raised on top of that, each plank split from a log with stone wedges, trimmed with a stone adze, meticulously fitted and bound together with coconut fibre, caulked with the same material, and payed with resin. The bigger Tahitian canoes were over sixty feet long (Cook measured one of over a hundred feet), and for ocean voyages they were lashed together in pairs with a space between, to form a catamaran. These twin canoes were very stable and could carry upwards of sixty men, with a mast and sail in each half and, if the chief or his ladies were travelling, a thatched cabin built on top.

The smaller canoes, used mainly for fishing, had a single outrigger and sailed equally well in both directions. They were always used with the outrigger to leeward; when they tacked, they let go the sail and sheeted it in at the opposite end, and sailed backwards on the second leg of the tack. Some had a sloping board on the windward side, suspended by a line from the mast, so that one of the crew could lie out on it to make the canoe more stable, like the crew of a modern racing dinghy. They were amazingly fast, much faster than any European ship or boat. The crew of one ship, under full sail and towing her boats, watched the canoes sailing in and out of their wake, underneath the tow ropes.

The age of migration during which the Tahitians found their island had long since come to an end, but they could still make voyages of a hundred miles or so. How they navigated out of sight of land is still a matter of discussion, but de Andia's early explanation is perhaps as good as any. He learned it first-hand from a Tahitian pilot, who went back to Peru in the frigate *Aguila*. Of course they had no magnetic compass, but they divided the horizon into sixteen points, each with a name, beginning at east with the sunrise; and they knew from past generations which segment their objective lay in. Once in the open sea, they observed the segment from which the ocean swell was coming, and in daylight they steered by the swell, which was more constant than the waves or wind. At night they were more exact, because they knew from the same ancient lore which stars rose or set above the island they were heading for, and steered by them. De Andia was himself an expert navigator, but the Tahitian experts, he wrote, could aim for an island, or even a particular harbour in the island, with as much precision as he could, provided their ancestors, however long ago, had at some time made the same voyage. What surprised him more was their weather forecasting. He took two Tahitians to the distant island of Raiatea, 'and every evening or night they told me the weather we should have the next day, as to wind, calms, rainfall, sunshine, sea and other points, and they never turned out to be wrong: a foreknowledge to be envied, for in spite of all that our navigators and cosmographers have written on the subject, they have not mastered this accomplishment.'

These peaceful people sometimes fought wars, which seems incongruous. Some Europeans, thinking of their own wars, imagined they were cruel and destructive, but in comparison they were harmless. The only weapons of war were stones and sticks, some pointed sticks like spears and some heavy ones like clubs. De Andia did not take them seriously. He witnessed two. One, when the Spaniards tried to intervene, turned out to be a mock battle which everyone was enjoying. The other was rather more serious, and houses were burnt or demolished; but only two warriors were killed, and as soon as that happened both sides broke off the battle by consent. Every war a European actually saw was much the same, and in the course of time there were at least a dozen. Most were caused by the rival ambitions of chiefs.

Neither de Andia nor any other visitor discerned the strict conventions by which the wars were fought. You hurt or even killed your enemy with the sticks and stones if you could, but if you saw things going against you it was correct and normal to run away to the hills with all your followers and hide until the tempers of both sides had cooled. The winners got whatever it was they had been fighting for, but the more honoured side was the one which first asked for peace. To be wounded was not considered heroic, but careless and stupid.

Perhaps the most peaceful of men need a fight from time to time, unless they are inhibited by moral considerations, to release some instinctive pride. Even two hundred years ago, European wars had grown too destructive, out of all proportion to the instinct they satisfied. Tahitian wars were better: they satisfied the instinct without outraging the soldiers' moral standards, or in reality doing much damage to anyone.

De Andia was on less certain ground when he wrote about Tahitian religion. As Cook once remarked, the mysteries of religion are dark, and they are especially hard to interpret from an unknown language. Even now, nobody can turn back the clock and enter the mind of a Tahitian born and brought up in his beliefs. De Andia observed some religious ceremonies, and was content with that.

The only people in communion with Tahitian gods, he noticed, were an exclusive class of priests. They presided at the nearest equivalent to temples or cathedrals, the vast solid pyramids, called *marae*, which were the Tahitians' only permanent architecture, and they were called in for their prayers and general wisdom when anyone was ill.

In the *marae* the priests offered up fruit and sacrifices of pigs, and occasionally – some people said every six months, while others said it was for the most important prayers – they offered a human sacrifice, a man who had been killed beforehand by hitting him on the back of the head with a stone. But because the people so revered their ancestors, the most important use of the *marae* was for funerals. They were such holy places that no Tahitians would enter their precincts or even pass near them except on ceremonial occasions.

Corpses were laid out on wooden platforms, wrapped in cloth and tended by their relatives until they rotted away and only their bones were left. Tahitians had an eloquent phrase for death: people 'went into night'. For their journey, food was put out to feed them ('or the maggots', one cynical Spaniard wrote). Finally, the bones were burnt or buried, and only the skulls remained. Some travellers, including Cook, thought the great number of skulls on the *marae* were a sign of frequent human sacrifices, but they were not. Most were the final relic of an ancestor who had 'gone into night' and joined the spirits. Likewise, some thought the roughly carved statues which adorned the *marae* were idols, but again they were wrong; these were the statues of departed chiefs, whom the people revered but certainly did not worship.

Most explorers were content, like de Andia, to judge Tahitian religion by its results, without bothering much about the details of its dogma. It was clear to them that Tahitians never had the slightest doubt about the spiritual belief which had been handed down to them through unrecorded generations, if only because they had never heard any suggestion that other beliefs might exist. Their gods were part of the reality of nature, like their mountains, seas, or skies; and if it is right to judge a religion by the society it fosters, the Tahitian religion was good.

Don José's long, observant report had offered Europe a glimpse, unbiased and uncritical, of how life went on in Tahiti before the foreigners came. It could have been useful, but it aroused little interest in Peru.

NINE

The First Preachers

————— ••❧ ❦ ❧•• —————

THE TWO PRIESTS LEFT by the Spaniards in 1774 were the first Christian preachers on the island. They were left there in the hope of converting the people – an experiment which was not repeated for twenty-two years.

The names of these two pioneers were Fray Narciso Gonzales and Fray Geronimo Clot, or Clota. They were astonishingly ill-chosen, as everyone from the Viceroy downwards admitted afterwards. 'They were terrorized by the most trivial events,' he wrote. From the very beginning, they had the misfortune to strike most Tahitians as hilariously funny, and with the greatest respect for the Church they represented, it is still very difficult not to laugh at them, and yet to be sorry for them in their timorous ineptitude, which was summed up by a minute the Secretary for the Indies wrote in reaction to their long report: 'Nothing but grumbles – file.'

There is something tragic in the list of equipment they took with them, which happens to be preserved in the Spanish archives. It reveals an optimistic expectation of domestic comfort and of huge congregations, while in the event they had little comfort and no congregation at all. There, nakedly catalogued, is every item of food they took with them for a year: their cooking pots and frying pans, their tools for carpentry and gardening, their medicine chest with seventy-five different drugs, their underclothes and tin-plated chamber pots – one each – their weaknesses for tobacco and snuff, six jars of wine and two of brandy, and some inexplicable items: 2000 sail needles, for example, but apparently no thread, and one 'rough case of 300 rockets'. There also are their silk and satin vestments of many colours – blue, green, crimson, black, and gold – their portable altar draped with crimson satin picked out with dark violet flowers, their crucifixes, chalices, illuminated missals, bells, ampullae, pictures, and eight-branched candlesticks, all for a chapel that was never built; and for the converts, a gross of rosaries, half a gross of medallions, and half a gross of crosses. The store-ship *Jupiter* also brought for them a prefabricated two-roomed house and a wooden cross three metres high, with the inscription

CHRISTUS VINCIT
CARLOS III IMPERIT 1774

The Spaniards had landed in the smaller, south-eastern part of the hour-glass shape of Tahiti, and by good luck the first people they met were the two highest hereditary chiefs of the island: Vehiatua, who was supreme chief of the smaller part, and Tu, the supreme chief of the larger part, who happened to be there on a visit. At that moment, the men who held these high offices were both very young: the Spaniards guessed they were between seventeen and twenty. Both impressed the Spaniards as men of noble presence, gentle, affectionate, and courteous, who wore their dignity with youthful nonchalance. Vehiatua was distinguished by fair skin, apart from his sunburn, and blonde hair which was almost red at the tips. Tu was dark, and conspicuously tall even among the Tahitians. Later visitors measured his height as six feet three inches.

Tu in particular had a status that was held to be holy, something equivalent perhaps to the Divine Right of early English kings; and each man had absolute authority in his own sphere. Each had a retinue of family and servants, and everybody did what he was told without any question. It was Tu's right – and duty – to be carried on a man's back wherever he went, because it was held that any ground he trod on instantly became his property, and by custom any house he entered was abandoned and never used again. But no European ever saw him exercise these rights. Vehiatua had built a house for him, but he walked about quite freely among the rest of the people; and he seldom wore anything more regal than a loin-cloth. As soon as the frigate was sighted both these chiefs came off to her in a canoe, as eager as any teenager for adventure and laden with gifts of cloth, fine mats, and food. In exchange, the Spaniards gave them axes, knives, and shirts.

The *Aguila*, on this second visit, was the first ship to arrive with interpreters – two of the four islanders who had been taken to Lima (one had died, and another had decided to stay there), and

Maximo Rodriguez, the clever young private of Marines who had learned the language from the four islanders. So the commander was able to take the chiefs to his cabin and ask them right away to give the Spaniards a plot of land for a house to be built on, and to allow the padres to live in it. They cheerfully agreed, and promised to supply men to build it. Light-hearted conversation lasted most of the day. The first Tahitian word that all the Spaniards learned, like Bougainville, was *taio*. They also learned the custom of making a special *taio* by exchanging names with him, binding the two men together in mutual trust and help. The day ended with embraces all round. Next morning they met again on shore, a site was chosen and the building was begun.

It took a month. The two methods of building could not really be combined. The Spaniards could not have built a Tahitian house, and the Tahitians were totally baffled by the sectional house the Spaniards had brought with them. So they built both. The Spaniards put up their boarded bungalow, which had solid walls for the padres' defence and privacy, and small slit windows closed by wooden shutters on the inside – two or three men with muskets could have held it against hundreds with sticks and stones; and the Tahitians, having promised to help, built one of their open houses over the top of it to keep the rain off, just as they built houses for their canoes.

All through that month, the Spaniards were strictly formal, neither violent and dissolute like Wallis and his men, nor euphoric like Bougainville. The carpenters at work on the house were always guarded by armed Marines, and never allowed to wander from the site. Only three mishaps disturbed the job. The worst was when somebody stole a sailor's shirt. The sailor chased and attacked the man he thought had done it, and the man threw a stone at him which hit him on the head and so nearly killed him that he was given the last rites. Tu and Vehiatua and their families fled from the district, followed by all their people, for fear that the Spaniards would take revenge. They had to be coaxed back, and even when it was proved that the sailor had chased the wrong man, they still remained nervous. They fled again when a Spaniard was killed by a tree which fell on him while he was cutting it down. Indeed the chiefs, so autocratic among their own people, were extremely timid with the Spaniards, who were outside their authority, overwhelmingly powerful and visibly ferocious in the punishment of their own malefactors. When a Spanish

Marine left his sentry post and spent a night with a woman, he was lashed to a gun to be flogged. Vehiatua burst into tears at the sight, as the Tahitians always did, and begged Commander Boenechea to forgive him. The commander refused.

On New Year's Eve 1774, the dual house was finished, the padres' crates of equipment were landed, and the two of them moved in, together with two of the Tahitians who had been baptized in Lima and were supposed to be Christians and the interpreter Maximo Rodriguez, who was ordered to stay with the padres. On the first day of the new year, the wooden cross was taken ashore with reverent ceremony, carried in solemn procession to the house, and erected in front of it. The Spaniards celebrated mass for the first time on the island, sang the *Salve Regina* and fired volleys of musketry, while 'an infinite number' of Tahitians watched them.

Four days later, all the naval officers assembled at the house with the padres and the interpreter, and invited the chiefs and other important islanders to a formal meeting. The chiefs promised again to look after the padres, but prudently said they might not be able to guard them against attacks from other islands or visits by other foreign ships. Maximo tried to make them understand 'the greatness of our Sovereign, the indisputable right he holds over all the islands and his wish to befriend and instruct their people'. Boenechea promised in the King's name that Spanish ships would often visit them, provide them with tools in plenty and defend them against their enemies. The Tahitians 'acknowledged His Majesty as King', and a legal document of surrender was written and signed by the paymaster of the frigate. It still exists in the archives of Sevilla, but it had no value because the Spaniards, in their growing weakness and poverty, could not keep their side of the bargain.

That was on 5 January 1775. On 7 January, the *Aguila* and the *Jupiter* sailed for a fortnight's cruise to neighbouring islands, leaving the padres ashore.

From the very beginning, these two men disliked and distrusted the islanders, and were mortally scared of them. In their first report, written during the fortnight the frigate was away, they referred to them as arrogant, overbearing, high-handed heathen, prone to stealing and every kind of vice, and taking satisfaction with their own hands, whether justly or unjustly, for any wrong they received.

The padres were especially furious with the two baptized Tahitians who had come back from Lima, where they had been christened Thomas and Manuel. Apparently the padres had expected them to take the lead in converting their countrymen – though one was the small boy who had been presented to the Viceroy, and he was no more than thirteen years old by then. It was unreasonable to hope that these two would uphold a foreign faith against their own families and priesthood. But when they both said they wanted to go back to their families, the padres made a stand-up row of it, accused them of ingratitude and apostasy, and demanded repentance. When they had gone, the padres declared them to be special enemies.

Through most of that first fortnight, the Tahitians were having a *heiva*, one of the tremendous periodical parties led by the *arioi*, with dancing, singing, play-acting, eating, and sexual games. Thousands of people from distant parts of the island turned up for the festivities, men, women, and children. All of them wanted to see the novel and comical visitors, with their tonsures and long black habits and their air of solemn self-satisfaction. The padres became a side-show, and it terrified them. The Tahitians in festive mood could not resist the temptation to make fun of them, and hundreds crowded round the house like children at a zoo. 'They called out to us through the screen "*Guariro!*", which means thieves: "*Neneva!*", which means fools: "*Poreho!*", signifying shell-fish, but used among themselves to express the privy parts, making grossly obscene mockery of us the while; and others called us "*Harimiri*", which means old gaffers. These terms we caught the meaning of ourselves; the rest, which no doubt were equally opprobrious, we did not understand. Meanwhile the women looked on with roars of laughter: the boys took their cue from the rest. We offered no retort.' Of course it was unkind of the Tahitian crowd and mortifying for the padres, but nobody meant them any harm. If only they had shown good humour and friendliness, a touch of humility, walked round among the crowd embracing people as the Tahitians did and using the one word *taio*, sharing the feasting, watching the plays and dancing, and choosing a moment there and then to stand up with their interpreter and tell their gospel story, they would have had a congregation ready-made. But they lacked that sort of courage. The more the Tahitians laughed, the more the padres displayed their affronted dignity. 'More than five hundred heathen collected at the hospice in the morning,' they reported with all solemnity, 'and left us no room to have our breakfast.'

The two men were Franciscans, and their founder would surely have known that the best way to get on with Tahitians, who owned nothing, was to own nothing themselves. Their rich European possessions, holy and domestic, were a fatal mistake; they set an unbridgeable gulf between them and the people they hoped to convert. They spent all day and most of the night guarding their property, but their diaries were full of minor robberies: chickens and piglets disappeared, sometimes the sheets off their beds, and once their shaving gear, four razors, the hone in its case, a handkerchief, a towel, and a napkin. Whenever this happened, they summoned the chiefs to make bitter complaints and lectured them on their people's wickedness. Almost always, the chiefs discovered who had the things and gave them back; but the constant petty recriminations must have strained the patience of those highly respected men, and done less than nothing to warm their hearts to Christianity. Tu only once showed a hint of impatience. 'He came to the hospice worrying us morning and afternoon,' the padres reported, 'begging us for plantains out of the few we had. Although the heathen gave offence to us by word and deed in front of him, he made no move whatever to check them. However much we asked him to send away the people who left us no peace, he took no notice beyond picking up a stone from the ground and handing it to us to throw at them . . . It seemed the chiefs had no recourse of any kind against the commoners.'

All these events were reported when the frigate *Aguila* came back from its fortnight's cruise. The padres complained to the commander that they had to do 'menial tasks not appropriate to our ministry', and they requested two servants from the crew. That request was received by the first lieutenant, who was distracted because his commander, Boenechea, was sick and dying. The padres were called off to the frigate to support him, but on 26 January he died, and was buried at the foot of the cross outside the house. The first lieutenant refused to give the padres two servants but appointed one, a grommet or ship's boy named Francisco Perez, who was said to be handy at gardening, looking after stock, and jobs around the house. This lad, whether willingly or not, joined the padres ashore, and two days after the funeral the *Aguila* sailed again.

From the beginning of February until the beginning of June,

the padres shut themselves in their house. Their novelty had worn off, and no more Tahitians came to stare or laugh. Tu had gone back to his home, and Vehiatua seldom came to see them. They celebrated mass with proper regularity, attended by the boy Francisco and sometimes by Maximo, though he spent a lot of time travelling round the island. No Tahitian was ever invited to watch these services, nor to a bible class. Terrified to go out, the padres did not try to learn the language or to tell their gospel story to anyone.

What lured them out in June was the news that Vehiatua was seriously ill, not in his house, which was close by, but in a small holy island dedicated to Te Atua – 'the false god these heathen worship', as the padres called him. Fray Narciso went with Maximo to persuade the chief to come to them for medical treatment, and not to entrust himself to the native priests. A week or so later, Vehiatua was carried back to his house, ill of a calenture or fever, with catarrh, and unable to use his arms or legs.

It is impossible to guess what disease he had. The early explorers did not think the Tahitians had any infectious or contagious diseases, except perhaps yaws, which is a fly-borne infection common in the tropics. Generally, they lived in perfect health and died of old age. But of course they were very susceptible to whatever germs or viruses the explorers brought with them. There had been an outbreak of something like influenza soon after the Spaniards came, and Vehiatua had been more exposed to infection than anyone else: he often had meals on board the frigate, where he learned to sit at a table and use a knife and fork, and he had done the same with the padres. He had probably caught something from carriers among the Spaniards who were themselves immune. Fray Narciso himself had periodic fevers, and once an attack of jaundice.

Anyhow, the padres gave him warm drinks which made him sweat and reduced the fever, and they rubbed his knees with some kind of embrocation from their medicine chest, and after a fortnight he began to feel better, and got up.

Unluckily, this recovery was celebrated by another *heiva* or feast, and again the yells of the crowd were 'such as to inspire us with dread . . . We stayed inside the house in great anxiety.'

But early in July, Vehiatua had a relapse. The *heiva* continued, but with a different tone. The Tahitian priests had taken it over;

the drumming and singing were interspersed with sermons or prayers for the chief's recovery, and the shouts of the crowd changed to cries of grief. It came to the ears of the padres that human sacrifices were to be made to emphasize the prayers. They jumped to the conclusion that they were to be the victims, and their terror turned to panic. They made Maximo get out their muskets, which so far they had hidden, and fire them into the air. That had the effect they intended: it frightened everyone. Next, to complete the chaos in their minds, a small boy told them he had heard that if the chief died, they would be killed in revenge.

In fact, according to the padres' report, three men from other districts were abducted and killed, and their bodies taken to one of the *marae* or temples to persuade Te Atua to spare the life of the chief. But at dawn on 10 August, the padres heard loud shouts from the island priests, and a man came to tell them Vehiatua was dead. They sent Maximo to the chief's house, and he found it was true. He came back in a hurry to hear mass, because it was the day of the Transfiguration of Our Lord. Even at this moment of tragedy, when the Tahitians were overwhelmed by grief, the padres were concerned with trivialities. 'Scarcely was mass over,' they wrote, 'when we heard that a thief had broken through the fence of our hen-yard. The interpreter set off running in pursuit. The thief, as he was being overtaken, dropped one hen he had stolen but continued his flight. The mother of the dead chief heard of the pilfering thief's effrontery, and there and then she sent her other son to the hospice to stay with us, so that if the people should come against us they would be deterred by his presence. This little lad [he was eight or ten years old] told us to load our muskets and stayed inside with us. The afflicted woman also sent all her servants and others to climb the trees round the house and keep watch.'

This was in fact the padres' final and most ludicrous misunderstanding. They thought the little boy had been sent to protect them and their miserable hens by his presence. On the contrary, he had been sent so that they could protect him. Nobody had dreamed of threatening the padres: it was all their imagination. With their muskets inside their walled house, and under the promised protection of Tu, they were the safest people on the island. But the little boy needed protection because he was the heir apparent to the chiefdom. Vehiatua had had no son of his own, so the inheritance was indirect, and his mother feared rival claimants from other districts.

Sure enough, as soon as the chief was dead, shouting gangs appeared, armed with sticks, from three other districts, some by canoe and some running overland. The quaking padres watched from their slit windows, with their muskets primed. But the invaders were met by men waving plantain leaves or seedlings, the emblem of peace; and instantly their threats evaporated, in the manner of Tahitian wars, and peace was declared before a blow had been struck. There was friendly discussion, and the boy's accession was agreed.

There is a gap of two months in the padres' diary after that, only broken by a story of how they climbed a hill, with the heir to the chiefdom and a good many other people, to hoist a flag on a palm tree as a signal to the *Aguila* when it returned. One would like to think they had realized they were not in danger and never had been; but even after that they went on writing lurid stories of their narrow escapes from death. In October, the boy's accession was celebrated. The padres did not attend, because, as they explained, they could not leave their house unguarded with so many people about. But one of them must have witnessed the feast that followed, and taken a final opportunity to sneer at it. Twelve hogs had been baked, but there was no organization. 'People got annoyed while the food was being portioned out, and the banquet came to a pause in such a clamour that more blows than meat were served to the bare backs of the guests. Nobody who succeeded in grabbing any would give up his prize, in spite of the hard knocks he got, so that at last no more of the meat was left, although it was half raw.'

On 30 October, the *Aguila* was sighted again, and four days later she anchored in the harbour. She had brought another year's supplies for the padres, but to the surprise and chagrin of her new commander they adamantly insisted on being taken home. He had to agree, but made the condition that they should write a thorough explanation for the Viceroy. The house was left empty, and the new chief and his mother promised to take care of it until new padres arrived.

The apologia the padres wrote put all the blame for the failure on the islanders' inherent wickedness and the apostasy of the two young people who had visited Lima. Tahitians, they said, would never be converted unless they were first moved from their scattered houses and made to live in towns, where they could be put under proper legal discipline. They must have been specially asked why they had not offered baptism to Vehiatua when he was dying, because they explained at length that he was living in mortal sin and had shown no special contrition. Their own conduct had set a good example: they had never allowed any woman into the hospice unless the chief's mother was present. They had taught the new young chief, who had lived with them for most of two months, to make the sign of the cross and pronounce 'the sweet names of Jesus and Maria', and that was the only success they claimed for their ministry.

In parallel with the padres' diary, and in stark contrast to it, is the diary of Maximo Rodriguez, the young Marine who had become their interpreter. He could not have been a more different kind of man. He was probably only just over twenty, and he was kind, friendly and sociable, and (according to himself) uneducated. So far as he was capable of hating anyone, he heartily hated the padres, and was ashamed of himself for doing it. He revealed that they not only quarrelled with everyone else, but quarrelled endlessly with each other.

He had an insoluble problem. He had been ordered by his senior officers, whom he deeply respected, to interpret for the padres but not, as the padres claimed, to be their servant. Of course he was a Catholic too, and given a chance he could probably have explained the essentials of Christianity to the Tahitians in words they would have understood. But that was the padres' job, certainly not a job for a humble private of Marines. Yet he saw all the time that their unbearable behaviour defeated their whole object and put them always in the wrong. It hurt him very much to see his religion made unattractive, indeed repulsive, by two such bad-mannered and untypical exponents. He had an inescapable loyalty to the men as priests, and he always defended them whatever they did, and never spoke against them to the Tahitians; but he always understood the Tahitians' wounded feelings and found himself secretly in sympathy with them. Try as he might, he could not bear the company of the padres except in small doses. To escape from it, he spent a lot of his time travelling about the island and living in perfect amity with the islanders. It is very likely that he was not a pure-bred Spaniard but part Peruvian Indian, and that may have made him more sympathetic.

His diary is thorough, in so far as he seldom missed a day; but it is simple and naïve, as he evidently was himself. It tells very little about Tahitian life, except that (in contrast to life at the mission house) it was happy and kind, and he was happy sharing it. He travelled like a Tahitian, taking nothing with him except the clothes he was wearing, knowing that they would give him whatever he needed; in return, he did them whatever small service he could and entertained them in long conversations. From a historian's point of view it seems a pity he was not more analytical. But he was not a historian: he accepted whatever he saw without wonder or surprise, and he wrote exactly the sort of diary a Tahitian might have written, if any Tahitian could have written. What it reveals is that a friendly young foreigner who was unpretentious and easy-going could enter into Tahitian life and be welcomed as one of themselves. He was the first who ever did it.

Maximo says nothing about his amorous adventures, if he had any; he just made friends with everybody, from the supreme chiefs down to the fishermen. The only hint of a special affection appears on the very last page, when the *Aguila* had come back and he did not dare to ask a favour of his captain: 'Fearing a denial, I refrained from begging His Honour the Comandante to allow me to bring away with me a boy of thirteen or fourteen years old, handsome and of great promise, for he was first cousin to Tu, the principal chief of the island.'

Poor Maximo: he seldom asked for anything for himself and was never rewarded except by slow promotion. Twelve years later, he was commissioned as sub-lieutenant of infantry in recognition of what he did in Tahiti, and that seems to be the highest distinction he ever reached. Those months in Tahiti were the only adventure in his life. He married, however, and had two daughters; and at least four manuscript copies were made of his diary. In 1835 his daughter gave one of them to Captain Robert Fitzroy, who is best known now as the captain of HMS *Beagle* when Charles Darwin made his famous voyage in her. Soon after, Fitzroy gave it to the Royal Geographical Society in London; and there it lingered for seventy years, until the historian B. G. Corney found it in 1908, translated it, and published it in 1919. By this devious route, young Maximo achieved a sort of immortality.

The padres' failure was not only farcical but tragic. It should have been perfectly possible to make a happy blend of Christianity and the Tahitians' old-established religion, and Catholics would have been the best people to do it. The creeds were not wholly dissimilar. Te Atua, after all, was a synonym for God, and the two concepts were more alike than unlike. The spirits whose aid Tahitians invoked were very like Catholic saints, and the rough wooden statues in the *marae*, which they venerated but did not worship, were only another version of the wooden cross outside the padres' house, or the images within. The Tahitians might well have been delighted, if they had been told with sympathy, to learn that Te Atua, in a distant country, had sent his son to earth.

The greatest difference was in the method the two religions used to induce moral principles – the Christians with their variety of sins and prohibitions, and the Tahitians with very few, but both with a positive idea of virtue. In the complex civilization of Europe, sins had to be defined, but in the simple life of Tahiti they did not. The only specific sins the padres observed (apart from cruelty and greed, which sprang entirely from their cowardly imagination) were infanticide and human sacrifice. They never mentioned sexual licence, and one can only suppose that, shut away in their house, they never noticed it.

Again and again in the padres' story, one wants to write 'if only': *if only* they had preached the Sermon on the Mount, *if only* they had approached the task with Christ-like humility – 'I did not come to abolish, but to complete' – they could have succeeded. It is questionable whether the Tahitians could have been any happier for it; but at least a knowledge of Christian morality could have protected them against the future onslaught of Christian immorality. But no: the padres wanted above all to abolish, to destroy, to deny all Tahitian belief and impose every Christian prohibition. They took it on themselves to judge the whole people of Tahiti and to condemn them all, and it never entered their heads to compromise, or try to understand, or admit that anyone else might reach acceptable standards by routes that were different from their own. Te Atua was a false god, his priests were charlatans and all the rest were wicked, and that was that.

The senior Spaniards who learned of the padres' failure put the blame where it belonged, and they hoped to send another expedition and begin again with wiser men. But the *Aguila* was old and rotten and had to be scrapped, and she was the only frigate in Peru. The Spanish Empire was crumbling at the edges, and no other Spanish ship ever came to Tahiti.

TEN

Cook's Last Visit

————— ••✠)(✠•• —————

WHEN COOK LEFT TAHITI in June 1774 he did not expect to see it again; but while the Spanish padres were plotting to leave the island, Cook came back to England and another voyage was already being discussed. He left home again after only eleven months, in July 1776, taking his same ship, the *Resolution*, and another North Sea collier, *Discovery*, as her consort.

The principal aim of this voyage was something new. Cook had proved that the great southern continent, Terra Australis Incognita, did not exist, or at least that it was covered with ice and uninhabitable. Now he was ordered north, to survey the west coast of North America and search for the western end of the North-West Passage.

For two hundred years, on and off, people had hunted for a navigable passage from the Atlantic to the Pacific round the north of Canada. The Elizabethans Martin Frobisher and John Davis tried to find it, and they were followed after the death of the Queen by Henry Hudson and William Baffin. Baffin came back in 1615 convinced the passage did not exist, but gullible people went on believing it did – and up to a point, of course, they were right: it did and does exist, but is permanently blocked by ice. In the 1740s there was a fresh spate of rumours, and Parliament offered a reward of £20,000 for its discovery, which by the 1770s nobody had claimed. Cook was now to search for the western end, while another expedition started from the east. It was hoped they would meet in the middle, though Cook himself and the navigators he had trained were always sceptical.

There were three reasons, or excuses, for calling at Tahiti on the way. One was simply that Cook wanted to; the second was to get supplies; and the third and most pressing was the King's command that Omai should be taken home.

Cook therefore embarked Omai at Plymouth, with a most extraordinary collection of presents his rich friends had given him: gunpowder, muskets and pistols, a great many bottles of port wine, English clothes of the latest outrageous fashion, a suit of armour made to measure, a barrel organ, a compass, a globe, and a regiment of tin soldiers. Cook also took on board a menagerie of livestock which the King ('Farmer George') wished to present to Tu: cows and a bull, mares and stallions, sheep, goats, chickens, geese and ducks, and a peacock and hen contributed by Lord Bessborough. The birds and animals were an appalling nuisance on board, but Omai was not: during the voyage, Cook's opinion of him improved. He grew sorry for him. Omai or somebody in England had said he was a prince, and he had begun to believe he was. He expected to come home as a hero, and to become some sort of potentate in Tahiti: in New Zealand he provided himself with two Maori boys as a nucleus of a royal staff. But Cook could not see how, with his new property and his new ambitions, he could ever find a place again in Tahitian life.

They made land at the anchorage Cook had used before in Vehiatua's territory. Here, from the people who came out to greet him, he learned the latest news: two ships had been in since his previous visit, left four men ashore and then come back and taken them away again. He guessed, rightly this time, that they were Spanish. Oberea was dead, and so was the young Vehiatua he had met, the man who had died when the padres were there. The new Vehiatua was the boy who had sought refuge with the padres. The Spaniards had warned him and his people to have nothing to do with the English, who they said had no right to be there, but that made no difference to anybody. Cook exchanged names with the boy, the first time he had done this in Tahiti, and supplies were lavish. When Cook went ashore, he inspected the padres' house, and the rather pathetic sticks of furniture they had left in it; a bed, a table, and some stools. What concerned him more was the cross outside, and especially its inscription:

CHRISTUS VINCIT
CAROLUS III IMPERAT 1774

He understood it marked the grave of the Spanish commander, and he had nothing against it as a Christian symbol; but he could not let the claim of discovery stand. The *Dolphin* had been there before 1774, and so had he. He had it taken down, and carved on the other side the British claim:

GEORGIUS TERTIUS REX ANNI 1767 69 73 74 & 77.

Then he had it put up again. The story scandalized the Spaniards when they heard a garbled version of it: they were told he had desecrated the cross and taken it away.

Cook soon moved on to Matavai Bay; there, in three years, almost nothing had changed. Tu, whom Cook still regarded as king, turned out to receive and give presents. Cook gave him, among other things, a linen suit, a gold-laced hat, and a Tongan bonnet of red feathers, and he thankfully put ashore King George's farm stock and Lord Bessborough's peacocks. Omai knelt at Tu's feet, embraced his legs and presented more feathers and a length of gold cloth, and Tu ignored him. More food was provided than the crews could eat, and the girls flocked back on board.

Omai's trouble was twofold. He was not a prince, not even a junior member of the chiefly class, and nothing in the world was going to make him one. He was an ordinary middle-class Tahitian – or rather Raiatiàn, for Raiatia was the island of his birth; and no such person had ever moved up to the aristocratic class, who were distinguished once and for all by their descent from gods. And, more subtly, he had come back imbued with the European concept of private property. That set him apart from his own people and left him stranded half-way between the islanders and the Europeans. He was a native of the islands, but he was rich, and no Tahitian had ever been rich before. He was an obvious target for the Polynesian sport of thievery, and he made things worse for himself by giving presents to his low-class friends which not even the chiefs had been given by Europeans. In particular, he was the only Tahitian who had fire-arms and powder and shot for them. It grew sadly obvious that not one of the chiefs was going to have him strutting around, much better armed than they were; and Cook decided to land him in the island of Huahine, where he may have hoped his old friend Uri would take care of him.

There was one bit of evidence that the chiefs themselves were getting into the same dilemma. Tu in particular had been given so many prized – though mainly useless – presents that what he wanted now was chests to keep them in. He had seen such chests in the Spanish padres' house. Cook had his carpenters make some, big enough for two men to sleep on top as guards. It was a sign – though Cook did not seem to recognize it – that the social system was starting to break down under European teaching. Before, Tahitians never dreamed of stealing from each other, and especially not from their holy chiefs. Now, it appeared, they had learned, and no number of chests would make things the same again.

But this evolution had a passing benefit for Cook. Very little was stolen from him on that visit, largely because Tu put his own guards round the camp on shore. Tu, now a property-owner himself and therefore fearful of theft, had begun to see things from the European point of view. And possibly there was also a change of public opinion, which was the only thing that really controlled Tahitians' behaviour. When somebody stole something from the rich Europeans – even though it was only for sport – everybody else, including the chiefs, expected retaliation and was *matau* and had to retreat to the hills, and bartering therefore ceased until the scare had worn off. That was as annoying for the islanders as it was for the visitors: both sides equally wanted to barter, and the opinion may have begun to spread that stealing from the Europeans, fun though it might be for the people who did it, meant too much loss of trade for everyone else.

The fleet of canoes was still there, and the war against the island of Eimeo was still going on, if it could be said ever to have started. When Cook had left the time before, Towha, the warlike chief, had said he would attack Eimeo five days later, and Tu had been hesitant. After three years, Towha was still saying it, and Tu was still hesitating. Towha tried hard to persuade Cook to take part in the attack, but of course Cook refused. Possibly he had a thought for Magellan, who met his own death by involving his ships and men in a local war in the Philippines. But Towha took the first steps by arranging a human sacrifice to the god Oro. He insisted Tu should attend. Cook asked if he could come, and Tu agreed. Cook went, with his surgeon William Anderson, John Webber the artist, and Omai to explain what happened.

That ceremony, and Webber's drawing of the scene, became a matter of controversy in England. People who thought the Tahitians had been praised too much, and wanted to find fault with them, argued that it showed they had a cruel and blood-thirsty streak, and that Cook should not have seemed to condone such an evil practice by his presence. But Cook would have been unrepentant. He seems to have had no profound religious beliefs of his own; he very seldom held a church service on board, and in his voluminous journals he very seldom if ever mentioned God. But his mind was open to sympathize with anyone else's belief. He

Cook attended a human sacrifice: from the controversial
painting by John Webber

was passionately interested in Tahitian life, and an occasional
human sacrifice, as he very well knew, was a part of that life, an
expression of Tahitian religion. The mysteries of religion, as he
said, are very dark, and it was one of those mysteries that the
sacrifice was offered to Oro as god of war, when Oro was also the
god supposed to have founded the *arioi*, who preached peace. It
may be a clue to the explanation that the *arioi* spoke of 'Oro whose
spear is now at rest'. The lesser Tahitian gods – perhaps anyone's
gods – held the views their worshippers gave them.

The scene itself was eerie, in a *marae* on a point of land to the
southward, but it was not bloodthirsty. The victim was already
dead when he was taken there. If one can judge by custom – or
what the Europeans were told was custom – he was a man in exile
from some other district who had been found alone in his canoe
and quickly dispatched by hitting him on the back of the head
with a rock. Cook's boat's crew were not allowed ashore in that
holy place. He and Anderson and Webber were asked to take their
hats off, as they would have been in church. There was a big
congregation, a great many priests, a few boys, and no women.
Drums were beating. The dead man lay on the ground, trussed to

a pole, apparently so that he could be carried more easily. Dead sacrificial pigs and dogs lay on a wooden dais, and behind, on a wall, was a row of human skulls – nearly fifty, Cook believed. Prayers and invocations the English could not understand went on and on, punctuated only by drumming. Symbols one after another were offered to the god – red feathers, the entrails of a dog, a few of the victim's hairs. An eye of the corpse was offered to Tu, who made a symbolic gesture of 'eating' it. A grave was dug and the dead man was buried in it, and a boy addressed the god in a loud shrill voice. At the height of the ceremony there was a screech from the woods: 'It is the god,' Tu whispered to Cook. Cook thought it was a Tahitian kingfisher: perhaps they were equally right, for the kingfisher was a sacred bird through whom the gods could speak. In the midst of the *marae* was a fence to hide the holiest secrets. Cook was not allowed inside it, but he made a hole and peered through, without seeing much. There was also a parcel or bundle containing something too sacred for him to see, which was carefully unwrapped and wrapped again with fresh red feathers in it: he had a glimpse of something simple made of woven and twisted coconut fibre, perhaps an image of the god.

The prayers and offerings went on through a second day, which was rather too much. But when the three Englishmen came away, they were not inclined to scoff: they were curiously awed by the intense emotion of all who took part. But it was not for Cook to encourage war. On the way back to the ship, Towha asked him how he liked the ceremony, and he answered – through Omai – that he did not like it at all, and thought the god would reward it with defeat, not victory. Omai, never tactful, added that a chief in England would be hanged if he treated a man like that. Towha was often angry, and that remark made him furious – and no wonder: it was one thing to ask the opinion of Cook, a chief in his own right, but quite another to be lectured on English customs by a lower-class Tahitian.

Perhaps that fury pushed Towha into action. Having propitiated the god, he set off to Eimeo in his fleet, and was defeated – or at least, he failed to win whatever sort of battle he expected, and had to make a truce on terms that did not please him, which was always the speedy end of Tahitian wars. He sent a message to Tu for help. Tu's fleet was lying ready, but he refused to budge. There were recriminations. Towha blamed Tu; Tu's father, the retired chief, blamed Cook; Tu said nothing. Very soon after, there was a second ceremony in the same *marae*, the celebration of peace. Everyone was invited, but Cook could not go. He had a very bad attack of some kind of rheumatism, and while peace was being declared he was being massaged by Tu's wife, three of his sisters, and eight other women. It was a painful performance, but it cured him.

In spite of the talk of war, this was a perfectly peaceful time in Tahiti. Cook and his officers led a social life, dining with Tahitians on terms of equality, even intimacy. Cook and Captain Clerke of the *Discovery* went riding on King George's horses. (Omai had tried to demonstrate the art, but he always fell off.) Riding horses, Cook thought, 'gave them a better idea of the greatness of other Nations than all the other things put together', and perhaps they were right to see horses as a symbol of power. Communication and travel, from village to village, town to town, or country to country, was one of the fundamental differences between Polynesia and Europe, and in Europe communication and travel meant the horse. The crews, meanwhile, pursued adventures of their own. There were many entertainments and erotic dances and, as ever, there was plenty of work to do; casks, sails and ironwork were taken ashore and mended, and so was the *Discovery*'s mainmast.

But all Cook's biographers have said he was not his old self on this final voyage. He may have been chronically sick – many sicknesses could go unnoticed then – or perhaps he was merely worn out by the strain of years of voyaging. Nobody can doubt it was a strain. A sailing ship's captain had more personal authority – and responsibility – than anyone in other walks of life. He was never off-duty, night or day, year after year; there was nobody he could turn to for advice or orders; he and his crew were entirely cut off from the world, and never entirely out of danger; and not only success but the safety, discipline, health, and happiness of all of them depended on him. And prime exploration multiplied every strain. Perhaps, after nine years of it, no man could have remained unscarred. At all events, on his final voyage, his young officers still admired him greatly, but now went in fear of his anger and sometimes, in the privacy of their journals, were critical of his treatment of the natives. It did not show in Tahiti because this time there were hardly any thefts, and stealing was the only thing the islanders did that really provoked him.

It was not so peaceful in the nearby islands: there, theft was rampant again, and Cook took action with a kind of rage he had never shown before. When the ships left Matavai Bay they went first to the island of Eimeo (Cook had never been there before, although it was only ten miles away); and in Eimeo it was a goat, of all things, that caused the trouble. Cook still had a few on board, and he put them ashore to graze, and two were taken. One was brought back the next day, and the thief explained that the man in charge of them had forcibly taken something from him, and he only took the goat in revenge. To retrieve the other goat Cook led a punitive expedition across the lovely island, threatened the chief, burned houses, and smashed up canoes.

It must be said that the islanders recommended more violence: a party of elders said he should march round the country and shoot every man he met (and so did Omai). That he would not do, but before he finished his destruction he regretted he had ever started it. So did some of his officers. James King, the second lieutenant, wrote, 'I cannot think it justifiable; less destructive measures might have been adopted and the end gained . . . I doubt whether our Ideas of propriety in punishing so many innocent people for the crimes of a few, will ever be reconcilable to any principle one can form of justice . . . In future they may fear but never love us.' Among the wreckage, the worthless goat was returned.

The same sort of thing marred the visit to Huahine, where they went to set Omai ashore. Cook's old friend Ori had retired as chief and gone to another island; the new supreme chief was a boy of eight or ten. During an entertainment, somebody took a sextant. Everyone knew who had done it: the man was calmly sitting in the audience. Omai drew his sword and threatened to run him through. Cook had the man taken on board and put in irons: 'a hardened Scounderal,' he wrote. During the night he confessed, and the sextant was found undamaged where he had hidden it. It would seem to have been a typical dare-devil deed, like the theft of the quadrant from Fort Venus; but Cook had the man's head shaved and his ears cut off, and then let him go.

Before that episode, Cook had set about making a possible home for Omai. He asked a meeting of headmen to provide a plot of land. They answered oratorically that the whole island was his (Cook's, that is, not Omai's), and invited him to take whatever he wanted. Between them, they settled on a plot about two hundred yards square. Cook paid them fifteen hatchets for it, planted a garden with the seeds he always carried, and set his men to build a house on it, a solid wooden house with walls. Some of the timber came from canoes he had broken up in Eimeo. Really, the problem was insoluble, and in trying to solve it Cook fell into the trap the Spaniards had met with the padres: you could not introduce private wealth to the islands and hope to protect it with walls. Private wealth was like a sore on a healthy body: like healing, social forces would eradicate it, smooth it over until it vanished. Omai was rich, and he was sure to be robbed until he was no richer than anyone else, when he would be left in peace. Cook knew it would happen, but there was nothing he could do beyond building the walls as strong as he could and leaving Omai inside them to work out his own salvation.

He did give Omai one bit of good advice, to share his belongings with the senior chiefs; and he let it be generally known that he would be very displeased, when he came back, if Omai had been badly treated. But he did not expect to come back. The only true advice he could have offered was to give away everything as quickly as possible, and perhaps he thought of it: but that would have been to expect too much from Omai, with his dreams of being a hero and a prince.

So Omai was installed in his house, with his toys and clothes and furniture, his suit of armour and his barrel organ – and guns. Before the ship left, he was giving dinner parties there for the officers, who were more than willing to help him finish his wine. At the last moment, Cook gave him the remaining livestock, a stallion and mare, goats and English pigs. He also gave him more powder and shot for the firearms. That was a strange breach of his principles: the guns were sure to be stolen, and whoever got them was going to use them.

Omai's farewell was rather less emotional than Odiddy's, but when he said goodbye to Cook he embraced him and burst into tears; and no European ever saw him again. He remained cut off from his people by his property and pride, as Cook had foreseen. But in later years some kind of a war broke out between Huahine and another island. Omai joined it as a warrior with his muskets, and the muskets won the war – though by then their flintlocks were broken and they had to be aimed by one man and fired by another with a glowing stick. Soon after that, Omai died – it was said of some natural cause – and all his property vanished.

There were other troubles in those final days. The threat of mass desertion rose again, to the extent that Cook mustered all his crew on deck and lectured them sternly. They might run off if they pleased, he declared, but wherever they went he would bring them back: dead or alive, he would have them. In the upshot, only three men ran. One was a rather simple-minded Marine, who vanished with his musket. He was found again with two girls in a native house, wearing native dress. The others were a sixteen-year-old midshipman and a gunner's mate. They departed with a Tahitian in a canoe, and had to be chased from island to island. A few others had the same idea, but got no further than the beach before giving up. A more serious plan was discussed by William Anderson the surgeon and no less a person than Charles Clerke, the captain of the *Discovery* – though Cook never heard of it. Both these men had consumption: they had come aboard with it. Anderson knew, and Clerke at least suspected, that neither of them would survive the far north where the ships were bound; but in the perfection of Tahiti's climate they might have a chance of life, or even cure. This of course was not a question of desertion: they meant to ask Cook for leave to resign their ranks and stay. They talked about it for weeks, but kept putting if off, and they left it too late. The last chance went by: both of them stayed at their posts, and both died in the Arctic.

The threat had been scotched by Cook's authority, but the temptation was strong and real. Many men – most, perhaps – had been begged to stay by the girls they fancied they were in love with, by the *taios* they were attached to, or by general friends and well-wishers. Wherever they looked, they saw idyllic sites for building a simple hut beneath the trees, by a steam or fronting a still lagoon. A life of love and leisure, simplicity and kindliness and dignity, an escape from the labour and oppression of life on board and the poverty and degradation of their lives at home – it seemed to be theirs for the asking. They longed just to lie down and rest, and watch the ships sail away, and sleep and wake up again to peace. Perhaps it was illusion, a kind of dream, but it appeared to be true, and they believed it.

But no: there were scores of beautiful, loving girls on board who had come all the way from Tahiti, and scores more who had come aboard in Huahine; and all of them were put ashore in tears, leaving men who thought themselves broken-hearted.

This time, when he left – and this was the final time – Cook did not express any sorrow in his journal. Was he, one wonders, disenchanted by the final outbreak of thefts? Was he seriously worried that his command would break up as a result of desertions? Or was he perhaps remorseful, knowing, as he certainly did, that he had launched a course of destruction that would never end? He put his foreboding in two well-known and eloquent passages in the journal. First he mentioned the shame of civilized Christians: 'We debauch their Morals already too prone to vice and we interduce among them wants and perhaps diseases which they never before knew and which serves only to disturb that happy tranquillity they and their fore Fathers had injoy'd. If anyone denies the truth of this assertion let him tell me what the Natives of the whole extent of America have gained by the commerce they have had with the Europeans.'

He wrote that earlier, in New Zealand. It was even more appropriate to the smaller Pacific islands. Now, leaving Tahiti for the last time, he was more prophetic: 'I own I cannot avoid expressing it as my real opinion that it would have been far better for these poor people never to have known our superiority in the accommodations and arts that make life comfortable, than after once knowing it, to be again left and abandoned.'

ELEVEN
Mutiny

————— ••❊)(❊•• —————

COOK HAD RIGHTLY THOUGHT that once the Tahitians had been discovered they should not be abandoned. But abandoned they were, for eleven years after his last voyage. His death in Hawaii in 1779 put an end to the first great phase of Pacific exploration, and the next ship the Tahitians saw had nothing to do with exploration. She was a stray, almost derelict, from the English penal settlement which had been founded in Botany Bay in 1787, and her name was the *Lady Penrhyn*.

It was said afterwards that the governor of the settlement, Captain Arthur Phillip, had sent her to abduct a cargo of Tahitian girls as 'wives' for the convicts. If that story was true it was one of the ghastliest crimes ever planned against Tahiti, and worse than the African slave trade. The *Lady Penrhyn* was a merchant ship which had been chartered to take a cargo of convicts in the first of the convoys that went to Botany Bay, and she had taken 102, all of whom were women. In all, that convoy took 558 male and 220 female convicts, and a few children, most of whom died very soon; and of the 212 Marine guards, 28 had their wives, with 17 children. There was certainly a shortage of women, and probably a vocal demand for more. But there is no indication in the original journals that Phillip, who was not a bad man, planned a raid on Tahiti, and he deserves the benefit of the doubt.

The *Lady Penrhyn* was paid off from government service when she had delivered her load, and left to find her own way home. So were several other transports. They were therefore no longer under Phillip's orders, but three of them, of which the *Lady Penrhyn* was one, were supposed to go to Macao in China, in the rather vague hope of picking up a cargo of tea for the East India Company and taking it to England. The other two went more or less directly there; but the *Lady Penrhyn* strayed all alone into mid-Pacific. There, her crew suffered a dreadful attack of scurvy.

Probably, on the diet of Botany Bay, the crew had started

scurvy before she sailed, and they had no anti-scorbutic food on board except some very old sauerkraut, which they all refused to eat until they were actually dying. Six weeks out, 'the people were in a very deplorable state, for with every person on board, including the captain, they could only muster ten men able to do duty, and some of those were in a very weakly state . . . Swelled gums, the flesh exceeding black and hard, a contraction of the sinews, with a total debility, were the general appearances.' Yet for some reason their journal did not explain, they pressed on eastward into the open ocean, beating against a squally wind and almost constant rain. On 24 June, after seven weeks, they reckoned they were in 32 degrees south and 207 degrees west of Greenwich – nearly a thousand miles south of Tahiti and almost as far from anywhere else. There they picked up a westerly wind and altered course to the north in the hope of finding the island. A fortnight later, they saw it.

Why on earth had they wandered thousands of miles off course, in the teeth of the weather? The journal gives no hint of a cause; but perhaps one ought not to look for logical cause in a crew who were desperately ill and had every prospect of getting worse until there were not enough men to sail the ship and they would drift in mid-ocean till after the last was dead. Clearly they were not heading for Macao; they must have given up that idea very early. Nor, until the last fortnight, were they steering any recognizable course for Tahiti. It looks as if they meant to go home the other way round, by Cape Horn. They were more or less on course for that, and were almost half-way to the Horn when they turned to the north.

The captain, whose name was Sever, seems to have been a nonentity. The journal was written by John Watts, who was the first mate and had been to Tahiti before, as a midshipman with Cook in the *Resolution*. One of them must have been a capable navigator. After six weeks of beating without any sight of land, they finally approached and found Tahiti from the south, which argues – since it could not have been luck – that they knew not only their latitude but their longitude; and to do that, since a merchant ship would not have had a chronometer, they must have been able to observe and calculate lunars.

It may be that Watts had been trying to persuade the captain from the very beginning to go to Tahiti for a holiday before the long voyage home; but there is no sign that he succeeded until it became an urgent matter of life or death. It was a narrow escape. When they sighted the island, they had only three men in one watch and two in the other, beside the mates, two of whom were 'ailing'. They made land on the south-east end, and men came off in canoes and made signs that they should come in and anchor there; but Watts insisted they should go on to Matavai Bay, because if they let the anchor go they would not have enough strength to raise it. Entering the bay, they sailed over the Dolphin Bank. They needed one more tack to reach the *Resolution*'s berth, but they missed stays and had to anchor where they were. A vast crowd of people was waiting on Venus Point, where Cook had built his fort, and a fleet of canoes came off to them with shouts of '*taio*' and '*Patri no Toote*', meaning 'Cook's ship', and life-saving gifts of fruit, and pigs and fowls. Watts began to see old friends, among them both Tu and Odiddy.

The apparition of this ship must have increased the Tahitians' puzzlement. She was very different from the naval ships they had seen before. The *Lady Penrhyn* cannot have been much of a ship before she left England, or her owners would not have chartered her as a convict-carrier. Probably, like many shipowners, they hoped to see the last of her and claim compensation from the government. Now, she had not been refitted or even properly cleaned since the 102 imprisoned women had been taken out of her hold. She must therefore have been filthy and stinking, besides being manned by a hideously dying crew. When Tu came aboard, he 'was astonished to see so few people, and the greatest part of them in a debilitated state, and enquired if they had lost any men at sea'. Nevertheless, the ship was made as welcome as ever.

None of her company took more than a short walk on the beach, but they picked up some news of what had happened in Tahiti in all those years. It was they who first heard the fate of Omai. Odiddy and Tu both told them that the chief of Eimeo, still resentful of Tu's favour with the English, had landed and killed off all the farmstock the King of England had sent him, except goats, which had bred and were scattered all over the island, and some ship's cats, or rather the descendants of some cats that Cook had put ashore. Some vegetables that Cook had sown were still growing, but the Tahitians did not eat them. The moral was that you could not introduce even animals or new kinds of food into Tahitian life: the Tahitians did not need them and were satisfied with what they already had, but were too polite to say so. A more successful gift was a framed portrait of Cook which Webber had painted for Tu. Tu still had it and cherished it. It was carried wherever he went, even on board the *Lady Penrhyn*.

One thing Cook had foreseen was that the islanders had run out of iron tools and forgotten how to make their old ones of stone or shells – or else could not be bothered. This was not entirely due to improvidence. Most of the tools Cook had given them were made on board by the blacksmith out of any old iron, and would soon have rusted away or been hopelessly blunted, bent or broken. The Tahitians no longer wanted red feathers: what they urgently asked for were boat-building tools, hatchets, knives, nails, gimlets, files, and scissors. The *Lady Penrhyn* had no special stock of these, or of any trade goods, but her crew scraped together enough to barter for food at what they called a very good rate of exchange, and what they could not pay for they were given – especially by Odiddy, who came on board every day, as amiable as ever, with offerings ready-cooked.

It astonished everyone then, and is still surprising now, how quickly men at death's door were cured of scurvy when they got fresh food. After a fortnight in Matavai Bay everyone on board was able to work and the ship was fully stocked for a further voyage; and Sever decided to go. For fear of getting a flock of people on board, he tried to slip out before dawn: but the breeze slackened, and the canoes caught up with him, all bringing gifts. 'We had the satisfaction', Watts wrote, 'of leaving this Island in perfect amity with the natives'; and indeed, the ship's visit, short though it was, had been more successful than most. In their weakened state, and with no armed Marines to guard them, they had not made any demands, and most were too sick to take any notice of girls. The Tahitians were sorry for them. Odiddy was in tears again when he saw they were going, and Tu came out beyond the reef before he put off in his canoe, saying he hoped it would not be so long before another ship came. No mention is made of a plan to abduct any girls: if any such plan had ever been made, they certainly did not do it. Nor had they any intention of going back to Botany Bay. They went to Macao after all, calling on the way at the uninhabited island of Tinian, where the Spaniards were known to have landed cattle which had bred and gone wild. On that voyage, 'no material circumstance occurred'; and reaching Macao, five-and-a-half months from Botany Bay, they found one of the other transports still there.

Exactly a week after the *Lady Penrhyn* reached Macao, HMS *Bounty* reached Matavai Bay, coming by a more southerly route. The *Lady Penrhyn*'s had been the shortest of all the English visits: the *Bounty*'s was to be the longest – five months, and that was too long. Of all the visits, this had the most profound effect on the crew and also on the Tahitians. It revealed the common man's opinion of Tahiti.

In modern times, the blame for what happened to the *Bounty* has been heaped on her captain, William Bligh. But it is risky to blame a man for events so long ago – by what standard is one judging him? – and all the evidence against Bligh was given by men on trial for their lives, so it is not without prejudice. He cannot be proved to have been exceptionally cruel or wicked for a naval captain of his era. He had been a success as master of the *Resolution* under Cook, which speaks well for him, and he survived to be one of Nelson's captains at Copenhagen and in the end a vice-admiral. But this was 1788, before Nelson had proved that the most efficient way to run a ship was with some sympathy and kindness, and before Wilberforce had argued against slavery and cruelty in general. The worst one can say of Bligh is that he was insensitive, tactless, rude, unreasonably stern, and given to childish rages: and the same could be said of many sea-captains then. Certainly he and Cook were very different. Cook looked for and brought out the best in men: Bligh looked for and brought out the worst. On the other hand, Fletcher Christian, the master's mate who led the mutiny which was to follow, seems neurotic and childish in the grudges he bore, and John Fryer the master, who refused to join it, was certainly a weak, mean-spirited man who hated Bligh simply because he was strong.

All of them had suffered a longer and closer confinement than most before they reached Tahiti. The *Bounty* was a very small ship, ninety feet in length overall and twenty-four in beam. The object of her voyage was the most extraordinary use that had yet been made of a naval ship and crew: to collect a huge number of seedlings of the breadfruit tree and transport them to the West Indies, where it was hoped they could be grown to feed the slaves. Her main cabin had been fitted to carry the seedlings in flowerpots and extended to take up a third of her length, and the whole ship's company lived in the remaining effective length of her, about forty feet: Bligh himself, eleven warrant officers and midshipmen, thirty other hands and two gardeners: forty-four men in all.

Bligh had intended to sail by way of Cape Horn, and he tried; but it was too late in the season, and the ship could make no headway against the westerly gales. So he turned and went round the world the opposite way; and in all that tremendous outward voyage, 27,086 miles by the log and a little over ten months, he touched land only three times, in Tenerife, the Cape of Good Hope and an uninhabited bay in Tasmania. His crew were therefore more astonished and impressed by Tahiti than most – its space and freedom, its shaded groves and rivers, and the uninhibited welcome of its people.

Bligh loved the Tahitians as much as anyone. 'I left these happy islanders in much distress,' he wrote in his first dispatch to the Admiralty, 'for the utmost affection, regard and good fellowship was among us during my stay. The King and all the Royal Family were always with me, and their good sense and observations joined with the most engaging dispositions in the world, will ever make them beloved by all who become acquainted with them as friends.' But his long journal revealed him only too clearly. It was well written, detailed, observant, but it was entirely concerned with his own experience and scarcely mentioned the experience of his crew. It was not that he was blind to what they were doing. In such a small ship, he could not have avoided knowing that every bunk and hammock had a girl in it every night, but he only admitted it obliquely. 'At sunset all our male visitors left the ship,' he wrote on the second day. The thoughts and emotions of his men did not concern him.

The snobbish pleasure he betrayed in writing of the king and the royal family was a repetition and exaggeration of Cook's. It was true they had to find and identify the highest chiefs they could, but it was pure invention to give them European titles. In reality, Tahiti still had nothing like a king. It had several chiefs who were or claimed to be a step above the rest. But Bligh followed Cook in treating Tu as king.

Tu was married by the time Bligh was there, to a lady named Iddeah. He was still lethargic, though perhaps less timid than he had been; but Iddeah was a very forceful person, large and strong and reputed to be a warrior, a surf-riding champion and an expert wrestler. When she had a chance, she quickly became a crack shot with a pistol, and she thought nothing of paddling off to the ship alone in a canoe on a day of storm. They had had four children, but the first had been allowed to die at birth, according to custom, because Tu was a member of the *arioi*. After that, perhaps because they both wanted children, he left the society, and – again according to custom – he abdicated in favour of his eldest son. The boy, who was six when Bligh saw him, took not only his father's title of *arii rahi*, supreme chief, but also his name, Tu. The older Tu, after that, was known by a series of names, the last of which was Pomare. As regent, Pomare, as he must now be called, exercised the practical power, largely pushed and guided by his wife. He remained on the friendliest terms with her although, at his own suggestion, she had left his bed for one of his servants, and he took her younger sister as a second wife.

This was the royalty whose favour Bligh enjoyed. Tu's, or Pomare's, father, brothers, uncles, and their wives dined with him on the ship nearly every day, or he with them; so did many lesser local chiefs. He often gave them all lavish presents, according to what rank he thought they held, and they fed the whole ship's company with pigs and fruit. But he was not allowed to visit the new Tu, the boy chief, because he refused to show his respect by stripping to the waist, which everyone else did, even the father and mother. Bligh offered to take off his hat, which he pointed out was how he would salute King George of England; but that would not do, and he was only allowed to speak to the boy across a river, and to send over presents for him and his younger brother and sister.

That may have been a double disappointment for him, because he was a family man and adored the Tahitian children. 'They are very handsome and sprightly,' he wrote, 'and full of antic tricks. They have many diversions that are common with the boys in England; such as flying kites, cats cradle, swinging, dancing or jumping in a rope, walking upon stilts, and wrestling.' Droves of them followed him on his walks through the woods – largely because of the sweets and toys he carried in his pockets. Strapping boys and girls of ten contrived to get themselves carried to him pretending to be infants in arms – which made him laugh as much as they laughed themselves. The stern and dreaded man could be seen off-duty playing these childish games. He did not have many attractive traits, but this was one.

Bligh certainly enjoyed his long stay in Tahiti and thought he had done well. He persuaded Pomare that the tools and clothes he gave him were presents from King George; and when Pomare asked what King George would like best in exchange, Bligh told him he would value breadfruit more than anything, and that he himself would do Pomare the favour of transporting them. So the two gardeners, with the Tahitians' help, dug up and collected and potted 774 seedlings, which filled the whole cabin in the ship. Yet all the time Bligh unwittingly sowed the seeds of disaster for himself and his crew, and also for the Tahitians. For himself and the crew, the disaster was caused by his own absorption in the 'royal' friends and his lack of interest in what the crew was doing. It never crossed his mind that they might be under a temptation some could not resist. Even when three men tried to desert, he was unconcerned. That had happened to Cook, and like Cook he set the chiefs to work to chase them to a neighbouring island where they were hiding and bring them back again. He flogged them and put them in irons.

For the Tahitians the pending disaster was less direct. Bligh continued what Cook had begun. By insisting that Pomare was king, by making him a favourite and loading him with gifts that nobody else possessed, Bligh persuaded him – or more probably his wife Iddeah – that he was, or ought to be, all-powerful, and created intense resentment in other neglected chiefs. That began to undermine the whole old-established structure of Tahitian society, the casual delegation of power from the supreme chiefs to lesser chiefs, and from them to the grandfathers of families. It made a centre of power where none had been before, and introduced jealousy. Grandfathers could no longer make their patriarchal judgements for fear they would be quashed by rulings from above. Family opinion could no longer be the arbiter of law when a new law, the king's, might contradict it, and when one man had the power to enforce his opinion.

Of course, it was not an instant change. It took time, largely because Pomare himself was reluctant and afraid to exercise the power the English offered him. Bligh became dimly aware of this near the end of his stay, when Pomare confessed he was afraid for his life. As soon as Bligh had gone, he said, he would be attacked by jealous rivals, and if they combined he would not be able to beat them. He begged Bligh to rescue him, to take him and his wife and two of his servants to England, where he was sure King George would be glad to see him. Possibly Odiddy had something to do with this request. He was still in Tahiti, and still had an ambition to go to England, and he had won himself some authority by marrying one of Pomare's aunts. To keep Pomare quiet, Bligh promised to ask King George for permission to take him the next time he came to Tahiti; and he let it be known that when he came again he would take revenge on anyone who harmed Pomare. But these threats and promises were hollow and insincere: he never expected to come back again.

He had raised Pomare to a position of power which Pomare could only sustain by fighting, a position that had never existed before; and having done it he left him to fend for himself. His only thought was to give him even more of the instruments of power, now including muskets, a brace of pistols, powder and shot. Pomare, still somewhat timid, looked askance at these dreadful weapons and remarked that his wife Iddeah would fight with one pistol and Odiddy with the other: Odiddy was already known to be a marksman, while the mannish Iddeah had 'learned to load and fire a musquet with great dexterity'.

In retrospect, it seems like appointing a new head of state to a peaceful, small, and backward country, and giving him a supply of atomic bombs.

On the verge of the most famous of mutinies, Bligh had no suspicion at all that trouble was brewing. He never admitted any blame himself. Long after, he blamed the attractions of Tahiti: 'The women at Otaheite are handsome, mild, and cheerful in their manners and conversation, possessed of great sensibility, and have sufficient delicacy to make them admired and beloved. The chiefs were so much attached to our people, that they rather encouraged their stay among them than otherwise, and even made them promises of large possessions . . . It is now perhaps not so much to be wondered at that a set of sailors, most of them void of connections, should be led away . . . when they imagined it in their power to fix themselves in the midst of plenty, on one of the finest islands in the world, where they need not labour, and where the allurements of dissipation are beyond any thing that can be conceived.'

Perhaps he wrote that to shift the blame from himself; but it was another admission of the grudging sympathy Cook had begun to feel towards deserters. And it was certainly right; the charm of Tahiti was the main cause of the mutiny. Naval sailors in those days were a mixed bunch: some willing volunteers who had chosen a naval life, some rounded up by press gangs, and some minor criminals, sentenced to the ships instead of prison. By any standards, their life was extremely hard; but by naval rules mutiny was a crime as bad as murder, and they were always very reluctant indeed to think of it. Mutiny at that time was perhaps more in the air than at any other; the great mutinies of Spithead and the Nore were only eight years in the future. Certainly some of the *Bounty* crew intensely disliked their captain. But they would never have done what they did if they had not seen in Tahiti a kind of life which was really much better than life in a ship or life at home in the purlieus of English cities.

Nothing happened until they were three weeks out from Tahiti and had covered 1500 miles to the westward and reached the Tonga group – the Friendly Isles, as Cook had called them. Fletcher Christian, the master's mate who led the trouble, had intended to desert alone in the ship's boat. Nobody knows how long he had had the idea, but he put it off until there were plenty of islands nearby, so that he could easily row or sail ashore and take the chance of life with the natives. Bligh had a high opinion of Christian and regarded him as a friend – this was the third voyage they had made together; he had appointed him an acting officer of the watch, which was unusual for a master's mate. On 28 April 1789, Christian's watch was from four to eight in the morning. In those secretive hours, he told two or three other men what his plan was, and found they wanted to come with him in the boat, and the idea was born of taking the ship and putting Bligh in the boat. By noon that day they had done it. Everyone quickly had to make up his mind whether to go or stay. The crew was equally divided. Eighteen men went with Bligh in the boat and twenty-five stayed with Christian in the *Bounty*, including four who said they did not want to, but could not find room in the boat.

There was plenty of threatening behaviour that morning, and many men took the chance to tell their captain what they thought of him, but there was no bloodshed. The boat, twenty-six feet long, was grossly overloaded with nineteen men in it, but it was not a murderous act to set it adrift. The weather was fine, and there was every reason to think that Bligh and the rest would quickly reach somewhere they could live until another ship was sighted – perhaps a matter of years, or perhaps the rest of their lives. They rowed to the nearest island the same afternoon: it was not much more than twenty miles away. What the mutineers did not expect was that Bligh would then show the strength of the discipline they disliked by keeping the men on the strictest starvation ration, and sailing the boat 3600 miles farther to the nearest European settlement, which was on the island of Timor. But that was what he did, through awful privations, in forty-one days. In less than a year, he was back in England with his story.

Most of the mutineers meant to go straight to Tahiti, and they made no secret of it: 'Huzzah for Tahiti' was the last of the shouts Bligh heard as they sailed away. But not Christian. He had the sense to know that Tahiti, and Matavai Bay in particular, were visited more often than anywhere else in the South Seas. Moreover, when the *Bounty* was long overdue and given up for lost, the navy would send a rescue ship, and Tahiti would be the first place it went. With a crime on his head, Christian had no intention of being captured. He chose to try to settle on a much smaller island called Tubuai, 550 miles to the south. He found it, the crew brought the *Bounty* to anchor, landed, and began to build a fort.

That was a failure. Tubuai was inhabited, but it had no livestock, or not enough. The mutineers were violent and antagonized the natives, who then refused to barter the little meat they had. Even more to the point, they refused to offer their girls. The mutineers took pigs and girls by force, and it was said a hundred natives were killed in fights. Christian soon had to make for Tahiti for food.

No European, mutineer or not, ever seems to have thought it was wrong to tell lies to the Tahitians, who were only too easy to deceive. By then, Cook had been killed in Hawaii, but Bligh had ordered his crew not to tell the islanders. In fact, they had heard of it, probably from the *Lady Penrhyn*. Now Christian, back in Matavai Bay, told them the *Bounty* had met Cook and his crew on a newly-discovered island, that Bligh was still with him, and that Cook had sent the ship to fetch a supply of animals. The Tahitians were delighted to hear that Cook was all right and had not forgotten them, and they eagerly competed to load the ship with gifts for him. By this swindle Christian received, in the course of a week, 460 of the islanders' pigs, 50 goats, and uncounted fowls, dogs, and cats. The islanders even ferried on board the bull and cow that Cook had given them. Christian also collected eleven girls, and after the ship had sailed again he found that thirteen Tahitian men had stowed away on board, among them the irrepressible Odiddy. So equipped, he went back to Tubuai.

Begun by force, the settlement there could not be made to prosper. Christian was surrounded not only by affronted islanders, but also a rebellious crew. The crew did not try to depose him – he was almost certainly the only man who could navigate – but demanded that he take them back to Tahiti, where most of them had a *taio* and had had a girl. Three months later, in September 1789, the *Bounty* was seen for the third time in Matavai Bay.

In those three months, a rather mysterious armed ship had come in and gone again. She was said to be Swedish, but her captain's name was J. H. Cox, which sounds nothing but English, and the only named member of her crew was Brown. Brown was certainly English or American, a 'shrewd and active fellow', it was said; and he was mentioned because he had assaulted somebody else on board and the captain put him ashore and left him there. He attached himself to Pomare, who was glad to acquire a foreigner who could care for his muskets; and so Brown became the first of hundreds of deserters or castaways who settled like flies on Tahiti. Cox also gave Pomare more muskets and the British Union Jack.

Sixteen men from the *Bounty* were landed and stayed, in spite of Christian's warning that they would be captured. That left him – assuming all the mutineers were still alive – with a crew of only eight at most. With that meagre remnant, scarcely enough to get the ship under way, he sailed again in the dark one night, and neither he nor the ship was ever seen again in Tahiti. He also took with him Tahitians, men, women, and children: some reports said thirty-five of them, some eighteen. He said he was going to settle on an uninhabited island far from the usual tracks of English ships, and this time he succeeded. He chose the empty island of Pitcairn, two square miles of land without a harbour, 1200 miles away to the east-south-east; it had been sighted only once, from an English ship twenty-two years before, and named for the midshipman who saw it first. There they burned the *Bounty* and were left in peace. Eleven years later, in 1800, all the original men were dead except one sailor called Alexander Smith, who had taken the patriarchal name of John Adams. But a second generation was growing up, and the settlement survived. It was eighteen years before they saw a ship, and she was American and meant them no harm. Twice in the nineteenth century well-wishers could not believe they liked their isolation and took them all away, but they went back. After a century they became Seventh Day Adventists, and they await the coming of Christ.

The sixteen men left in Tahiti landed their shares of all the stores on board the *Bounty*, including a good supply of tools and weapons. They tried to fit into Tahitian society, and some succeeded; but on the whole it was a disappointment. For transient · visitors Tahitian rules of conduct, such as they were, had been suspended by hospitality, but prospective permanent residents had to conform. Those who had thought themselves in love found now that the islanders blamed the English for the promiscuity all sailors had enjoyed. Among themselves, promiscuity was a teenage privilege, and of the sailors only the midshipmen were teenagers. Older men were expected to marry unless they were *arioi*, and marriage was not the romantic solitary idyll the Europeans imagined. The girls, or some of them, could be loving, kind and faithful wives; but a marriage was expected to unite two families, and as the sailors had no families they were not universally welcome as husbands. They also had to learn to share their wives with their *taio*s, and to share family life and family responsibilities with scores of relations. A few – the gentler, younger and more sensitive ones – succeeded and proved it was not an impossible dream. The rest ran wild.

Pomare saw them all as useful allies in the power struggle he could no longer avoid, and he gave them plots of land round Matavai Bay, had his people build them houses – a job that took only a day or two – and fed them all. But most of them were restless, and the first thing they did – the only thing they combined to do – was to set to work and build themselves a schooner. One does not know what they meant to do with it: perhaps they felt they must have a line of escape, or perhaps they could not instantly settle down to idleness and needed something to occupy their hands and minds. The schooner was not to be very big: 'about the size of the passage-boats between London and Gravesend'. But it was a colossal and brave undertaking to build any ship in Tahiti, where nothing but a canoe had ever been built before. To begin with, they had to find suitable trees and fell them and haul them down from the mountains, saw them and split them into keel, stems, frames, planking, masts, and spars. Presumably they had to make the nails, and improvise all the rest of the ironwork in an English ship, not to mention the caulking and pitch, the ropework, blocks, and sails. The Tahitians marvelled at their perseverance, and sometimes helped with the heavy jobs. In the end she was finished and launched in Matavai Bay, a monument to the self-sufficiency of sailors in that era.

Before then, however, a few of the mutineers had abandoned

the rest. One was Charles Churchill. He had been master-at-arms, and was one of the three who had tried to desert before the *Bounty* sailed. Now he left Pomare and Matavai Bay and went to join Vehiatua in the south-eastern part of the island. A seaman called Matthew Thomson, said to be one of the most ignorant and brutal of the crew, went with him.

Churchill had exchanged names with Vehiatua and become his *taio* in the early days: now, soon after Churchill joined him again, Vehiatua died without an heir. By custom, if a chief died childless, his *taio* had a claim to the chiefdom, and so Churchill became an *arii rahe*, supreme chief of that part of Tahiti. Whether it was a popular choice or not – one can hardly believe it was – it was a position he could hold with his muskets against Tahitians; but not against Thomson. Thomson, enraged with jealousy, shot him. To murder a supreme chief was a crime unheard of and unforgivable, and Vehiatua's people turned on Thomson with their weapon of war and stoned him to death. Later, they found a four-year-old nephew of the original chief and appointed him to rule in the old-fashioned way.

In return for his hospitality, Pomare asked the rest to help him in his long-standing quarrel with the island of Eimeo. They refused, but offered to clean his muskets and pistols; and those weapons, in the hands of three or four Tahitians – including Iddeah no doubt, and Odiddy, who had come back with the *Bounty* – were enough to change the precarious balance of a Tahitian war. Pomare won. Next, with all his ambitions aroused, he wanted to conquer Vehiatua's country; and this time the remaining mutineers agreed to take arms. They relaunched their schooner, which had been hauled ashore for the windy season, and some of them led a fleet of canoes. The others attacked overland. It was a walkover. In wars where it was honourable for frightened men to run away, and both foolish and shameful to be wounded, the fear of muskets made victory easy and immediate. Vehiatua's people made for the hills and Pomare became the ruler of all Tahiti, the first there had ever been. The victory parade was a curious scene. The Union Jack which Captain Cox had given Pomare had been accepted as a royal and holy emblem, replacing the pennant which Wallis had planted. This national flag was paraded right round the island, not by the English but by the Tahitians; and it was respected and revered by all, not because they welcomed Pomare's rule but because they were terrorized by fourteen men with muskets and wanted peace.

Another ship narrowly missed witnessing this celebration. She was HMS *Pandora*, Captain Edward Edwards. Two years after the mutiny, she was bringing the navy's revenge. Tahiti had not been everything the mutineers expected, but for most of those two years they had at least known gentleness and kindness and enjoyed a degree of freedom they had never known before. By contrast the price, when they had to pay it, was a very terrible example of European inhumanity.

The mutineers' schooner was still at sea when the *Pandora* came in, and only four mutineers were in Matavai Bay. All four of them went aboard, not knowing what to expect, and probably not believing their deed could be known so soon. All four were hand-cuffed and put in chains. Bligh was not on the *Pandora*, but a man called Thomas Hayward was: he had been a midshipman in the *Bounty* but had made the opposite choice that fateful morning and gone with Bligh in the boat. He and another officer, with their armed Marines, scoured the island, chased and captured the schooner and followed fugitives into the hills, while according to later visitors the 'usual course of festivity, amusements and debaucheries' was seen on the ship and around the bay. It was only a matter of time; in the end, they rounded up all the fourteen remaining mutineers. All of them gave themselves up when they were surrounded.

Among the festivities, there were other much more distressing scenes on the *Pandora*, and one was specially remembered. One of the first mutineers to go on board was a midshipman, George Stewart. He was probably a more desirable young man than the old lags among the mutineers, and he had lived 'in a most tender state of endearment' with a girl and her family in Matavai Bay. He incongruously called her Peggy, Peggy Stewart, and they had a baby girl. When he vanished on board, she put off in a canoe to see him, taking the baby, and when she found him imprisoned, the meeting was 'so afflicting and affecting that the officers on board were overwhelmed with anguish'; so were the crew, no doubt – but not Captain Edwards.

Peggy was removed by force, with the baby. Left on the beach, speechless with grief, she lost the will to live and refused to eat, and in a month or two she died of what was called a broken heart. In the Tahitian way, the baby was lovingly brought up by aunts, and later visitors met her as a growing child.

Edwards can perhaps be excused for his apprehension at

taking mutineers on the long voyage home, but the precautions he took were worse than barbarous. He had a box built on deck. It was eleven feet long, and the only way in or out was through a locked hatch in the top. Into that box he crammed the fourteen captives, still manacled. On the voyage he ran his ship aground in the Torres Straits. She sank, and he gave the order to abandon ship; but he refused to unlock the box. At the last moment, somebody opened the hatch, and the master-at-arms dropped the keys of the manacles through the hole. Ten of the men succeeded in climbing out: the other four were drowned. With the crew, the ten escaped from the wreck in boats. Then, in captivity again, they were reshipped to England, where they were put on trial. Bligh had meanwhile gone on a second breadfruit expedition, which was successful. In his absence, and on his written evidence, four men were found innocent and six guilty: and of the six, three were pardoned and the other three were hanged.

PART III
ORIGINAL SIN
1796–1842

———— ••❧❦❧•• ————

TWELVE

The Mission of the Duff

AT SIX O'CLOCK on the morning of 10 August 1796, a ship named the *Duff* dropped down the Thames on the ebb tide, with a flag at the mizzen top-gallant which bore three silver doves on a purple field with olive branches in their beaks. On board a hundred voices were singing the hymn 'Jesus at Thy command, We launch into the deep', which the sailors in the ships they passed heard 'with silent astonishment', as well they might. The London Missionary Society, newly founded, was sending a mission to Tahiti.

Nobody now could write about this expedition and hide his own prejudice, for or against it. The only honest thing is to let the prejudice show when it must, but not to let it distort the recorded facts.

The directors of the London Missionary Society were said to hold 'the doctrinal articles of the Church of England in the sense usually termed Calvinistic'. Of course they were learned theologians, but inevitably the missionaries they sent on the first of their missions were not of the same intellectual calibre. They represented the most primitive, inflexible end of the range of eighteenth-century Calvinism. They meant well, they worked without sparing themselves for what they thought was right, they were often brave, and they soon came to like the Tahitians; but one has to add that they were fearsomely narrow-minded. All their thoughts came from literal reading of the Bible, 'that inestimable book, compared with which all beside is pompous ignorance'. They believed unshakably that they knew the only and absolute truth, and were bidden by God to take its blessing to heathen idolators. One of them wrote, 'the real Christian in every situation of life possesses peculiar excellence'; and in that confident self-esteem they were ready to destroy whatever the Devil put in their way. They most firmly believed in original sin: mankind, since the fall of Adam, was essentially wicked; every baby was born in sin, and the only possible way to redemption and the mercy of God was through true repentance, baptism, faith and the sacrament of the Last Supper. In their view, since no Tahitian had followed that way all Tahitians must be wicked, and condemned to eternal hell-fire unless they could be rescued by conversion. It was a view extremely opposed to Rousseau and the theorists of the innocence of the Noble Savage; and it was a doctrine the Tahitians for many years found quite impossible to credit.

There were thirty missionaries altogether, with six of their wives and four children, one of whom, a boy of ten, died of consumption when they came to Portsmouth. Only eighteen, and five of the wives, were destined for Tahiti – the others chose to try Tonga or the Marquesas – and only four were ordained ministers. All the rest were artisans from the poorest of London parishes – carpenters, smiths, weavers, bricklayers, shoemakers, tailors, one hatter, one cooper, one surgeon, one butcher, and one buckle and harness maker. They had been chosen by a church committee mainly for their piety, but also in the hope that their useful arts would be welcomed by the heathen. The heathen, however, turned out to have no iron for the smiths to work on, no woven cloth, no barrels, bricks or shoes, hats, harnesses or buckles, and did not want anything except the iron which the missionaries had brought in rods and bars on the ship. On the other hand, they did have a religion of their own which satisfied them completely, and their faith in it was every bit as strong as the Calvinists' was in theirs.

The *Duff* had been chartered by the Society, and her crew had also been chosen for their moral quality, though moral sailors were rare. The captain, James Wilson, had been captured by the French in India. He escaped by swimming a river full of crocodiles, had been recaptured and kept in a dungeon by a rajah and had escaped again; and then had seen the light and confessed his sins. The chief officer was his nephew William, who was equally devout and wrote his own journal of the voyage of the *Duff*.

While they were waiting for a wind in Portsmouth, they sent a communal letter to the directors of the Society which revealed their mode of thought: 'When, in our imagination, we conceive ourselves landed on our destined islands, surrounded by multitudes of the inhabitants, earnestly enquiring, "From whence do you come? and what is your errand?" we answer, "From a distant shore: the friends of God and human kind; touched with compassion at your unhappy state, as represented by our countrymen who have formerly visited you; moved by the Spirit of our God, we have forsaken relatives and friends, braved storms and tempests, to teach you the knowledge of Jesus, whom to know is eternal life . . . Though Satan and all the host of hell should be stung with indignation and resentment at our boldness in the Lord, and fire the hearts of their deluded votaries with all the fury and madness which brutal ignorance and savage cruelty are capable of . . . yet, trusting in the faithfulness of the Most High, the goodness of our cause, the uprightness of our intentions, the fervency of our affection for Christ our head, and the elect of God, our hearts remain undaunted . . .' There was a lot of rethinking to be done before this could be put into words to charm the Tahitians.

It seems that not one of the missionaries, who were the only passengers, had ever left England before. They had scarcely left their own parishes, which of course was less unusual then than it would be now; and they started, like so many newcomers to the sea, by being dreadfully seasick. The butcher's wife was so bad that they both gave up and went ashore in Portsmouth, but the others all suffered on, naïvely amazed by everything and marvelling at the hand of the Lord that protected them. It was indeed a perfectly successful voyage. They stopped in Rio and were disconcerted by the signs of popery there, and then they sailed non-stop by the route that Bligh had taken, south of Africa and Australia and north of New Zealand, 13,820 miles on their log and further, Captain Wilson believed, than anyone had ever sailed before without a sight of land. Only six months out of Portsmouth, on Sunday 5 March, they were in Matavai Bay. Coming more than half-way round the world, their calendar was a day wrong. They never put it right, and fifty years later they were still observing the Sabbath (one of their strictest rules) on the day everyone else said was Saturday.

Tahitians swarmed on board that Sunday – or Saturday – morning, pleaded to be their *taios* and deluged them with presents of cloth and fruit and pigs, which they rejected because, as they tried to explain, it was God's day, when they could not do any transaction. The refusal of gifts of women caused even more hurt and surprise. Instead, the brethren proposed Divine Service on the quarter deck. Hymns were chosen for their harmonious tunes, 'O'er the gloomy hills of darkness', 'Blow ye the trumpet, blow', and finally 'Praise God from whom all blessings flow', and one brother preached, in English, with peculiar solemnity and eloquence, on the text of the First Epistle General of John, chapter 4 verse 8, 'God is love'. The service lasted an hour and a quarter. Forty or fifty Tahitians were present, mostly *arioi*, and everyone seemed 'charmed and filled with amazement', except that they talked and laughed in the hymns and had to be brought to order. It was the first of very many incongruous scenes.

It was a pity these men brought such a dour and cheerless creed. Tahitians were always merry. The missionaries – one can only judge by what they wrote – seldom laughed, never made a joke or understood anyone else's, never enjoyed what they condemned as unseemly levity, and never let themselves forget for a moment the awful burden of the sins of the world. The word 'gloomy' in the first line of the first of the hymns they sang was a summary of their view of life – or at least of how it appeared to others – and the clothes they wore were a conscious symbol: black top hats, black frock coats, black boots and trousers, and their wives in bonnets, if not black then decently obfusc, and respectable dresses that hid and disguised their bodies from chin to toe. Perhaps it was also symbolic that they never seem to have used their Christian names, but always referred to each other by surnames and titles: the Reverend for the ministers, Mr, or more often Brother, for everyone else – Brother Nobbs, who was the hatter, or Brother Cock, a carpenter – and Mrs for all the wives, even their own. They very much valued the fraternal love that united them, and took care to preserve it by formal politeness to each other.

From the moment they anchored in Matavai Bay – or rather, from the Monday morning when they were ready to listen – they were overwhelmed by the Tahitians' ebullient, indiscriminate love and kindness. Their first individual contact was with an elderly man they called Manne-Manne, who they understood was the head priest of Tahiti and an ex-chief of a neighbouring island, and they also soon met Pomare, the chief regent, and his son, the young chief Tu. They thought Tu was about seventeen, but Bligh,

The first landing from the *Duff*, by R. A. Smirke: a
huge painting commissioned by the Missionary Society
for presentation to Captain Wilson

six years before, had thought he was eight: seventeen or fourteen,
he was tall and well-built like his father and was already married.
Luckily, two Swedes also turned up in a canoe – beachcombers
who had landed from two separate ships; they both spoke English
and Tahitian and volunteered to act as interpreters, though the
missionaries were, quite reasonably, wary of trusting them. When
the missionaries managed to explain that they wanted to live
ashore, they were instantly given a very large house on Point
Venus, which had been built for Bligh and never used except to
store his seedlings. When they asked for a plot of land to go with it
they were invited to take the whole district of Matavai Bay.
Captain Wilson and several others went ashore and made plans to

divide the house into compartments – bedrooms for the married couples, others for the bachelors, a library, a store-room and a place for the surgeon and his medicines, and at the other end a large open space for a chapel – and the Tahitians joined in with vast enthusiasm and bundles of bamboos to do the building. More food was given to the visitors than they could possibly eat, and all the while the building went on the *arioi* entertained everyone with wrestling matches.

It was probably a happier, more cheerful, and less inhibited scene than the missionaries had ever encountered, as exotic in its human elements as in the tropical surroundings and the warm blue sea after the riverside parishes of London. But they were not surprised by the evidence of love and kindness. Some of them had read the journals of some of the earlier discoverers, and all of them knew the official story of the *Bounty* mutineers. So they were warned of the allure of Tahiti. They had a short period when they could not believe it. The plan had been for the *Duff* to leave the Tahiti volunteers, go on to drop the others in Tonga or the Marquesas, and then come back to Tahiti before going home. As the time approached, those who were staying took fright and suggested that all of them should stay, with the ship to protect them: they suspected the kindness was only a ruse and might suddenly turn to plunder and massacre. It was not surprising they felt exposed. But they were not short of courage, as the Spanish padres had been, and a committee of senior members talked them out of their fears. It was resolved to stick to the plan and pray. The *Duff* went away, and left seventeen men, five wives and three children. One man, the surgeon, had refused to stay.

Their mistrust faded fairly quickly, and they began to find themselves, unexpectedly, respecting the heathen, thinking of them with affection and comparing them favourably with the nominal Christians who had been there before. Of course nobody attacked the visitors. Nobody even tried to rob them in Tahiti, though there were thefts in some other islands. Not even the girls were importunate, though there was one upsetting incident right at the beginning, before the *Duff* had gone. Manne-Manne, the high priest, persuaded Captain Wilson to be his *taio*, and then brought five girls on board, all apparently under fifteen, who the missionaries understood were his wives. He invited the captain to take his pick, could not believe him when he declined, and even asked them all in the morning which of them had been chosen.

The old priest was given a lecture on the evils of polygamy, and 'did not at all relish this doctrine'. But it must have been a misunderstanding. Nobody in Tahiti, not even a priest and ex-chief, could possibly have had five wives in their early teens, and the girls can only have been young willing friends of his.

After that, the Tahitians seem to have understood very quickly that these men in black were quite different from any Englishmen they had met before, except Captain Cook himself and a few like Dr Forster: they were as hungry as anyone for food, but not hungry for sex. Some supposed there was something wrong with them, that they had the misfortune to be incomplete; but when they further understood it was a religious principle they began to excuse the girls' previous behaviour: they claimed it had been the English sailors who insisted. In their own minds, that may have been true. Confronted by sailors, the girls had only done what they always did with men, made themselves as alluring as they could; but with frustrated sailors, it had let loose an outburst of lust far beyond what they expected. It had surprised the girls, but they did not deny they had enjoyed their success.

However, they made no massed assault on the missionaries, as they had on the other English ships they had seen. Only a few individual offers of seduction were recorded. One of them, in the Marquesas, so upset Brother Harris, a cooper, that he ran away in the dark and spent the rest of a stormy night sitting on his sea-chest on the beach. Brother Harris and his chest had to be hauled off through the breakers the next morning, using ropes from a boat.

Right from the beginning, it was an arduous life on Point Venus – and not least for the wives. Apart from their presence, it was much as one imagines life must have been during the founding of a medieval monastery, and utterly unlike the surrounding life of Tahiti. A bell was rung at six in the morning; at half past, everyone assembled for prayers; after that, they laboured at their 'various occupations' till ten. The period from ten to three was allotted to mental improvement; and from three until dusk for more of the 'various occupations'. The bell rang again at seven for prayers and the reading of the journal.

The 'various occupations' were their respective trades, so far as they could be applied in Tahiti. They planted a garden of seeds of familiar vegetables, and built a shed for a blacksmith's forge; they built pens for the pigs and fowls they had been given, and a flat-bottomed boat for carrying goods and passengers in through the river mouth, avoiding the need to land on the open beach. In between times they wrote their sermons and endlessly discussed their many problems.

When, after fairly long experience, the missionaries came to make a joint report on Tahitians, it was full of the word 'surprising'; what surprised them was that they found so much to approve or even admire. 'Their generosity is boundless,' they said, 'and appears excessive: the instances our brethren record are surprising. Not only cartloads of provision more than they could consume were sent in for the whole body, but individuals have received the most surprising abundance, without any adequate return even expected or suggested. To one of the missionaries was given as a present a double canoe, with a travelling house, three large pearls, a fine seine, a beautiful feathered breastplate, two large hogs, sandal wood, cloth and fine mats in abundance.' And again they said: 'all are friendly and generous, even to a fault; they hardly refuse anything to each other . . . Poverty never makes a man contemptible; but to be affluent and covetous is the greatest shame and reproach . . . They will give their clothes from their back, rather than be called *peere peere*, or stingy.'

They had special praise for the girls. They were disappointed in their physical beauty: like some other Europeans, they thought them too masculine. 'Yet they possess eminent feminine graces: their faces are never darkened with a scowl, or covered with a cloud of sullenness or suspicion. Their manners are affable and engaging; their step easy, firm, and graceful; their behaviour free and unguarded; always boundless in generosity to each other, and to strangers; their tempers mild, gentle, and unaffected; slow to take offence, easily pacified, and seldom retaining resentment or revenge, whatever provocation they may have received . . . Many are true and tender wives. Our European sailors who have cohabited with them have declared, that more faithful and affectionate creatures to them and their children could no where be found.'

The brethren had nothing to say about the girls' promiscuity, except that 'their ideas, no doubt, of shame and delicacy are very different from ours; they are not yet advanced to such a state of civilization and refinement.' On the other hand, they gallantly believed what the girls said about themselves and the sailors; 'It is too true, that for the sake of gaining our extraordinary curiosities, and to please our brutes, they have appeared immodest in the extreme. Yet they lay the charge wholly at our door, and say that Englishmen are ashamed of nothing, and that we have led them to public acts of indecency never before practised among themselves. Iron, here more precious than gold, bears down every barrier of restraint: honesty and modesty yield to the force of temptation.' The brethren were being too credulous; but many other unexpected people, for many reasons, felt they had to come to the defence of Tahitian girls.

Even these stern Calvinists found only three specific sins in Tahiti. Two were the same that many other visitors had reported: infanticide and human sacrifice. The third was something new: what they called 'onanism', which to them meant any kind of homosexual activity. This was probably common in Tahiti. The women, as the brethren had observed, were not so purely feminine as European women were supposed to be: nor were the men so purely masculine. After the way they were all brought up, nothing was likely to be uncommon or disapproved of unless it was harmful or unkind. Probably it had passed without comment from most of the visitors for two reasons: they had not noticed it in the deluge of women, and in the late eighteenth century, as in the nineteenth, homosexuality was a thing one mentioned only obliquely in writing. The missionaries wrote of 'many unnatural crimes, which we dare not name, committed daily without the idea of shame or guilt'. They closed their eyes and minds to it, except among 'a set of men of the most execrable cast, called *mahoos*, affecting the manners, dress, gestures, and voice of females, and too horrid to be described.' Nevertheless, other people did describe the *mahoos* or *mahu*s, but without discovering whether their odd behaviour was mainly sexual or mainly a social convenience, a way of getting a desirable place in the household of a chief. Tahitians showed no disapproval of them at all. But how widespread and commonplace true homosexuality really was must remain an inquisitive question that cannot be answered, because nobody answered it clearly at the time.

Nor is it clear what standards the missionaries used in their judgement of Tahitians. Much later, they said it was the Ten Commandments. If so, they must have found that rules made for Jews in the time of Moses were hard to apply to Tahiti. In those that could be applied, the Tahitians showed well. No doubt there were bad men among them, but in general they coveted nothing,

honoured their fathers and mothers, did not steal except, as a kind
of sport, from Europeans, and bore no false witness. They were
adulterous by the European definition of adultery, but not by
their own. If they made graven images they did not worship them,
and they committed no murder except (like the Christians) in
war, and in the two circumstances of sacrifice and infanticide. Nor
did they take the name of their god in vain: on that, the missionaries quoted Cook with approval: 'Captain Cook does the
Otaheiteans but justice in saying, they reproach many who bear
the name of Christian. You see no instances of an Otaheitean
drawing near the Eatooa [Te Atua] with carelessness or inatten-
tion; he is all devotion; he approaches the place of worship with
reverential awe; uncovers when he treads on sacred ground; and
prays with a fervour that would do honour to a better profession.
He firmly credits the traditions of his ancestors. None dares
dispute the existence of deity.'

That left only two Commandments. The Tahitians did not
observe the Sabbath because they had never heard of it and
besides, did no burdensome labour on any day of the week, let
alone the Sabbath. More fundamental was the first Command-
ment, 'Thou shalt have none other gods but me'; that was
where the Tahitians failed. Undeniably, Te Atua was not a deriva-
tive of the Jehovah of Moses. He was not the Christian God –
although the likeness was remarkable; the missionaries even learned when they enquired that Te Atua could be conceived as a
trinity: god the father, god the son, and god the bird or spirit.

On the other hand, if the missionaries judged by St Paul's
three criteria, they found the Tahitians had perfect faith, though
in their own version of God; they had not much need of hope,
because they were not threatened by gods or men; and of charity,
the greatest of the three, they had an abundance.

Perhaps less stern and more forgiving Christians would have
left well alone, and found some way of combining the different
faiths and preserving the best of both; but the doctrine of original
sin stood in the way. In that view, a man could not claim to be
virtuous if he had never been tempted. Virtue had to be achieved
by battle against the devil. The creed required the Devil as well as
God, Hell as well as Heaven, a constant war in which one had to
take sides. The missionaries found a semblance of God in Tahiti:
what they had to import was the Devil.

They longed to preach, not only to each other, which they did at least twice a day, but to the crowds. They could only do it, in the beginning, by using the Swedes as interpreters; and they could not know how much of their careful thought survived that ignorant and possibly malicious rendering. They did not make the mistake the Spaniards did, of shutting Tahitians out of their services; on the contrary, they welcomed them, except to the sacraments. Their makeshift chapel had no door and was always open; crowds hovered round outside it, especially for the hymns, and sometimes ventured in. There was a tragi-comic scene when Manne-Manne, the high priest, made his way into a communion service and lined up with the communicants, hoping to share the bread and wine; and when they passed him by, he nipped round the back and joined the line further down for a second try.

The Swedes were a constant bugbear; so were other castaways and deserters the missionaries met from time to time. All of them had homes and women somewhere, and some had children; so they were always disappearing and were seldom there when they were wanted as interpreters. Obviously, back in Europe, they would have been sinners and gaolbirds of the deepest dye, who could only be expected to undo what the missionaries were trying to do and to mislead the Tahitians whenever they could.

It was their unwelcome dependence on people like this that began to make the brethren see their task on a new timescale. The naïve vision they had expressed in Portsmouth began to fade. These were no ignorant heathen, consciously miserable, eagerly awaiting the glad tidings of the knowledge of Jesus; on the contrary, these were people with minds and a god of their own, who were consciously and visibly happy. To reach them and begin to change them, the missionaries would first have to become as fluent in Tahitian as the Swedes; and beyond that, they would have to translate the Bible, the source of all they believed. They were embarked on a labour no single lifetime could complete. But still they were not daunted. They gave up any idea of making the quick conversions some missionaries claimed in other lands, and began to put together a printing press, first to print a Tahitian dictionary and grammar for themselves and then, God willing, to print the Bible in Tahitian.

Meanwhile, however, there were opportunities to explain what they thought of the sins that came to their notice. The first was when Manne-Manne was having dinner with them and drank rather a lot of red wine. When he wanted yet another glass, he felt he had to offer an explanation: he was going to officiate that afternoon, he said, at a human sacrifice, and the wine gave him courage. A Swede hastily told him he had made a gaffe, but also told the brethren what he had said. They mulled over it for a week, then told Manne-Manne that if he did such things, he would forfeit their friendship. He said he would reform, but the brethren 'informed him, that our Lord knew his heart, whether he was sincere in his promises'. And he certainly was not.

Against such sins, the brethren had only two arguments. One was the threat of their own displeasure, amplified by a threat that they would go away to another island. They used it against Pomare when they found he also approved of human sacrifice, and he was 'evidently affected'; though it was hard to say whether he really wanted them to stay or was only being polite. The other argument was that the British God detested such practices, but that was less effective: the Tahitians answered with amiable logic that the Tahitian god liked them.

Infanticide was an even more pressing problem. Iddeah, the manly wife of Pomare and mother of the young chief Tu, was pregnant again, and announced that she meant to let her baby die, because its father was not Pomare but her current lover, who was one of her servants. The missionaries accepted her marital eccentricity as something based on a concept of marriage unlike their own: 'Pomare and Iddeah had for some time ceased to cohabit; he had taken another wife, and she one of her servants; but they lived in the same state of friendship, and with no loss of dignity.' But they could not understand or condone the family logic which meant that any babies she conceived with the servant would not be allowed to live. They confused the two cases which made the deed essential in Tahitian eyes: the *arioi*, who did it to fulfil the society's oath and preserve the society, and the chiefly families, who did it to preserve their holy lineage. Iddeah's case was the latter. If the baby had been Pomare's, she explained to the brethren, it would have been all right; but it was quite unthinkable for her or her family, or anyone else, that young Tu, the chief, should have a half-brother or half-sister who was base born, with a servant as father. In two or three generations, such a thing would dilute the family blood till it ceased to exist.

The brethren used everything from bribes to threats to persuade her that killing the baby would be a dreadful crime. They even made a kindly offer to adopt the infant themselves and have their wives look after it. But that was not the point, she said: she was quite able to look after it herself. The point was that it could not be allowed to live. They offered her three shirts and other gifts; 'Yea more, that we would report her conduct to Queen Charlotte and the British *arioi* ladies, to whom nothing would more endear her.' They 'failed not to open the wrath of God', and Brother Lewis, one of the ordained ministers, preached from 'Thou shalt not kill'.

They could not change her mind, because they did not yet understand what they were up against. They were asking Iddeah to defy a respected belief, to defy the whole of her extended family, destroy its sanctity, and probably also forfeit Pomare's power and her son Tu's right to the chiefdom; and all at the whim, as it seemed to her, of an unknown foreign god. She was highly offended, and said she had a right to do what she pleased with her babies and would observe the custom of her country in spite of the brethren's displeasure. And so she did.

Her unnatural crime did not go unpunished, the brethren recorded: 'a dreadful milk abscess brought her under the surgeon's knife, and repeated sharp rebukes'. They ostracized her, and refused to give her any presents or accept any from her. But they had to forgive her in the end – she was a very influential person whose support they needed – and there is a glimpse of her three months later taking a dish of tea with Mrs Cover, a minister's wife, as if they had been in an English vicarage.

The *Duff* had first arrived in early March. It left to take small parties of missionaries to Tonga and the Marquesas, and came back on 6 July. Between then and the *Duff*'s final departure for England on 3 August, the brethren in Matavai Bay reported their progress to Captain Wilson, and wrote the letters on which their joint report was founded.

The progress had been meagre. Once in a while, when a Swede had translated a sermon sentence by sentence, a Tahitian had said he had understood it and it was *my ty*, which seemed to mean very good. One, who had learnt English phrases, said the British God was a good fellow, and several that they would change their religion if the chiefs did it first. These reactions lifted the brethren's spirits for a moment, but the chiefs showed no sign of giving a lead to the rest. Everyone was ready to listen politely; but it was their nature to be polite. The brethren could only say that the people seemed to be teachable, but were 'rooted in the traditions and prejudices of their ancestors'. If they themselves persevered and learnt the language, they hoped to have a great effect on the rising generation.

Meanwhile they could only claim four things with satisfaction. The Tahitians had given up having feasts or *heivas* within the missionaries' hearing; they behaved with decency round the mission house on the Sabbath; their dress and manners showed 'a great improvement on the side of modesty'; finally, a most pathetic and revealing claim, their own example had 'already restrained the natural levity of the natives'.

They had discovered they could not destroy the Tahitians' creed simply by offering them another. Tahitians were quite unaware of sin, or of themselves as sinners: there was nothing to attract them to a god who threatened to burn them eternally in hell. Nor was there anything attractive in the brethren's life of religious melancholy. There was only one other thing the brethren could do, and they set to work with awful determination to do it: destroy the contentment and happiness the Tahitians' belief had brought them and reduce them to the misery of the poor in England, to whom the message of preachers could be joyful news.

So, at the end of the first four months, the missionaries' opinion of Tahitians was the same as everyone else's: they were good people, generous, kind, and happy. The report which expressed this joint opinion was put together by the Society when the *Duff* brought back their letters to England, and it was published in 1799.

Very much later, in 1845, another report was published, with the directors' blessing, in a history of the Society, and it said exactly the opposite: the Tahitians, before the missionaries came, had been mean, cruel, malignant, oppressed by their rulers, dishonest, untruthful, depraved, ferocious, quarrelsome, and warlike. They were idolators sunk to the lowest possible depth of moral degradation, whose 'system of superstition was one of the most absurd and sanguinary that ever prevailed among mankind'.

Beyond any reasonable doubt, this was a string of lies; yet the directors of the Society were not the men to tell deliberate lies. They must have been persuaded by the passage of forty-six years that it was true. What then had happened to make them so contradict their predecessors, and contradict everyone who had seen and described Tahiti in its early days?

The answer is not perfectly simple, because many things were changing. The whole principle of missionary work was changing: it was becoming rather gentler, and less self-righteous. In the meantime, also, the missionaries had fundamentally changed the Tahitians. There were still a few people alive who remembered the Tahitians as they had been – Joseph Banks for one – but there were not many. Nearly all the original thirty brethren were dead or retired from active life, and only two were still in Tahiti. Mission work had come under widespread criticism, especially for what it had done to the Tahitians. The Society was prepared to admit mistakes had been made in Tahiti, which was its first experiment; but it could not admit, as some people were saying, that its results were entirely evil. Tahitians in 1845 were certainly unsatisfactory people, to themselves and everyone else. But the missions could not admit they had made them so; they had to maintain they had been even worse before the missionaries came.

In the first year, the missions suffered many disasters. The *Duff* got safely back to England, and the Society turned her quickly round and sent her out again, just before Christmas 1798, with another party of twenty-nine volunteers for Tahiti, of whom nine had wives and some had children. But this time, off Rio, she was captured by a French privateer. The French took her into Montevideo and sold her there, and dumped the missionaries ashore.

Montevideo was not unfriendly. It was Spanish, and Spain was still neutral in the war between France and England; but the missionaries were unwillingly stuck there for a couple of months. Then they found a small packet that could give them a passage back to Rio. On the way they were captured again, this time by a Portuguese warship. Portugal was also neutral, so it is not at all clear what offence the packet had given; but the mission party was divided into groups in a Portuguese convoy and taken to Lisbon. There they found several ships that were bound for England, and they arrived home, still in small groups, after a year at sea, ragged, broken and sick of adventure. And the Society had lost its ship.

But things were settling down in Tahiti. The excitement of the *Duff*'s arrival had worn off. The Tahitians continued to look after the brethren and their wives, and they loved their children; but they could not imagine what they had come for. Not trade apparently; not women; not conquest or land. It had sunk into their minds that the brethren wanted to make them believe in the

English God, but that did not seem to them an adequate reason. They thought there must be something else behind it, and they waited to find out what it was. Since the brethren ate voraciously, some guessed they had only come for food, and that England must be starving. They enjoyed it when the visitors sang hymns, but that could not compare with the religious exaltation (which Cook had described) of the ceremonies in their own *marae*, much less with the prayer meetings of their revivalists, the *arioi*, which culminated in all the fun of humorous plays, mock battles and erotic dances.

As for the brethren, they came to an impasse. They had made friends with the people and had tried their best to explain that the Christian God was the only real one, but nobody was impressed. It was a fact so obvious in missionary circles that nobody had really thought of having to prove or explain it, in a language they did not know, to people who had a satisfactory god of their own. Certainly it was a problem far beyond the powers of pious bakers and weavers.

They tried to impress the natives by showing their superior skill in 'useful arts', as if to prove that better shoemakers, weavers, or hatters must have a better god. They set to work to build themselves a new house with solid boarded walls and floors and lockable doors, in the hope that Tahitians would copy them and spend less time in useless amusements. But the Tahitians saw no point in it. They preferred their own airy houses, which they could build in two or three days, to a solid house that took months. In all the arts that were really useful in Tahiti, the brethren were sadly inept, as only townsmen could be. They were not resourceful, like eighteenth-century sailors; they were incompetent Robinson Crusoes. They could not manage canoes, and when they tried they had to shout for rescue – as, for example, when they put to sea in a canoe and forgot to take the paddles, sailed downwind and could not get back again. Probably, although they never exactly said so, they could not swim: in any case, when Tahitians were merrily bathing in the rivers or surfing on the reefs, the brethren were too prudish to take off their clothes. They could not climb trees, least of all coconut trees. They were not much good on rocks: time and again, when they undertook long walks, they found themselves spreadeagled on a rock and shouting for help, while even pregnant Tahitian women passed the same way. They asked to be carried over the least of rivers. They could only light fires with matches.

They were always making themselves look foolish, and, far from admiring their skill, the Tahitians pitied their clumsiness.

A particularly risky enterprise was their hospital. The only one of them listed as a surgeon had already gone home in the *Duff*, but they set up a hospital near their house and invited everyone for treatment. Hardly anyone came. Of the few who ventured in, some expected to be given a present if they took the foreign medicine; others would only take it if it was sweet. All expected a miracle cure, if any, and if they were not well the following day they went away in disgust. The brethren explained to themselves that native medicines were administered by priests, and depended on prayer to be effective. People were afraid to take the European doses for fear of offending their own god and making things worse. The brethren condemned this as superstition; but really the same could have been said about European medicine in the 1790s, especially when it was prescribed by people without any medical training at all. They were putting faith to an unequal test. If one of their cures seemed to work – and instantly – the patient gave credit to his own god, to whom he had also prayed; if it did not, which was much more likely, he blamed the British god.

So for a year the missionaries mystified the Tahitians, but they did not antagonize them and did not wear out their generosity. The crisis came in an unexpected and really rather ludicrous way. In March 1798, exactly a year from the day when they landed, a ship came in to Matavai Bay, the first that had been seen since the *Duff* departed. She was the *Nautilus*, bound from Macao in China to the north-west coast of America for a cargo of furs. No ship on that route and in that trade would be a high-class vessel, and she had an English captain and a motley crew, probably mostly Chinese. She was so short-handed that she had hijacked six Hawaiians; she had been driven thousands of miles off course by bad weather, and had run out of stores; and she had nothing to barter for food except muskets, powder, and shot.

Those were the only things the Tahitians wanted by then; the old, innocent days of beads and red feathers had gone. They were also the only things the missionaries did not want them to have; they had too many already, though most of them did not work. So the missionaries decided to supply the *Nautilus* themselves, with the pigs and fruit they had already been given. The six Hawaiians deserted and joined Pomare, and the captain appealed to the missionaries to get them back. They agreed to help the captain with that, too, but only partly succeeded: one of the deserters was taken by the mission's Tahitian servants and forcibly put on board again, but the others stayed. To everyone's relief the *Nautilus* departed.

A fortnight later she was back in even worse distress, after another storm. She had abandoned her voyage and now was demanding supplies to get her to the penal settlement at Botany Bay. Two more sailors deserted, and men were another thing Pomare wanted: muskets to fight with, and sailors to teach his followers how to fight. Again the captain went to the missionaries for help, and again they agreed: they did not want more dissolute sailors on the island. Four of them went to see Tu and tell him he must send the deserters back. He refused, so they went to look for Pomare.

This was straining the Tahitians' patience too far. The missionaries, it seemed to them, had unfairly stopped them trading and taken the trade for themselves. Now they were claiming the right to decide who should visit the island and who should not, and demanding that Tu should turn out men who were willing to help him. On their way to find Pomare, the four were set upon, 'their clothes were forcibly torn from their bodies', and all of them thought they were being murdered. They were not. 'Stripped as they were, except a small girdle of native cloth,' they were taken to see Pomare and his wife Iddeah, who 'expressed their utmost distress at the calamity', dressed them more thoroughly in native cloth and sent them home by canoe – but kept the deserters. Back home, the missionaries found all their companions expecting murder and preparing to sell their lives dearly.

It was not a very serious assault. Removing a pompous person's clothes, especially his trousers, has always been a popular sport and revenge – for example at universities, where it used to be called 'debagging' – and the Tahitians' sense of humour was always youthful. Two days later, the clothes were returned, and the high priest came to call with a plantain shoot and a chicken as a sign of peace. But the brethren were utterly outraged; so much so that eleven of them, including four who were married, decided then and there to abandon the wicked island and its heathen. They took passage in the *Nautilus* to Botany Bay, where they found, according to the Society's historian, that 'they had rushed upon the very evils from which they fled at Tahiti': that historian was very critical of them. They ought not to have tried to usurp the chiefs' authority, and their alarm was unwarranted by any real or apparent danger. It was just as well they had gone, he concluded.

Anyhow, only six of the seventeen brethren were left to carry on. One of them was Brother Harris, who had been so frightened by the threat of seduction in the Marquesas, and he too gave up and went home soon afterwards. Another was the Reverend Mr Lewis, one of the ordained ministers, who soon announced that he was going to marry a Tahitian, and left the mission house to live with her. His case was tragic. After he had gone, he spent his time gardening and trying to help the chiefs and the people, and he continued to read the Bible and pray. The Tahitians liked him, and his perhaps was the best way to approach them – to become as nearly as possible one of them. He might have had more success than anyone else. But the missionaries refused him a Christian marriage although the affair had not yet been consummated, and they excommunicated him: his course, they said, was directly opposed to the word of God (but why?), and was therefore sinful. Four months later, he was found dead in his house with marks of violence on his body. His wife said he had done it himself, but the brethren decided, without any special evidence, that he had been murdered. They were sorry afterwards they had not treated him better. Perhaps they thought they had driven him to suicide, and did not want to think it.

About the same time, both the other missions, to Tonga and the Marquesas, were abandoned, and not a single soul in any of the three had been saved from damnation. The seven men who had gone to Tonga fared worst. Among the first people they met were two escaped convicts from Botany Bay, called Ambler and Connelly, 'men who seemed ripe for every crime', and very soon afterwards seven more sailors deserted from an American ship – probably a whaler – men who 'seemed if possible even more depraved and vicious'. Ambler and Connelly had been there for eighteen months, enjoying all the delights of what Cook had called the Friendly Islands; and of course the very last people they wanted to see in their sensual paradise were missionaries, who would disapprove of everything they were doing and try to stop them doing it, and would also, they may have surmised, have got them re-arrested by any British warship that came in. Yet the missionaries had to depend on these men as the only interpreters, and the only people who could tell them who was who in the islands. The two of them had won a lot of influence among the islanders, who of course neither knew nor cared if a man had a criminal past, but judged him entirely by what he did when he was with them. Very likely the pair had muskets and knew how to use them, an accomplishment every islander admired.

Within scarcely a week of landing, one of the brethren, Brother Veeson, a bricklayer, went native. He dressed himself as a Tongan, lived with the Tongans and acquired a Tongan girl. This was a different matter from Lewis's well-considered desertion: it can only have been that seven months' celibacy on the voyage had been too much for Veeson. He wanted a Christian wedding. There was only one ordained minister, and he had only been ordained when the ship was in Tahiti; but he agreed to regularize the union. When he explained to the girl, through Ambler or Connelly, the meaning of the Christian marriage vows she refused them with scorn, though she went on living with Veeson. Veeson then cut himself off entirely from the mission, and in the brethren's words 'embarked on a course of fearful apostasy, vice, and peril'.

Next, an elderly female chieftain died, and the missionaries were told – again presumably by the two gaolbirds – that they were suspected of causing her death by their prayers. They began to be robbed and abused. Next the supreme chief was murdered by his brother, and the islands were racked by civil war. The missionaries, who had weapons, were requested to fight, but they refused. Then everyone's hand was against them, they were plundered of all they possessed, their guns and even their clothes, either by rival gangs of fighters or by the sailors. They lost their houses, and were driven for food to follow the wake of the fighters, who sometimes fled in defeat. Once they saw Veeson fighting among the rest, but he ignored them. They longed to escape, and had built themselves a boat, but they built it so far inland that they could not drag it to the sea, and nobody would help them. Naked and hungry, they spent a long time hiding among the rocks on a deserted coast. At last, in a skirmish, three of them, and a sailor who lived with them, were killed. Nobody ever said where the sailor had come from.

The war ended, but the peace was not much better. The surviving missionaries were put to work at their own forge, turning out weapons and tools for one or another of the chiefs, sometimes threatened with death, sometimes offered friendly protection. An earthquake, followed by a typhoon, destroyed the fruit trees and brought everyone to the edge of starvation. After almost a year of constant horror, they heard a gun and saw a ship: an English privateer, which took them, destitute, to Botany Bay.

They were too far gone to denounce the two escaped convicts, or the other deserters. But they blamed them for most of their troubles, and they were probably right. Certainly Ambler and Connelly had good reason to want to get rid of them, and it is only surprising that they stopped short of murdering them all.

Of all three missions, only the one in the Marquesas was perfectly peaceful, perhaps because only one of the brethren landed there. This was Brother Crook, who was left alone when Brother Harris took fright at the assault on his virtue. Crook was a very young man, only twenty-one, who was listed as a 'gentleman's servant, and since tin-worker'. The trade of a tin-worker could not have been more useless in a South Sea island, but perhaps his time as a gentleman's servant had given him a broader view of the world. At all events, he was evidently likeable, sensible, and brave.

Alone in the Marquesas, everyone treated him with the utmost kindness. The chief adopted him as his son, Nobody there had much to eat, often only a paste made from last year's breadfruit. They shared it all with him. But they simply could not see any reason why they should abandon their faith in their god and accept another.

Crook stayed a year on that island and only left it by chance. He was paying a visit to an American ship in the offing when she was blown out to sea. He could not get back, and was landed on another island sixty miles away. There he stayed seven months. It was just the same story: there were more people there and they had rather more food, but they were equally kind, equally fond of Crook, and equally devoted to their own god. When a ship came in that was going to England, he went with it, intending to confer with the Society and then come back. But he never did. Possibly, to judge him by his actions, he may have put forward a feasible interpretation of God's will which had not been mentioned by any of the others: that the happiness of the islanders was also God's creation, and it was impious to disturb it.

THIRTEEN

Muskets and Mercenaries

————••€)€3••————

THIS WAS the year 1800 – a convenient date to look back at the thirty-three years since the *Dolphin* fired her broadside, and to see what changes the Europeans had so far brought to Tahiti.

The changes were remarkably small. Visually, there were none. Even Matavai Bay, where most of the visitors landed, still seemed the beautiful, virginal place it had always been, and people landing for the first time still felt 'imparadised'. Any marks they made on it were soon obliterated by its verdant growth, as surely as their footprints on the sandy beach were obliterated by the winds and waves. A botanist might have noticed one or two new species of trees; but to anyone else's eyes the hectic adventures of those years might never have happened. The Tahitians imposed on the island the patterns of their ancient way of living, which were unchanging: their houses fell down but were built again in the same way, scattered haphazardly in the shade of the trees and joined by meandering, footworn paths. There were still no other kinds of tracks. Probably somebody had tried to explain about wheels, but nobody yet had made one; and the horses and cattle the Europeans had left there, thinking they would be useful, had all died out. The only foreign animals were goats, which flourished in flocks in the mountains, untamed and of no practical use to anyone.

But the Tahitians themselves had begun to change. It was not a drastic change so far, no more than a seed of change which was germinating in their minds, as new diseases were germinating in their bodies. From the very day they learned that there were other people in the world, things could never be quite the same again. Primeval innocence had been shaken for ever by the *Dolphin*'s broadside.

The only thing that protected them from sudden change was their confident satisfaction with things as they were. They knew the Europeans were cleverer than them, but they did not envy their skill. So far as they could see, it only made life needlessly complicated. One of them put it neatly when he was dining on a ship and was told that the Tahitians ought to work harder. 'What for?' he replied, in effect. 'You people need so much. Just to eat, you need knives and forks, plates, chairs and tables. It costs work to make these things and eternally wash them. But we eat without them, so we save the work.' All through the years they stuck to this attitude of mind. They really thought their kind of life was better – as indeed it logically was.

Bartering had been going on all the time, whenever a ship was in. The Europeans were always in need of food, and usually of women, and they offered everything they could think of in exchange. Tahitians often took a passing fancy to some novelty, but in the end there were only three European possessions they coveted. One was iron, the second was muskets, and the third was rum.

By 1800 they may already have been – they probably were – less sure of themselves, less trustful of their own institutions; but it did not show. Superficially, they were as kind, carefree, and happy as they had always been, and no visitor could have noticed the incipient mental change. But one change, the most drastic and cruel of all, was growing obvious. They were dying.

Guesses at the population of the island were very vague, but there was no doubt it was falling fast. When the *Dolphin* sailed along the coast searching for a way through the reef, her master, Robertson, thought it was the most populous country he had ever seen: men, women, and children lined every yard of the shore, watching the ship that had come from outer space. Cook estimated in the 1770s that there were 200,000 Tahitians, but his way of making the estimate was very rough, and most people afterwards thought it was too high. Dr Forster, with more of an air of exactness, made it 121,500. During the *Duff*'s visit in 1797, the first officer, William Wilson, with two or three others, walked the whole way round the island counting the houses, and multiplied the count by an average number of people for each kind of house, which was probably more accurate than Cook's or Forster's guesses. The difference was astonishing. The new figure was of the order of one tenth of the original; to be precise, 16,050. Nine out of ten Tahitians had vanished. During the next fifteen or twenty years, while the missionaries were active, the numbers continued to fall, until there were no more than six or seven thousand

Tahitians left. If the figures were right, twenty-nine out of every thirty people had died without any child to take their place; and however far wrong the figures were, there was no possible question that the race was being driven to extinction.

The missionaries put it down to the people's sins – specifically idolatry, infanticide, and sacrifice. The Tahitians knew it was happening too, and in their philosophy the explanation was probably much the same: they were giving offence to Te Atua. Factually, the only possible primary cause was disease, though the psychological assault of the European presence may perhaps have been a secondary cause.

It was not only the 'venereal distemper', though that had become so widespread it might almost have been called universal. Tahitians, hitherto free from almost all infection, had no immunity from any disease the ships brought with them. Of course there was nobody there who could diagnose them, but it seems likely that diphtheria, tuberculosis, smallpox, viral infections, and pneumonia were among the fatal diseases. Tahitians said the sailors had infested their houses with fleas, and no doubt they brought lice and rat fleas too – sailors always had them – and hence typhus, which was commonly known as 'ships' fever'. When any of these diseases got a grip ashore, there was nothing to stop it. Whole families were commonly wiped out. One remote valley, which originally had four hundred people, was infested first by smallpox and then by tuberculosis, and in less than a year two survivors, one man and one woman, fled from its desolation. But the missionaries flourished, either blessed or immune.

The psychological effects came later. The most intelligent Tahitians thought of their race as doomed, but people in general were not despondent. Explorers of the Americas since Columbus had observed that some of the native races had the ability to lie down and die if they felt that life was not worth living. They showed no symptoms of sickness: it seemed to be an act of will. The Spaniards found it annoying: they wanted the Indians alive as slaves. It seems likely that Tahitians also had this enviable faculty: when they gave up wanting to live, they died. But not yet: in 1800 they still had hope and vitality.

Most of the missionaries, on the other hand, had lost the hope that had brought them there. They were certainly prudes, but one cannot think most of them ran away to Botany Bay just for fear of losing their trousers. That episode must have been a catalyst that started them admitting their doubts to each other. Their Christianity was unchangeable, but there was simply no way of passing it on to the Tahitians, who had a faith of their own and did not know a word of English. The whole plan had been wrong. It ought to have started with a few men who were scholarly enough to learn Tahitian quickly. Most of the humble artisans did not know how to begin. They were slow to criticize the men who had sent them out, but they could surely have been forgiven if they felt, and even said, that somebody ought to have thought of this before.

At any rate, only a few missionaries – six at first, then five, then four – were willing to look at the problem afresh and set themselves to master it.

When all the rest, and the wives and children, had packed their numerous boxes and bags and been taken off in boats to the *Nautilus*, those who were staying wrote a hasty letter to the directors of the Society. It began with a dutiful prayer, but wasted no time in explaining what had happened. Its main purpose was to beg the Society never to send out another large party, untrained, with masses of stores and provisions, and especially not to send wives and children. Missionaries ought to need nothing, they said, except a few hatchets or axes to give away as presents. The island provided 'food and raiment suitable to its climate . . . The more we are encumbered with wordly things, the less concern we have for the conversion of the heathen.' On the other hand, they promised 'the right hand of Christian brotherly friendship' if the Society would send four or six more Christian men, 'void of worldly encumbrances'.

On the day the *Nautilus* sailed, the missionaries began to put these ascetic ideas into practice. They had always been well armed, but equally had always resolved not to take any part in Tahitian wars and only to use their weapons in self-defence. The four survivors saw this was illogical. If the Tahitians attacked them, they could not possibly defend themselves, and it would be foolish and wrong to try. It would mean they had ultimately failed, and martyrdom would be their refuge. So they sent all their weapons on board the ship to be taken away, with the exception of two muskets, which they gave to Pomare and Tu.

Then they thought of all their other possessions. The forge was the first. The Society had provided it, but for the Tahitians, not for them. Between the four of them – two parsons, a bricklayer, and a carpenter – they did not know much about forges, and, moreover, they wanted to spend their time in learning to preach, not trying to hammer out axeheads. So they gave the whole forge to Pomare, and the stocks of iron. And while they were at it, they also gave him all the contents of the mission's stores, and offered him all their own personal possessions, which he declined.

It was wise of them, and in good Christian tradition, to get rid of their worldly goods; but it was a mistake to give them all to Pomare and Tu. It perpetuated Cook's mistake in thinking Tu was a supreme ruler: in fact, nobody in Tahiti had ever been supreme, unique, above all others. There were always several *arii rahi*, equally holy, whose temporal power waxed and waned and who periodically quarrelled and fought their own peculiar kind of war. The whole thing mystified the Tahitians, who had no conception of supremacy among their chiefs. Pomare knew the other *arii rahi* were jealous, but by the time the *Duff* appeared he had begun to believe he was something special, solely because the Europeans said he was; and his son had revived the old privilege, which had lapsed some generations back, of being always carried on his servants' backs. The two of them, father and son, had formed a policy of pride, totally foreign to Tahiti: to behave as king and regent, collect all the wealth they could from the Europeans and all the weapons, and use them to defy the other chiefs and either buy them off or beat them in battle.

In truth, such wealth and power had never before been in the hands of one family. Wallace's and Cook's mistake, carried forward by their successors and now perpetuated by the immensely valuable gifts given by the missionaries, had destroyed the old balance of power which had kept Tahiti peaceful and – within its limits – prosperous for longer than anyone remembered. But the other *arii rahi* did not give up their own hereditary rights without a struggle. The next decade, from 1800 to 1810, was a history of unprecedented wars as the other *arii rahi*, in ever-changing alliances, fought to overthrow the pretensions of Pomare and Tu.

So the English had created a perennial cause of civil war; and next they introduced the means of making wars more dangerous and bloody than they had ever been: muskets and mercenaries.

By the middle of that same decade, Tahiti had become a famous place. Most Englishmen in any walk of life must have heard of it, many North Americans, and certainly all Protestant churchmen and sailors. Consequently, all ships that passed anywhere near it found some excuse to put in to Matavai Bay to see for themselves. In a rather later period, the majority were American whalers; but in the 1800s most were still English, and most were sailing between the home country and the penal colonies, thousands of miles west of Tahiti, first at Botany Bay and later elsewhere in Australia. A few were naval ships, some were privateers, and most were merchantmen on government charter which had taken out a cargo of convicts by way of the Cape of Good Hope and were trying to make the homeward voyage by Cape Horn. So it came about that most of Tahiti's contact with the outside world was by way of Botany Bay, and most of the ships that came in were infected by an atmosphere of crime and punishment. They were the toughest of ships with the toughest of captains and crews. The news spread among them that you could trade old muskets for anything you wanted in Tahiti; so old muskets were what they brought.

Some of the trade in muskets, powder, and ball was an official affair organized by successive governors of the penal colony. (One of these was Captain Bligh, who was appointed governor in 1805 and lasted three years before he caused another mutiny, this time in the army garrison, who put him in his own prison.) These representatives of the British Crown often sent ships to Tahiti specifically to barter for pigs to feed the garrison, and they paid for the pigs with muskets. The missionaries recorded figures for one of these ships in 1803. She was the *Harrington*, a privateering brig of fourteen guns and fifty men. She sailed from Botany Bay for South America to attack Spanish shipping, picked up a prize there, and came in to Tahiti to trade on the way back. For an old musket worth ten shillings in Australia (fifty pence in decimal currency), the Tahitians gave her pigs worth fifteen or twenty pounds. She also supplied three hundredweight (say 150 kilograms) of powder, and on top of that 'even the wretched females whom the king sent off to the ship for the vilest of purposes were ordered to take nothing as the price of their debasement and vice but gunpowder . . . and it was reported that property to the amount of 700 pounds was expended for the purposes of prostitution while the vessel remained at Tahiti.' It was possible that the stories of girls being abducted for the penal settlement began at this period. If a pig was worth thirty or forty times what it cost in Tahiti, there was obviously an even greater profit to be made on the side in girls. Nothing would have been easier, when they came on board every night, than to sail away in the dark with a shipload of girls for the comfort of the crew on the voyage, and then to sell them to senior officers or rich settlers or the brothels of the garrison or the convicts. It was not long before the Royal Navy was applying its strength against the slave trade in the Atlantic and the Indian Ocean, but there was nothing to stop it in the Pacific.

Muskets, especially old second-hand ones, were inefficient weapons, impossible to aim with any accuracy. Lord Nelson was killed by one in the middle of this decade at Trafalgar, at a range of about fifty yards, but a shot like that was exceptional and needed more luck than skill. But muskets were much more efficient, and above all more frightening, than the sticks and stones the Tahitians had used in their wars before. They trans-formed the whole character of Tahitian wars; and mercenary European fighters changed it even more. These were sailors who had deserted their ships.

One cannot generalize about the deserters, as one can perhaps about the missionaries; some of them may have been good men in bad ships, victims of injustice who simply could not stand the life on board. But some were certainly very bad men indeed. Sailors in that era were not, on the whole, a high grade of humanity. The navy was a cut above the rest, but even a British naval crew had convicted criminals in it. Some of the *Bounty* mutineers meant well, but most of the men who jumped ship in the 1800s came from merchantmen; and most Europeans who found themselves mer-chant seamen in the far Pacific had something dark in their past that they were running away from. It was these men, good or bad, and not the heathen islanders, who became the missionaries' main opponents.

The reasons for their desertions were always the same: women and what seemed to them to be freedom. In the old days, the Tahitians would gladly have given them all they wanted of both, but now the chiefs expected something in exchange. It was easy for any deserter to find a chief who would promise him a hut, a willing wife and a life of plenty – and, most important of all, a chief who would hide him from his ship's search parties. All the chief asked was that he should fight for him in wars, and most sailors were happy to do that. It passed the time.

Of course they were far more expert at fighting than the Tahitians were. They laughed at the old-fashioned Tahitian rules of war, which made it honourable to run for the hills and hide when things were going badly, and most honourable of all to sue for peace. The deserters brought with them the ruthless conventions of Christian wars: the virtue of fighting to the death, of asking and giving no quarter. There were never very many of these men, perhaps forty or fifty at the most, but they terrorized everyone and transformed Tahitian life. Where people had lived in mutual confidence and kindness, they now lived every day in fear.

The only consecutive account of these years is in the missionaries' history, which of course is partisan and obscured by their own misunderstanding of what was going on. In particular, it is hard to discover who was fighting whom at any given moment. The missionaries always regarded Pomare and Tu as lawful rulers and everyone else as a rebel; but sometimes Pomare and Tu were on opposite sides and fighting each other. Also, the wars, like any other activity in Tahiti, had a religious element which the missionaries refused to understand. Thus, people were apt to say their leader was not a secular chief but a god, usually the god Oro; and sometimes both sides in a battle believed and said they were fighting for this god, just as opposing armies during the Reformation in Europe both claimed they were fighting for God.

Throughout it all, the missionaries continued to live in the mission house, pressing on with their 'great object, the spiritual benefit of the people', and taking as little notice as they could of the confusion of war around them. The Tahitians continued to give them more food than they could eat, and anything else they asked for. Their progress in learning the language was very slow, but in August 1801, after four-and-a-half years in the island, the first of them was able to compose a simple sermon and deliver it in Tahitian. This was Brother Nott. Soon after, Mr Jefferson could do it too. These two preached every Sunday, first at the mission itself, and later at meetings in the neighbourhood of Matavai Bay. But all to no avail. A lot of people turned up and listened carefully. Month after month and year after year, they persevered with their preaching. Ten more missionaries arrived and joined in the work when they had picked up enough of the language. But not a single Tahitian confessed that he was coverted. On the contrary, as time went on, the congregations became more argumentative, and the people 'cavilled at their discourses, or ridiculed their statements; ascribing all the evils they suffered, to the supposed malign influence of the God of the missionaries, and avowing their determination never to acknowledge his claims to their belief and obedience.' And, in a manner of speaking, it cannot be denied that they were right; for the Europeans who had brought the Christian creed had also brought all the evils, the wars and diseases.

Another evil they brought (though the Tahitians welcomed it) was alcohol. The English of that time were hearty drinkers, to say the least, and ships in particular were pickled in rum. The naval ration was so enormous that sailors could hardly avoid becoming alcoholics. Even the Calvinists saw some virtue in what they called 'ardent spirits', and physicians prescribed them as cures. Consequently, all captains and officers from the very beginning had entertained chiefs and their families at drinking parties – they laughed when their guests, to their own astonishment, got dead drunk – and probably the sailors had done the same with their humbler friends. At first, the Tahitians liked the officers' wines but disliked the brandy and rum; but they soon got a taste for those too, and the chiefs entirely gave up the chewed *ava* root which had been their only intoxicant. Things were not too bad while they depended on bottles of rum as gifts, or rewards for the services they rendered, but in the 1800s the deserters, needing more drink themselves, began to set up stills, and taught the Tahitians how to make a sort of brandy of their own.

The first man who succeeded was an armourer or blacksmith with the unusual name of Savary. He deserted his ship and lived for two years in Tu's entourage. He made a still, and kept the chief in drink until he was picked up by another ship and forcibly taken back to Botany Bay. Tu supposed the missionaries had insisted that he should be deported, and perhaps they had – they did not want Tahitians to get their drink too easily – but Tu of course resented losing such a useful man. His still broke down, but other Tahitians were able to copy it. Soon there were stills all over the island. The Tahitians were made a nation of drunks.

Until about 1810, everything went from bad to worse: for the Tahitians, ever-growing alcoholism, ever-growing terror in war, and ever-growing deaths from disease; and for the missionaries, no progress at all. The only people who got what they wanted were the deserters. The island was infested by roving armies, each led by these mercenaries, some nominally fighting for a specific chief and some running wild and fighting for nobody but themselves. Any of them could set themselves up as minor chiefs by brandishing their weapons and showing off their ruthless skill. All the armies killed without mercy or distinction, burned houses, and destroyed the fruit trees and crops. People were driven to hide in shacks in the forests.

In about 1808, Pomare died, suddenly and unexpectedly. The missionaries had always regarded him as a friend, although he was the leading exponent of human sacrifices – which greatly increased in number as rivals prayed for victory or tried in their terror to appease their gods – and although he had killed their other friend, Manne-Manne the high priest, who had indiscreetly disagreed with him. Soon after, Pomare's wife and Tu's mother, the forceful Iddeah, succumbed, so the missionaries said, to the excessive use of ardent spirits; and finally Tu's young wife, his only wife, died in what seems to have been an attempted abortion. The missionaries, who of course believed in the wrath of their own god, put all these disasters down to his just punishment of the family's wickedness; their 'frightful debaucheries,' they wrote, 'impious and prodigal destruction of human life, and direct promotion of drunkenness, profligacy, and theft, seemed almost to challenge the forbearance of the Almighty.' Tu himself, whom the missionaries judged to be the worst of them all, survived, and therefore became Pomare in his turn. He was left without any wife and without any obvious heir, and not long after his father's death he was decisively beaten in battle and fled from his enemies to exile in the island of Eimeo.

Just before that, the missionaries had had to share their house with the entire crew of a ship called the *Norfolk*. She was a small armed vessel which belonged to the governor of the penal settlement. Like so many others she had been sent to barter for pigs, and she drove ashore and was wrecked in Matavai Bay. She was so badly damaged that she could not be repaired, but her crew, her stores, and her armament were saved. The missionaries had to take them in, even though most of them were ex-convicts, released or on parole – not the sort of men the missionaries liked to associate with. Her captain's incongruous name was Bishop. The crew demolished the chapel, which was badly sited for defence, cut down the surrounding trees and built a stockade, and installed the ship's artillery. The mission house became a fortress, armed against the people the mission had meant to convert. When Pomare saw defeat approaching he asked for help. Captain Bishop sallied forth with his crew and guns to fight for him – and shared the defeat.

That action put a final end to the missionaries' pose as neu-trals in the wars. They were firmly identified with Pomare's party. Captain Bishop, of course, did not stay; as soon as another ship came in, he embarked with all his men to go back to Botany Bay. And when Pomare lost the final battle and was making for exile, the missionaries had to admit they were beaten, too.

One may think they were often foolish and nearly always mistaken, but for eleven years they had laboured earnestly towards what they thought, in their narrow way, was right, and they had absolutely nothing to show for it. They were doubly dejected because in all those years only two letters had reached them from the Society in England. They felt isolated on the other side of the world. They did not know whether the Society wanted them to struggle on or not, and in fact there was a strong opinion in England in favour of abandoning the Tahitians and spending the Society's resources somewhere more profitable. 'No success has attended our labours, so as to terminate in the conversion of any,' the missionaries wrote in a letter home. 'There is no apparent desire after instruction in the blessed truth of the Gos-pel: the news of salvation is an idle tale to them, and though they are visited as a nation with sore afflictions, they still reject and despise our message.' The Society added in its history that the missionaries 'deemed it, after humiliation before God, and prayer for Divine guidance, their duty to retire from the islands, at least, for a season'. In October 1809, all the missionaries except three embarked for Botany Bay: of those three, one went to Eimeo and two to the island of Huahine, where Cook had become the old chief's friend. The mission house in Matavai Bay fell into the hands of the mercenaries, and so did Captain Bishop's artillery. They burned the house, melted down the type from the printing press to make bullets and tore up the holy books for cartridge paper. A large picture of King George III, the Prince of Wales and the Duke of York was rescued by Tahitians, taken to a temple and offered to the god Oro.

'To all human appearance,' the Society's history said, 'the Tahitian mission was now at an end.'

FOURTEEN
Laws and Commandments

————— ••❧❦❧•• —————

FOR TWO YEARS, Tahiti was at peace: Pomare in exile, his father dead, and the missionaries gone. Pomare's rivals may have argued, but they did not fight each other. Even the deserters, with nobody left to fight against, began to settle down, some to a semblance of domesticity, and some in attempts to join the teenage promiscuity. The Tahitians, it was true, could never be independent again. As Cook had predicted, they had forgotten their ancient handicrafts and had to rely on European products, especially tools; but these they bartered from visiting ships, together with more muskets, powder, and rum. And by then they were irrevocably infected not only by European diseases, but by European sins – envy, greed, unkindness, covetousness. They had an unaccustomed amount of work to do in repairing the damage of wars, rebuilding houses and replanting trees. Nevertheless, they returned to many of their old ways, and they had never lost their old beliefs. Happiness and contentment began to seep back.

At the end of those two years, something quite unexpected happened. Pomare sent a message to the missionaries by way of Huahine. He wanted to be baptized. The request, they said, 'came like a breath of life'; they were astonished and delighted – 'even unto tears'. After their early admiration, they had come to think of all Tahitians as wicked, and had thought Pomare the most wicked of them all. In their eyes, he was a chronic drunk, cruel, a stubborn idolator, a murderer, and a fornicator – all the bad things he could have been. He was even suspected of the 'nameless crimes'. They knew his knowledge of the Christian faith could only be very crude. It was hard for them to believe he had truly seen the light. Several of them hastened to Eimeo, and found him insisting he was a Christian. They had to explain that they must be sure he repented of his past and understood the essence of Christianity before they could baptize him, but he accepted that. He said he would attend to their lessons, and they should baptize him as soon as they were satisfied. So they set to work on him, and on growing numbers of his domestic and political followers whom he told very firmly they had to be Christians – or else.

Pomare's portrait shows a stolid, heavy man, with all the signs of premature ageing (he must have been well under thirty) which can be caused by a dissolute life, and especially by alcoholism. But he must have been cleverer than he looked, because he had undoubtedly taught himself to read, using the written version of his language which the missionaries had devised in the last decade. The only things written in that language were the missionaries' simplified catechism, their Bible stories, and the bits of the Bible they had managed to translate – mainly the gospel of St Luke. Pomare must have read these again and again for practice.

To the missionaries, the conversion was plainly miraculous. It had happened while they were not there: it was the hand of God. This seemed to them the more evident when they heard that members of the Society in England had been praying for this very event. In fact, Pomare had been converted before they began their prayers, though news of it had not reached England. But that was no obstacle. The missionaries were seldom stuck for a biblical quotation, and now they recalled Isaiah: 'Before they call I will answer: and while they are yet speaking I will hear.'

However much he declared his penitence, it was sadly obvious that Pomare was the same man: he was certainly still drinking, and probably fornicating too. No sinner in England would have been welcomed into the church on the evidence he provided, and the missionaries knew they were stretching a point. It merely seemed to them that that was the path God had led them to. Nobody, then or now, could know what really went on in Pomare's mind, but perhaps it is not too cynical to mention the political advantage to him in saying he was a Christian. He was a high chief, and had been led to think he was the highest, by right, in Tahiti. He was in exile, and had no hope of getting his chiefdom back without wholehearted European support. The mercenaries were not enough: his rivals had them too. But the mercenaries were of junior rank, and despised by the European captains. Missionaries were senior: they talked to the captains as equals. It must have been clear to Pomare that if he was a Christian, the missionaries and all the captains in future would be on his side. By that means, and only by that means, he had a chance of going back to Tahiti and winning. He may even have thought King George, who had plenty of soldiers, would send a few to help him: his father had suggested it to Bligh.

If that was his plan – half-conscious perhaps – it worked perfectly, except for King George's soldiers. Soon, hundreds of Pomare's followers in Eimeo declared that they were Christians. Among them were the two chiefs of Huahine, who had always been on his side. The missionaries rejoiced, set up a school for them all and tried to tell them what their decision meant. A rumour spread that many more in Tahiti were willing to follow. In due course, Pomare ventured back to Tahiti. Two missionaries followed close behind – one of them the faithful Brother Nott. Their first intention was to take care of him: they were afraid he would be exposed to temptation. Pomare, on the other hand, was spoiling for war, and soon Tahiti was at war again, more bloodily than ever before: now not merely a war in which one chief fought against another, but in which Christians fought against the rest.

Until this final war, the missionaries' narrative of events, although it was partisan, was understandable. But now it degenerated, with so many contradictions and such evident self-deception that it represents nothing but the groping of their own uneasy conscience. People were to ask ever after if Christianity was imposed on Tahiti by force. The answer must be that it was. But the missionaries, to do them justice, had not wanted it to happen that way. Their avowed plan had always been to destroy the Tahitians's own religious faith, however cruel that process might have to be, in the hope of intruding Christianity into the void that would be left. But the Tahitian faith was too strong for them. They had failed to destroy it in eleven years, and had given it up as a bad job two years before Pomare offered – for whatever reason – to do it for them. It was Pomare who led the Christian throng, the missionaries following in its wake like army chaplains, answering each other's doubts with hollow arguments that this was the work of God.

Two pitched battles were fought in the autumn of 1815 – springtime in Tahiti – within a few weeks, as it happened, of the Battle of Waterloo. The missionaries' account of them tells nothing of the tactics or technique, nor of the pain, or fear, or horrors: it is only a set of the clichés that clerics had used for hundreds of years when writing about battles: stories of the enemy spending the night before the battle in feasting, while the Christians spent it in prayer; of the Christians praying and singing hymns as the hostile hordes advanced; of the commander addressing his men and ending with the words 'Now go, and may the presence of Jesus go with you.' Such tales go back at least to the Battle of Hastings.

The Christians won both fights, and after the second they gave their enemies a feast, and baked a hundred hogs for it. One has to imagine this scene: some thousands of people must have been there, but nobody described it; and it was very important, more important indeed than the battles themselves. The missionaries claimed it afterwards as an example of Christian forgiveness and mercy, but they were mistaken; feasting their enemies was not a common Christian or European practice – there had been no feast for the French on the evening of Waterloo. On the contrary, it was a reversion to old Tahitian manners, and all the Tahitians knew what it signified.

The feast was probably held at the head of a beach, where there was plenty of room and plenty of large round stones which could be heated for the cooking pits. It was a long, hot job to slaughter a hundred pigs, dig a hundred pits, and gather fuel for a hundred fires. Pomare's army and camp followers would have done the work, while, as guests, the beaten army waited, their apprehension slowly turning to pleasant anticipation, some of them hiding their wounds perhaps, because they had not yet learned to be proud of battle scars. And then a long wait again – three hours – while the pigs cooked out of sight, each under a mound of earth. There was plenty of time, when everyone knew he was to be fed, not massacred, to discuss what they had all been fighting about. It must have been dusk or dark when the ovens were dug open: starlight perhaps, cool and calm, a bar of moonlight motionless on the lagoon, the crowns of the coconut trees all black against the sky, and the savoury smell of the pork overcoming the scents of sea and earth and flowers.

The beaten warriors, it was said, were too bemused, and probably too tired, to enjoy the food; but every one of them knew what it meant. Pomare had won the battle, which was all very well; but he had the greater honour of being the first to offer peace. By accepting his feast, the others accepted his terms of peace. They accepted him as chief, and even accepted whatever version of god he chose to give them. Nobody in Tahiti had ever gone back on such a pledge.

And the idols he shall utterly abolish
Tahitian effigies were not really idols, but the
missionaries collected and destroyed them all the same

Next day, they all began an orgy of tearing down their ancient temples and burning the emblems of their gods.

The political struggle, and then the final battle and then the feast, broke down the Tahitians' old beliefs, and the whole of their method of government broke down with them. The old, cosy devolution of rule from the superior chiefs to the lesser chiefs, and from them to the heads of families, could not be made to work with a single king. What was more, Pomare – the king the Europeans had chosen – had no intention of surrendering any power to anyone: he wanted it all himself. Yet he had no idea how to set up a single-handed rule. He had never seen it done. He refused to consult any other chief. In some desperation, when everything was falling into chaos, he asked the missionaries how to do it: how did King George do it? There were a dozen of them on the island by then, and they racked their brains for all they had ever heard of English law and the English judicial system. It was very little, as little as one would expect from impractical men who scorned all knowledge that was not in the Bible. Governing was not their job.

Yet governing was what they had to do. They had fought for spiritual authority, and had won themselves secular responsibility too. It was a supreme opportunity – to create an entirely new social system even better, kinder, and fairer than the one they had destroyed. But it was also a very difficult job indeed, and one has to sympathize with them: it needed a genius, and none of them would have claimed to be a genius. Cook could have done it: Tahiti would have elected him king without hesitation if he had still been alive around 1800. He might have created a state on the lines of a well-run naval ship. Joseph Banks might possibly have done it, if he had been more patient than usual, and created some theoretical Arcadian state of his own. The missionaries, faced with a problem that was beyond them, turned to the Bible again.

Tahiti, they pointed out, had never had any formal legal system: the old conventions of behaviour and the two sins of unkindness and irreverence were not good enough. They told Pomare he must make laws. What laws? he asked. There was a moment perhaps when they might have chosen the teaching of Christ and turned that into civil law. But more to their taste was Mosaic law, which was ready-made in Genesis and in the catechism, which they had already simplified and put into Tahitian. They proposed the Ten Commandments, and those were instantly proclaimed as Tahitian law. It did not matter that Tahitians had not been in the habit of breaking those Commandments before the Europeans told them not to. They were certainly doing so now. First, introducing the concept of private property had introduced the concepts of envy and theft. Now it was not only the Europeans who owned things and were rich. The chiefs, and Pomare in particular, were also rich, and wanted to protect their riches from people who envied them.

Having chosen the laws, there was the problem of enforcing them. The missionaries vaguely recollected English courts, with their array of magistrates, judges and clerks, and the concept of trial by jury. First they created magistrates: themselves and some of Pomare's friends, the few he trusted. For a while there were no courts: the magistrates gave judgements wherever they happened to be, and whenever anyone came with a complaint. And punishments: it took time to make prisons and find prison warders. The first prisons were not buildings but stocks, two logs which could be clamped together over the ankles of a row of offenders. Meanwhile the magistrates levied fines in pigs, and people who had no pigs were condemned to labour. Pomare wanted a road, and men were sentenced to build so many yards of road, according to the gravity of their crime. The road started where Pomare lived, a few miles west of Matavai Bay – a place which became the centre of government, and finally the present town of Papeete – and after years of forced labour, yard by yard, it ran right round the island.

Soon, what had satisfied Moses was not enough for the missionaries. They confused crime and sin, and everything they disapproved as sinful was made illegal. No other parson had ever had such scope. They did not have to preach against sin and threaten punishment in a life to come: they only had to tell Pomare to make a new law forbidding each sin and they could punish it then and there. They themselves lived in perpetual melancholy remorse for the original sin of the world, and they expected everyone else to do the same. They equated beauty with sin, and suspected that any sign of happiness, such as laughter – 'unseemly levity' they called it – was a symptom of sin. If they heard anyone laughing, they asked what he had to laugh at, and whatever it was, it was likely to be wrong. Tahitians laughed a great deal.

So in a short time, all singing, except of hymns, was declared illegal. So were dancing and wrestling. So was play-acting. So were beating drums and playing the Tahitian flute, the most harmless of musical instruments, one would suppose, since they played it with their noses and it had only four notes. Sports the missionaries considered manly were grudgingly permitted, except on the Sabbath, when all work and all amusements, everything except going to church and reading the Bible, was forbidden not only by the Church but by the law.

The missionaries tried to stop sin by law, but sometimes failed. Distilling spirits was made illegal – not, they explained to themselves, because it was sinful in itself, but because it led to drunkenness, and 'the Bible declares that no drunkard shall inherit the kingdom of God'. Other people since then have tried to stop alcholism by law, and have always failed. All that happened was that the stills were hidden and people drank in secret: and so secretiveness and deceit were introduced to the open Tahitian character.

Next, this and other problems needed police. There was no organized police-force in England yet; the first was created by Sir Robert Peel in Dublin in 1808, and it is unlikely that the missionaries had heard of it. But they must have been familiar with the parish watchmen of London and especially the Bow Street Runners, who wore red waistcoats and were used by the magistrates to look out for crime, chase suspects through the streets, and make arrests. Similar men served the missionaries, and many visitors saw them, patrolling the beaches in old military jackets, armed with rusty swords, apparently listening for forbidden music, sniffing out stills, herding people to church and accosting illicit lovers.

Lovers baffled the missionaries. The Ten Commandments, of course, forbade adultery, but that did not mean much in a country where nobody was married in the Jewish or Christian sense. The missionaries longed to stamp out sex, except within Christian marriage, but they could not stop the Tahitians loving each other and expressing it in the way that seemed to them natural, harmless, and good. The new rulers seem to have had the sense not to declare all sex illegal – or perhaps Pomare refused to agree – he had a will of his own. Instead they very positively said it was a sin, and they set about discouraging it indirectly by trying to make each sex less charming to the other. Tattooing, and anything approaching nakedness, were sinful and illegal. It became fashionable for Christian girls to cut off their dark flowing hair and give up scenting their bodies and wearing garlands of flowers. The missionaries' wives were busied in sewing classes, and the art spread quickly; so Tahitian girls could now be dressed in the bonnets and standard, shapeless, long-sleeved frocks which were known in Africa as Mother Hubbards and had the merit, compared with the native dress, of being unbecoming and hard to take off.

But nothing could destroy the girls' smiles or the twinkle in their eyes, and nothing could fundamentally change the Tahitian habit. Sex became secretive, like drinking, and that was all; and the missionaries remained unhappily aware that every bush around them might hide a couple – perhaps only children – leading each other further towards damnation.

One has to add that the Tahitians were not unwilling partners in this transformation. When they took to anything new, they took to it wholeheartedly, and Christianity itself became a popular fashion. The missionaries knew that none of their converts really understood it, but the same could be said of most English people at home. They had a constant bad example in deserters and other visitors who claimed to be Christian but were shameless in their sins. But in spite of that there was no lack of outward signs of piety. Tahitians built churches everywhere and dutifully filled them on the Sabbath. Typically, they resolved to build the biggest church in the world. It was just like any Tahitian house, a thatched roof raised on poles; but it was 712 feet long and 54 feet wide (much bigger than the nave of Westminster Abbey). A stream ran through it, and it contained three pulpits from which, on the day of its consecration in 1819, three missionaries preached three different but simultaneous sermons.

When the process of converting Tahiti was well under way, it happened that several ships came in, bearing people who recorded what they saw. The first ships were Russian: two naval frigates under Captain Thaddeus Bellingshausen in 1820, and another under Captain Otto von Kotzebue in 1823. Their impressions were quite different.

Bellingshausen's frigates, the *Vostok* and the *Mirnyi*, entered Matavai Bay prepared for anything, with guns and small arms loaded and primed and sentries doubled; and they were surrounded at once, like any other visitors, by canoes. The view, their captain remarked, was enchanting, and the Tahitians, to his surprise, were kind and gentle. Two friendly deserters came on board, one American and one English, soon followed by Mr Nott and then by Pomare, with a wife and daughter and a retinue of girls. Pomare and his wife, of course, appeared as King and Queen: Pomare was known to the Europeans as King Pomare II. The Queen was a comely lady of twenty-five, and her daughter was ten.

Bellingshausen knew very little of Cook and apparently nothing of Tahiti; so he saw everything as it was at that moment, as if it were not undergoing any change. And everywhere he went, Mr Nott came too as interpreter, so Bellingshausen saw everything through missionary eyes. Only once did he notice that 'the presence of Mr Nott was unwelcome to the King'. On that occasion, Pomare took his hand and led him alone to a little hut, where he hastily shut the door. It was his bedroom, furnished with a double bed, several benches, a clock, a rolled-up map of the world, and some English books, among them a school geometry book. The King wanted a note, written in Russian, to say that the bearer should be given a bottle of rum. He provided ink, a pen, and a bit of paper, and Bellingshausen wrote it for him, making it three bottles of rum and six of Tenerife wine. And only just in time: the door opened and Mr Nott came in: the King quickly hid the note and began to show off his knowledge of geometry.

That was the only glimpse that Bellingshausen had of any rift between Tahitians and their new masters. They all seemed to him to form a homogeneous Christian community, and in his ignorance he naturally gave the credit for Tahitian gentleness and kindness to the teaching of the missionaries. On the Sabbath, when no natives came off to the ships, he went ashore and found them all in church, very attentive to a sermon Mr Nott was preaching. 'The strict observance of the religious law,' he wrote, 'in a people whose former savage instincts cannot completely have faded from memory, must really be regarded as exemplary.'

Two years after that, Pomare died of apoplexy, caused, it was supposed, by his excesses, especially drink: his profession of Christianity had not cured him, nor had the laws he made. His very young son succeeded him, a handsome and promising boy. He attended a mission school and the missionaries had great hopes of him. But very soon after he also died. His sister, Aimatta, was next in succession, and it was this unfortunate girl, known as Pomare IV, who bore the brunt of the changes still to come.

Bellingshausen's orders had been to sail right round the Antarctic in the highest possible latitude, and this he did, filling in some of the gaps Cook had left. The next Russian frigate, which arrived three years later, was bound for the Russian Siberian coast, to the north. Its captain, Otto von Kotzebue, took exactly the opposite view of the missionaries, and maintained they had done nothing much but harm – not because he was anti-Christian, but because he was a member of the Orthodox Church and believed that the religion the missionaries taught was 'a libel on the Divine Founder of Christianity, the benign friend of humankind'. He had read Cook and Bougainville, and echoed what they had said about Tahitians. They were, and always had been, 'gentle, benevolent, open, gay, peaceable and wholly devoid of envy: they rejoiced in each other's good fortune, and when one received a present, all seemed equally gratified . . . Oppressed by no care, burdened by no toil, tormented by no passion, seldom visited by sickness, their wants easily satisfied, and their pleasures often recurring, the Tahitians passed a life of enjoyment under the magnificent sky of the tropics, and amid scenes worthy of Paradise.' Now, von Kotzebue found the Tahitians confused by a creed they did not understand, and preoccupied with trying to adjust to its demands.

But left alone, they could still show their old qualities. Von Kotzebue arrived on a Friday, and was welcomed as usual by bartering crowds, whom he freely allowed on board. 'The deck was soon transformed into a busy market, where all was frolic and fun; the goods were offered with a jest, and the bargains concluded with laughter.' The next day, though – Saturday – was still reckoned by the missionaries to be the Sabbath, and no canoes came out. 'To our great astonishment, the stillness of death reigned among the dwellings of the happy inhabitants. They were celebrating the Sunday, on which account they did not leave their houses, where they lay on their bellies reading the Bible and howling aloud. All the doors were closed, and not even the children allowed to enjoy the beauty of the morning.' This must have been an exaggeration, but at the end of his stay Von Kotzebue's opinion was reasoned and firm. The religion of the missionaries, he agreed, had restricted theft and incontinence; but instead it had introduced bigotry, hypocrisy, and contempt for all other faiths. Especially, he thought it a shame that 'every pleasure be punished as a sin, among a people whom Nature destined to the most cheerful enjoyment'.

The next visitor was an English naval captain, Frederick Beechey, who in 1826 passed through in HM Sloop *Blossom* on another search for the Pacific end of the North-West Passage. Captain Beechey suffered from an almost indecipherable style of English, but one can discern through his verbiage an opinion somewhere between Bellingshausen's and Kotzebue's. He was used to the Church of England and sympathetic to the missionaries' creed, but he also wished, like Kotzebue, that they had not tried to abolish all the Tahitians' pleasures. When he went with his officers to call on the Queen, she arranged a dance to amuse them – 'an indulgence I had hardly expected, such performances being prohibited by law, under severe penalties. It was necessary that it should be executed quietly, and that the reed pipe should be played in an undertone, that it might not reach the ears of a policeman, who was patrolling the beach, in a soldier's jacket; for even the use of this melodious little instrument, the delight of the natives, from whose nature the dance and the pipe are inseparable, is now strictly prohibited.' The dance disappointed Beechey and his men. It was so tame that 'there was nothing at which any unprejudiced person could take offence; and it confirmed the opinion I had often heard expressed, that Pomarree, or whoever framed the laws, would ·have more effectually attained his object had these amusements been restricted within proper limits, rather than entirely suppressed.'

Nine years later, in 1835, Charles Darwin came there in HMS *Beagle*. As one would expect of a true scientist, he refused quick judgements: 'The prohibition of the flute and dancing is inveighed against as wrong and foolish; the more than presbyterian manner of keeping the Sabbath is looked at in a similar light. On these points I will not pretend to offer any opinion, in opposition to men who have resided as many years as I was days on the island.' Nevertheless, he was charmed by the island and its people, and it was clear that his private opinion, if he had expressed it, would have opposed the missionaries. He admired tattooing as an art. Although the missionaries had banned it, they could not remove the tattoos that people already wore. 'It requires little habit', Darwin wrote, 'to make a dark skin more pleasing and natural to the eye of a European than his own colour. A white man bathing by the side of a Tahitian was like a plant bleached by the gardener's art compared with a fine dark green one growing vigorously in the open fields. Most of the men are tattooed, and the ornaments follow the curvature of the body so gracefully, that they have a very elegant effect. One common pattern, varying in its details, is somewhat like the crown of a palm tree. It springs from the central line of the back, and gracefully curls round both sides. The simile may be a fanciful one, but I thought the body of a man thus ornamented was like the trunk of a noble tree embraced by a delicate creeper.'

He himself saw only one example of defiance of the laws, and that a trivial one. Typically, he made a two-day expedition up the mountains with two or three Tahitians, which few if any Europeans had troubled to do before, admiring the vegetation and the spectacular scene and enjoying his companions. He had taken a hip-flask with him. The Tahitians could not resist his invitation to share it; 'but as often as they drank a little, they put their fingers before their mouths, and uttered the word "Missionary".' But it was quite wrong, he wrote, to suppose that the Tahitians had become a gloomy race, living in fear of the missionaries: it would be difficult in Europe to pick out of a crowd half so many merry and happy faces. Evidently, after nearly forty years of missionary work, it was still possible for a cheerful and sympathetic young man – which Darwin was – to catch glimpses of the Tahitians as they had been.

Most of the changes forced on Tahiti in that period, 1815–35, had been purely negative, variations on the theme of 'Thou shalt not'. One was different, but had little success: the introduction of money. Everyone seemed to think the Tahitians ought to earn money and spend it. Deserters on the whole had nothing to sell, but a few of them had some Spanish dollars they wanted to spend, and they wanted the people to accept them, especially the girls. Merchants were also making their way to the island by then, with goods to sell for cash and sales talk to convince the people they wanted things they had never wanted before. And missionaries were convinced of the value of regular work for regular pay: if Tahitians could be persuaded they needed money, they could be pressed into jobs, which would leave them less time for the sins of idleness.

The wares the merchants brought were mainly printed cotton cloth for the women, and any old worn-out European clothes for the men. Both became a deplorable fashion. Men who had impressed everyone, in the old Tahitian clothes, by their dignity, bearing, and physique were persuaded to cram themselves into jackets or trousers, threadbare and bursting at the seams and for the most part (since Europeans were usually smaller) so tight they could hardly move. Merchants obtained these cast-offs from rag-and-bone men or even garbage dumps in Australia, America, and Europe, and sold them at a prodigious profit. Few Tahitians could ever afford more than one garment: they paraded to church in a jacket and no trousers, or trousers and no jacket, and Europeans laughed at their tragic pride.

The London Missionary Society spent a lot of money and took a lot of trouble to send out machinery for factories to extract the syrup from sugar cane and process and weave cotton, with men to teach the Tahitians how to earn money by doing it. This was a total failure. At first the Tahitians, men and women, liked to see the wheels go round, but when the novelty wore off they stubbornly refused to labour at it. A case in point was a man called Gyles, the overseer of a sugar plantation in Jamaica, who was sent out with a whole sugar factory and set it all up in Eimeo. The year after, an American sea-captain won Pomare's ear, told him the history of Jamaica and warned him that if the sugar succeeded it would lead to invasion and slavery. It was perhaps no business of his, but it was true that Gyles had been an overseer of slaves, and might possibly have looked on Tahitian labourers in the same light. Pomare insisted that the mission should send him away again. They did, and his machinery rusted away to nothing.

So it took at least a generation to force a money economy on the island. For years, the Tahitians could not, or would not, see the point of it. Different coins confused them. They thought a shiny new Spanish dollar was worth three or four old worn ones, and did not value either for its own sake. Anybody could swindle them: they did not even care. If they had a dollar or two to buy an outrageous garment that caught their fancy, that was all they needed. The girls could easily earn money by selling themselves, and men could borrow it or sell their surplus products.

But of course money had to come in the end, and when it did, it finally turned the girls into prostitutes. It undermined the old generosity, which had made everyone give anything to anyone in need. And it destroyed the communistic equality. A few people understood about money, and grew rich: the majority sank into poverty.

Reading everyone's diverse opinions, one is drawn to a comparison none of them exactly expressed: that the Tahitians saw the missionaries in much the same light as healthy teenage European children saw, and still see, stern, old-fashioned schoolmasters. These masters made arbitrary rules, unknown to church or state, and tried to enforce them by punishments of their own devising. They lived in a solemn world of their own and were always sure they knew best. Even their clothes and deportment were quite unlike their pupils', and so was their idea of good behaviour.

Yet the Tahitians, like the schoolchildren, were not really afraid of such authority. The Tahitians treated the missionaries with outward respect and awe, but made fun of them behind their backs. Like the children, they knew the masters would never understand their jokes. The rules were a bore. People kept them when they knew the masters were looking, and broke them whenever they thought they could get away with it. The great thing was not to get caught, and they blamed themselves if they did. The feeling is familiar to anyone remembering his school-days.

There was one great difference. Schoolchildren are never much oppressed by school because they can look forward to leaving; they know there will be a time when they will be free of its restrictions. Tahitians had no escape. But living from day to day, as they did, they had never been in the habit of looking ahead, and had never feared the future. Nor were they in the habit of looking back, and they soon forgot how well they had governed them-selves before the Europeans came and claimed the right to do it for them.

FIFTEEN

Into Night

——••⁊)(⁊••——

ONE OTHER WITNESS of that time deserves to be mentioned, because he wrote on behalf of people who were largely illiterate and could not tell their own adventure stories: the beachcombers and deserters. This was Herman Melville, the American sailor whose novels about nineteenth-century whaling are still famous – especially *Moby Dick*. Melville was in Tahiti in the early 1840s, and he wrote two autobiographical books, *Typee* and *Omoo*. The whalers he sailed in were as wicked as any ships that ever put to sea. Their job was cruel, exciting, and very dangerous; full of chases with hand-held harpoons and rowing boats, and the disgusting aftermath of a catch. Their food was appalling, and of comforts they had none. The ships followed no route, only the whim of the captain, and their voyages lasted until they had a full cargo of whale oil and had run out of stores, which was always a matter of years. The crews were often mutinous, and always apt to desert when they came to anchor. It was said that by 1840, 150 whalers, mostly American, put in to Tahiti every year. This meant about three thousand hard drinking, undisciplined men, starved of sex, who at their best could not be controlled except by curses, fists and the butt end of a handspike.

Melville deserted twice from his ships, the first time in the Marquesas Islands and the second time in Tahiti. The Marquesas, by chance, had been left almost unmolested: only a few explorers, a few missionaries, and a few ships in need of supplies had called there. The people were much the same as Tahitians, and spoke slightly different dialects of the same Polynesian language. But there was one important geographical difference. The islands had no continuous coastal plain like Tahiti, but many separate valleys, and these were inhabited by separate clans who had nothing to do with each other and often fought the Polynesian kind of war across the intervening mountains.

One of these valleys, on the largest island, Nukuheva, was

known to whaling captains as a refuge, and there Melville's ship, the *Dolly*, came to anchor. There also, to their astonishment, they found several naval vessels flying the flag of France, led by the sixty-gun frigate *La Reine Blanche*, Captain Dupetit Thouars. Unknown to the British or Americans, the French were laying claim to the whole group as a colony, and they had already put a hundred soldiers ashore. That made no difference to Melville, who had been six months on the *Dolly* without a sight of land and had made up his mind he could not stand her any more. He got ashore with a young friend called Toby, and, to avoid the French and their own shipmates, they made for the mountains. After three days and nights up there, wet and hungry, they lost their bearings and came down by mistake into a neighbouring valley, called Typee, whose people had the reputation of being ferocious cannibals – a reputation which had kept the valley free from any visitors. But Melville and Toby first met a beautiful young girl and boy who led them to their family's house; and there they were welcomed with the uninhibited hospitality Tahitians had shown to the first Europeans they saw. They were fed and clothed, slept on the family's mats and bathed with them in the streams; and Melville won a charming and gentle girl whose name he wrote as Fayaway. The whole tribe came to see them, and Melville, who had hurt his leg, was carried everywhere like a chief.

They stayed in idyllic peace for four months, but they never thought of staying for ever. It was partly the restlessness which afflicts most sophisticated people when they try to live a simple life, and partly that they still believed the Typees, in spite of their loving kindness, were cannibals who might change their minds and eat them. When they decided to go, the Typees tried to stop them, and their departure became an escape which left Fayaway in tears and everyone else disappointed and uncomprehending. But escape they did, and signed on again in another American whaler, the *Julia*, which turned out to be as bad as the first.

Four months later, Melville was ready to jump ship again, and this time sixteen of the twenty crew decided to do it too. They were approaching Tahiti, because the captain was sick and had to be put ashore. His orders were that the mate should take the ship on a further hunt for whales and then come back to fetch him. The crew was determined to take her into harbour and abandon her there.

They were a fearsome gang, and perfectly typical of a whaling crew: 'A wild company,' Melville called them, 'men of many climes – not at all precise in their toilet arrangements, but picturesque in their very tatters.' Melville of course was a highly literate man – he had been a schoolmaster – but only one other man on board could write his own name, a disgraced doctor known as Dr Long Ghost, because that was what he looked like. The rest, when it came to signing a document, marked crosses against their names – or rather, their shipboard names, for all of them kept their true ones secret. Melville was known as Typee, because that was where the ship had picked him up. Others were Salem and Liverpool. Most had names like pirates: Navy Bob, Long Jim, Bungs, Black Dan, Flash Jack, Jingling Joe, and Beauty. All of them proposed to join the floating population of scores of similar men in Tahiti, and to sample the island's delights.

But as the *Julia* approached the land they heard a salvo of guns and saw a frigate. They had caught up with *La Reine Blanche*, which was trying to claim Tahiti for France, as she had claimed the Marquesas, and Melville witnessed the beginning of the final assault on the island.

All shipping by then had given up landing in Matavai Bay. Instead, they used the bay of Papeete, a few miles further west. This was where Cook had seen the Tahitian war fleet and where the first Tu had his home in those early days. Papeete had always been a safer anchorage, but its two entrances through the reef were difficult before it had been surveyed: the first ship's captain to find his way in had been Bligh in the *Bounty*. Now, in 1842, it sheltered a pretty village, as European as it could be in the tropics. A road ran along the foreshore; the beginning of the track, built bit by bit as a punishment, which led more or less right round the island. Along it were a row of tidy white houses of European style, several churches, several prisons, and, conspicuously, the official houses of an American and a British consul, with mown lawns and national flags on flagstaffs. The British consul was a senior missionary named Pritchard, and the American one a Belgian or Dutch merchant called Morenhout, who had made a fortune by exporting pearl oyster shells. Queen Pomare also lived there, in a modest Tahitian palace, and most of the principal chiefs of the island had left their own chiefdoms and settled in this centre of power. Within the last decade, Queen Pomare's wealth had been greatly increased by gifts from foreign rulers. Queen Victoria especially had filled the Tahitian palace with antique furniture and had also sent Pomare a crown and a carriage and pair. She loved the crown and always wore it on her evening stroll along the road, touching it politely to important Europeans like ships' captains. She seldom used the carriage – only a mile or two of the road was fit for it – but it started a fashion for horses, which the Tahitians had reasonably called man-carrying pigs when Cook first landed two. Now all the chiefs and most of the missionaries travelled on horseback, which set them even further apart from the common people. Papeete also provided, hidden among its magnificent trees, what visiting sailors demanded: organized brothels and illicit grog-shops.

After Melville's months of pristine hospitality in the Marquesas, Tahiti was a sad disappointment. If he and his mates had landed anywhere else in the island, they would still have found friendly Tahitians who would have hidden them and looked after them. But in Papeete they found a chaos of rival people claiming authority and quarrelling among themselves. Here were the Queen and the remaining chiefs, bewildered and impotent. Here also were the English missionaries, still insisting on their dour code of behaviour, and the two foreign consuls. Here now were the French, with the power of their frigate's guns, and under their protection a handful of Catholic missionaries, preaching that the English protestants were wicked heretics. Here were European and American merchants, intent on making fortunes, and deserters of all nationalities, who took no notice of anyone's laws but their own. And here, finally, were the remnants of the ordinary Tahitian people, entirely confused by two foreign languages, two versions of Christianity and several sets of contradictory laws, and driven for their own survival into scorning all the laws, native, British or French, Protestant or Catholic.

Although the *Julia* was an American ship, Melville and his fellow-mutineers fell foul of the British consul: not the missionary Pritchard, who was on leave, but his deputy, who had been born and bred in Tahiti. He was the son of William Wilson, the first officer of the *Duff*, who had left the sea and become a missionary himself. The son came on board the *Julia*, but he was terrified – and no wonder – by the violent threats of the crew. He retreated and asked the French to send an armed boat to arrest them. They were put in irons and imprisoned in *La Reine Blanche*; but after a few days they were taken ashore and marched in handcuffs through the village to the British prison, which was known as the *Calaboose Beretanee*. *Calaboose* was roughly the Spanish word for a prison, and *Beretanee* was Tahitian for British.

It was one of the simple prisons the missionaries had devised, nothing but a set of stocks – two coconut trunks clamped together at the ends, with notches cut out for a long row of ankles. The man in charge was an amiable old Tahitian who called himself Captain Bob and did not take prison too seriously. He clamped the two logs together at night, with the sixteen pairs of ankles inside them, but by day he let the prisoners out. They did not run away, because they did not want to get him into trouble. Tahitians, men and women, wandered past to look at them and try to chat, and if anyone saw a European coming along the road the prisoners hastily put their legs in the notches and shouted for Captain Bob to come and lock them up.

They were always hungry. The official ration, supplied by the consul, was a bucket of hardtack a day; but when they found the Tahitians liked the stuff (they had better teeth than the sailors) the prisoners started giving it all to Captain Bob, who gave them fruit from his garden in exchange. After the *Julia*, it was an agreeable life.

Sitting there, in or out of the stocks with nothing to do, Melville learned some of the reasons for the surprising presence of the French – though he never quite learned that what he was seeing was the beginning of the final end of Tahitian culture. The French had only the slenderest claim of discovery. They had never been in Tahiti apart from Bougainville's ten-day visit three quarters of a century before and a few casual visits since. Their action was a far cry from the gentle hints the Earl of Morton had given to Cook in 1768, when he said the Tahitians were 'the natural, and in the strictest sense of the word, the legal possessors', and that they should be 'made sensible that the crew consider them the Lords of the Country'.

The French intervention had started back in 1836 with three Catholic priests, two Frenchmen, and a large, bluff, blue-eyed character called Father Murphy. They had landed on the southern end of the island and were allowed to go to Papeete because they said they had a message for the Queen. They travelled along the coast, which they remarked was part heathen and part heretic, telling the people that the Christian missionaries they already had were false, and that they themselves were the only true teachers. Of course they sincerely believed it, but for the Tahitians it was disruptive. The Queen told them no foreigner was allowed to land without her permission, and a council of chiefs confirmed it: this was in fact one of the early laws proposed by the missionaries and approved by Pomare, and it had been meant to keep out undesirable sailors and convicts from Botany Bay. The priests were ordered to leave, but when a suitable ship came in they refused to go, and barricaded themselves in a house provided by Morenhout, the consul. The Queen's retainers, urged on by the missionaries, took the thatched roof off the house and bundled the priests, with all their baggage, into canoes and thence on board the ship, which took them away.

It seems that one of them at least went all the way back to Europe to complain to the Pope and the King of France at this setback to the Catholic cause, and in 1842 they came again to Tahiti; this time with the royal support of the sixty-gun French frigate.

It is no use looking for right or wrong in the nineteenth-century scramble for colonies; in some places perhaps it did some good, but most people now think all of it was wrong. What happened in 1842 was simple. The British were busy establishing Australia and colonizing New Zealand, and they had no time for small islands in mid-Pacific. The United States of America remembered being a colony itself and had no wish to take colonies of its own. The Spanish Empire had fallen to pieces. But the French navy had several frigates at large in the Pacific. They saw the chance of a useful conquest, and took it; and by the standards of that age it was a legitimate thing to do.

By then Captain Dupetit Thouars of *La Reine Blanche* was an admiral; and one has to remind oneself that in colonization under sail action was normally taken by officers on the spot, who had no time to ask their governments for decisions. Dupetit Thouars was further out on a limb than most; if he asked for instructions, he had to expect to wait at least a year to get them. His orders were vague and all-embracing: roughly speaking, to claim for France and the Catholic faith whatever islands he found available. He was a dutiful officer, and believed he was right in what he did. The English believed he was wrong. The Tahitians had very little say in the matter. They were the victims of an unusual colonial rivalry: two nations competing for one very small plot of land – each of them urged on by religious belief, one Protestant and one Catholic, and each with unfortunate memories of centuries of enmity and its recent climax in the Napoleonic wars.

The British navy, of course, was also there. In particular, HMS *Vindictive* was often in and out of Papeete, but her commanding officer, Commodore Nicolas, had even vaguer orders. In particular, he had no instructions on what to do about the French, because of course the British Government did not know what the French were doing. He wrote letters of desperate protest to Dupetit Thouars and made a proclamation that no British citizen had to obey French orders. That was all he could do, short of opening fire on *La Reine Blanche* then and there in Papeete harbour; and it was certainly not up to him to start a war against France.

Dupetit Thouars therefore landed with no physical opposition, under cover of his guns, taking demands and threats for the Queen. The demands were for a letter of apology to his King, a recompense of 2000 Spanish dollars for the priests who had been ousted, and a signed agreement that the law should be changed and all or any Frenchmen allowed to settle in the island. The threats were to devastate the island with war. The Queen was humiliated and helpless; her own palace, the chiefs, and the whole of the village were cowering under the guns. She was rich by Tahitian standards, but she did not possess 2000 dollars in cash. The money was collected and paid by the even richer foreigners who lived there, and she sent her carriage and pair to Hawaii and sold it to help pay off the debt. She wrote the letter of apology and changed the law, and the priests landed again and requested houses for themselves and a plot of land in Papeete to build a Catholic church.

The English missionaries were outraged, and not without reason. They had been labouring there for forty-five years. Some of them had spent the whole of their working lives there, had English wives and families, and looked on Tahiti as their permanent home. Henry Nott, for example, had come out with the *Duff* when he was twenty-two and was still there and still preaching when he was nearing seventy. To their own satisfaction, they had made the island Christian and given it a system of law, which was operated under their guidance by the native rulers. What upset them most about the French invasion was not that it was

French instead of English, but that its primary aim was to make Tahiti Catholic instead of Protestant.

Of course there was infinite scope for misunderstanding. The French spoke no Tahitian, and the Tahitians had mastered a little English but did not speak a word of French. Dupetit Thouars, it seems, believed the Queen had willingly asked him for the protection of France. The English believed he had won what he wanted by trickery, by bewildering and frightening the Queen and bribing some of her chiefs to sign French documents they could not understand. It is true enough that Tahitians were always innocently easy to trick, and were quite out of their depth in the language and sophistry of international politics. The French, among many other things, laid claim to the 'exterior sovereignty' of Tahiti. Not even the English could understand what they meant by that, and who could begin to explain it to the Tahitians?

Looking back, it seems clear that the Queen had not intended to ask for French protection. When she wrote her apology to the King of France, she also wrote to Queen Victoria, begging for British protection against the French. All she got back was a vague and unpromising letter from Lord Palmerston: Her Britannic Majesty, he said, was 'strongly interested' in the prosperity of the islands, but 'must decline entering into any engagement of the kind suggested.' In fact, Queen Victoria was about to make a state visit to France, and Britain had no intention of risking the splendour of that occasion, or the precarious balance of power in Europe, by opposing France over anything so remote as the rights of Tahiti.

Whatever the Queen had intended, and whatever Dupetit Thouars had understood, he reported to France that Tahiti was now a protectorate, and declared a provisional French government to advise the Queen. At first, it comprised three Frenchmen with the title of royal commissioner, and its president was Morenhout. The salvo heard from the *Julia* as she approached the island was a salute, fired to celebrate this treaty or victory. Thouars also dismissed Mr Pritchard, the British consul, who had opposed him, and sent him out of the island.

These actions, especially the last, caused an uproar when news of them reached England. The British Government was furious but ineffective: it said the island had been seized 'partly by intrigue and partly by intimidation', but it decided not to interfere. In fact, it had no authority. The French believed the mis-

sionaries had been tools of the British Government, and that
Tahiti, all those years, had been some sort of British colony,
disguised by typical British deceit. But it was not so. The British
had been by far the major influence in Tahiti for eighty years, but
they had never made any claim on it since Wallis planted his flag.
It was a strange omission for an empire-building nation.

To calm the British Government, France repudiated Dupetit
Thouars' high-handed behaviour, but did not withdraw its formal
protection. On the contrary, it voted money and troops for the
purpose and, ever since, Tahiti has been under French control.

The chaos Dupetit Thouars let loose penetrated even to the
English prison. The *Julia* mutineers, lined up in the stocks, began
to realize that the British consul had lost interest in them. Finally
the daily bucket of hardtack stopped coming, which they took as a
hint that he wanted to see the last of them, and would be happy if
they disappeared. The *Julia* had scraped up another crew and left
port. Most of the mutineers wandered away from prison in ones
and twos and signed on in other whalers, but Melville and Dr
Long Ghost, adopting the names of Peter and Paul, had heard of
two men, a Yankee and a Cockney, who had a plantation in Eimeo
and wanted hands. They went there and asked for a job. They
never discovered what made the consul change his mind, but the
fact was that he was losing power to the French, who were taking
over everything, even the prisons.

The plantation the Yankee and Cockney owned was a relic
of the many plantations that had failed. They had tried employing
Tahitians and found it a waste of time and money: Tahitians did
not value regular pay or understand regular work. Peter and Paul
did not last long either: digging virgin soil with Australian hoes
was not their idea of fun, and they left for a leisurely stroll round
Eimeo. After Papeete, the smaller island was delightfully simple
and untouched. It had no French, and only one missionary – or
only one that they heard of. The people were Christian in name,
but they had not lost their old Tahitian ways. Some of the girls
made the ragged sailors welcome, just as their mothers or grand-
mothers had welcomed Cook's crews. Some rebuffed them.
One explained graphically that her eyes, head, and ears were
Christian, but some of the other bits of her were not.

Hospitality, as of old, was boundless. One family was
especially kind to the unprepossessing vagrants: a father named

Ereemea Po-Po, his wife Arfretee, four beautiful children, and several meek and pathetic aunts, besides a bald and portly sort of butler, whose jobs were not only housework and preparing food, but climbing the coconut trees. Ereemea was not a Tahitian name. A missionary had baptized the man as an adult and offered him a choice of Tahitian versions of biblical names. Ereemea was Jeremiah. Among the alternatives were Adamo, Nooa, Daveeda, Eorna (John), and Patoora (Peter).

This family seems to have made a happier blend of Christian and Tahitian virtues than any other reported. They went to church on the Sabbath, read the Bible, held family prayers and said grace before and after meals. Yet as soon as they saw the two mutineers the old Tahitian habit took over and they made them part of the family – which indeed was a virtuous act in either religion, but more often practised in Tahiti than in nineteenth-century Europe.

They were upper-class Tahitians, related to chiefs, but they lived in the old simplicity, a life like an endless picnic. Their house was what Tahitian houses had always been, a large thatched roof on poles and an earthen floor covered by grass or rushes. It had no partitions and no privacy; they had no secrets and nothing to hide. But, a sign of the times, they had some private possessions. Beside the usual mats and baskets, the house had several chests, which contained their Sunday clothes and a few assorted European treasures – knives, looking-glasses, beads. At meals, the guests were fed first and none of the family ate until they had finished – apparently to make sure the guests had more than enough, whether or not enough was left for themselves. After the first of these dinners, and the customary nap and swim that followed it, Arfretee exclaimed at the sailors' ragged and rotten clothes, delved in a chest and gave them each a brand-new suit of sailors' frock and trousers, which she must have hoarded just in case some destitute Europeans came along. The family was lucky to have survived so long; but such simple kindness could not last much longer.

The sailors stayed with them some weeks, straining themselves to be on their best behaviour. Through them, they met scores of their relations, all the congregation of the church and most of the neighbours. They learned that the Queen was also in Eimeo, where she had fled to escape the French, and that she was collecting an army to protect her independence. They thought

they would make good officers in it, and contrived to get into her
house to offer their services. That was a failure. They confronted
her when she came in to dinner, but she dismissed them without a
word, and her attendants hustled them out. Frustrated, Melville
signed on yet again in a whaler he liked the look of. He left Dr
Long Ghost on the island, and never heard of him again.

What had driven the Queen into exile were renewed threats of war
from Dupetit Thouars. It was bizarre. He had received the troops
that had been voted to protect the island, and presumably he and
his government expected to protect it against the British, or the
Protestant missionaries, or perhaps the American whalers. But
none of those showed any inclination to fight. The only people
who actively opposed him were the Tahitians themselves, or the
large majority of them who were loyal to their Queen. He had to
use his troops against the very people they had been sent to
protect.

It was true the Queen was forming an army, and she was
supported by all the chiefs of neighbouring islands. Yet none of
them had ever fought a European army, and none of them had any
idea of what they were up against. The civil wars of thirty years
before, even the Christian war, had not been much of a training.
All had been fought by one Tahitian force against another, each
led by a few mercenary sailors with a few serviceable muskets, and
even in the last the old Tahitians rules of war had prevailed. It was
a new generation of Tahitians who had to face the heirs of
Napoleonic tradition.

Yet they fought for two years. It has been proved again and
again – and is still being proved today – that regular troops can
never wholly defeat determined guerillas who fight on their own
ground, and it was that sort of war that was finally brought to
Tahiti. Such wars are often bestial, largely because the frustrated
regulars feel forced to be more cruel and destructive than they
intend or custom allows. Tahitians, of course, were practically
unarmed; but the French had no road for their guns except the
single track round the island, and their enemies could always
infuriate them by vanishing into the forests or retiring up the
mountains. So the destruction and suffering were intense, homes
were burnt, crops ruined, women seized or made hostage, children starved.

Tahitian culture had been faltering for years. Its deathblow was sudden. It was a mortal change from the old days when kindness and reverence had been the only rules, and a Tahitian had seldom met anybody he did not know, and never anybody unfriendly, and the groves that might now hide an ambush had the safety and familiarity of home.

It would be absurd to blame the French, in so many ways the most civilized of Europeans. The British were equally capable of cruelty to simple people, and so were the Americans. The British would never have done what the French did in Tahiti, because they had known the Tahitians for several generations and had almost always loved and admired them.

The French, on the other hand, would never have believed, even if they had been told, that the English missionaries had no official authority, that naval captains were the only representatives of the British Crown who had ever been there, or that they had never tried to win political control. The French did not want to fight Tahitians. They were astonished when they offered battle. Perhaps when Dupetit Thouars or the officers stopped to think, they understood they were fighting Tahitians only because they were Protestants and friends of the English, France's ancient enemy.

In the end, of course, the Tahitians had to give up. They had the most cogent reason men ever have for fighting – to preserve their homes and the only freedom they knew – but they were logical people, and it was obvious that what they were trying to preserve was being destroyed by the effort of preserving it. There was nothing left worth fighting for. Queen Victoria had refused to help them, the missionaries were on their side but impotent, the British frigates did nothing, and there was nobody else.

Naturally, they disliked, even hated, the French at that time. They called them *Wee-Wee*'s – perhaps because they said *Oui*, but it sounded insulting. They had to submit, and take the last chance of life under their conquerors: French soldiers, French bureaucrats, French judges, bishops, priests, and *gendarmes*.

Queen Pomare, as it happened, survived it all. The French either killed, imprisoned or degraded her chiefs, the last descendants of gods, and they took away all her power, but they let her call herself Queen until she died, an old woman, in 1877. A son succeeded her, but in 1881, with nothing to do, he abdicated, and Tahiti was formally proclaimed a colony.

Many visitors to Tahiti in the latter part of the nineteenth century were bitterly critical of the venality of French administration, especially Paul Gauguin, who lived in Tahiti and the Marquesas from 1891 to 1901. Of course he was French himself, but he was a rebel by nature and would probably have found as much to detest in the British rule of islands further west, or the American rule of Hawaii. The French did their best, but for years after peace was restored, the languorous temptation of Tahiti undid their efforts to be precise, efficient, decisive, or even just. Bishops, so Gauguin said, not to mention every judge and *gendarme*, had their teenage mistresses whom they callously won by their patronage and more callously discarded, and who absorbed too much of their attention.

A less partisan and much more perceptive visitor was a Scotsman, Robert Louis Stevenson, who went to the South Seas in 1888 in the hope of postponing his death from tuberculosis, and stayed there with his wife and stepson until he died in Samoa in 1894. A man much loved in his time and a master of English prose, he blamed nobody, but left scattered in several books the most eloquent obsequies for the Polynesian. 'He beholds with dismay the approaching extinction of his race,' he wrote. 'The thought of death sits down with him to meat, and rises with him from his bed; he lives and breathes under a shadow of mortality awful to support; and he is so inured to the apprehension that he greets the reality with relief.'

In the aftermath of the war, suicide was commonplace. A gentle death was enviable, the fulfilment of a gentle life; men and women cherished their own coffins, dug their own graves and lay in them, smoking, eating, drinking, and chatting to their friends, sometimes for a week or two while they waited and hoped to die. 'The Polynesians', Stevenson wrote, 'are subject to a disease seemingly rather of the will than of the body. I was told the Tahitians have a word for it, *erimatua*, but cannot find it in my dictionary.' There is a word that comes near it in English, but it is seldom used: accidie. It was this that afflicted the Indians Columbus captured, and it was fatal; it was meant to be. It was nothing so positive as despair or misery; rather, it was dispiritedness, resignation, a lack of will to live, a recognition of death as a refuge. One cause of it in Tahitians was boredom, for they were left with nothing whatever to do: no responsibility, no deep religion, no work (they still saw no point in labouring on plantations) and no

Papeete at about 1890

amusements or fun – not even the old-fashioned pre-European wars, which Stevenson rightly recognized as 'the most healthful, if not the most humane, of all field sports'. The importance of amusements, he said, could not be exaggerated. 'In a climate and upon a soil where a livelihood can be had for the stooping, entertainment is a prime necessity. It is otherwise with us, where life presents us with a daily problem, and there is a serious interest, and some of the heat of conflict, in the mere continuing to be.'

Tahitians in the 1840s did not want to 'continue to be'. They had often been afraid, *matau*, but seldom much afraid of death, and now after the slaughter and among the diseases raging more fiercely than ever, the living were far outnumbered by the recent dead. It was an island of ghosts. Every valley, every grove and stream and ruined house, was haunted: the survivors, sleeping or waking, were always aware of living among the dead. Of course, some obstinately clung to life, the ardent Christians and the youngest; but very many simply wanted to make the easy crossing they had always conceived death to be, to surrender and 'go into night' and be absorbed by gods and join the pressing multitude of spirits. 'Conceive', Stevenson wrote, 'how the remnant huddles about the embers of the fire of life; even as old Red Indians, deserted on the march and in the snow, the kindly tribe all gone, the last flame expiring, and the night around populous with wolves.' He quoted a Polynesian saying, and so did Melville, fifty years before him: 'The coral spreads. The palm tree grows. Man vanishes.'

SIXTEEN
A Different Dawn

———••❢❳❬❸••———

MODERN TAHITI gives emphasis to the Polynesian saying. Nothing drastic has happened there since the 1840s, when Tahitian society, already undermined by the English crews, the missionaries, and the American whalers, finally collapsed. The island people, those who were left, slowly evolved under French rule, and in the end achieved a different kind of balance. Tahiti now is a very different place, but it is a tolerably happy place again.

Given that it had to come under foreign rule, French rule was probably the best it could have had. At least, it saved it from the total destruction of islands further west in the Second World War, and from the fate of Hawaii, which became a huge American naval base and a holiday playground, overwhelmed by tourists. And beyond that, the French temperament was possibly best suited to the Tahitian. In the course of time, the French came to love Tahitians, as the English had, and the Tahitians extended their universal love to the French.

By degrees, the French relaxed their colonial rule: Tahiti is now the centre of French Polynesia, or Territoire d'Outre-Mers, governed by a statute that gives it a fair degree of autonomy. The Tahitians, for their part, loyally identify themselves with France – an attitude that showed in the Second World War, when over a thousand volunteers formed a battalion for the Free French Army.

The population grew again under French rule. It had fallen disastrously under the missionaries, from the hundred and forty thousand that Dr Forster guessed to six thousand – and fell further still, no doubt, in the early years of the French. Now it is nearly a hundred thousand again. But it is not all Tahitian: far from it. The French annual census lists 61% as Polynesian, 13% as European, 7% as Asiatic (mainly Chinese), and 19% as half-castes. But the statisticians who make the census admit these ethnic origins cannot be sorted out. Some people like to claim to be half-castes because they think it gives them a social advantage, or a better job. On the other hand, Tahitians do not look far back in their family trees, and even those who call themselves Polynesian can never be sure they have no foreign ancestors. After two centuries of the Europeans, there is probably no such thing as a pure-blooded Tahitian. They are extinct.

But the descendants still have the racial character. The men are still handsome and strong, the girls are still charming: they are cheerful, kind and hospitable to each other and to strangers. Tahiti has a considerable tourist trade – nothing like Hawaii's, but a hundred thousand visitors a year and always growing; and its Tourist Board informs them that tipping does not exist, and would be a denial of the people's habit of hospitality – a small but telling fact. There cannot be many tourist resorts in the world that could say the same.

Tahitian society was always stratified, and now it is more sharply so than ever, but with different strata. The Europeans – that is, the French – hold all the high posts in administration and provide the technicians. They are rich, and live in the town. The Chinese are businessmen, and may be richer. Those who are mainly Tahitian live in the country, and are farmers and fishermen, as they always were: in town, they have only the lowliest positions, as labourers and domestic servants. The half-castes of all mixtures fill the lower and middle ranks of administration or private trade.

Language is still a difficulty. It always is in the aftermath of a colony: any colonizer with a conscience wants to preserve the indigenous culture, which needs the indigenous language: and yet it also wants to educate the people for a place in the wider world, which needs another, more complex, language. It is worse when there are three languages. Tahitians learn Tahitian from their parents. French is the official language, and the language of schools. But for some reason they learn English more easily than French, and they need English too for international dealings and even to cope with their tourists; four out of five of these come from North America, Australia or New Zealand, and speak nothing but English. Three languages take up a lot of the time of Tahitian children, and a lot of their capacity for learning.

In spite of all this, Tahiti seems a happier place than most in the modern world. The people are strongly religious, as they always were, and no doubt that helps them to recognize their blessings. But one strange gap remains in the influence of France. The French took over complete political control, and one of the reasons for doing it, probably the strongest, was to win the Tahitians for the Catholic Church. But the Catholic priests never took over completely: at least half the people are still Protestants, and only one third are Catholics. In part, this may be a later influence: there are Mormons and Seventh Day Adventists, too. But largely it derives from the emphatic faith the old missionaries planted so firmly, before the French were there.

Physically, the island has not changed very much, except in the town of Papeete. Everywhere else, its verdure is so prolific, its climate so benign, its mountains so high and steep, that its beauty is almost indestructible. Matavai Bay, where its history began, is still much the same. There is a lighthouse on Point Venus now, and a spur of the island road leads down to it. There is a discreet memorial on the spot where Cook built his fort, and a small Museum of Discovery; and the river which used to run along the back of the beach – so handy for watering – has changed its course and now runs straight into the sea. One can still find exactly the place where Cook first jumped ashore and strode up the black, sandy beach, and one can see the place substantially as he saw it. To feel imparadised there, as his sailors did, one would have to close one's mind to the town which lurks just behind the headland to the west, and close one's ears to the roar of the jets taking off from the airport beyond the town. Nevertheless, it is still a lovely bay, and the French have preserved it by law.

The rest of the island, further away from the town, has changed even less. Most of the houses have walls now, and doors and windows, but they are still scattered haphazardly among the coconut and breadfruit trees. There is still only one road, the one started by Pomare and the missionaries as a means of punishment in the 1820s, which runs right round the larger part of the island and half-way round the smaller part. Somewhat primitive buses, called by the English word 'trucks', and locally built of wood on lorry chassis, ply along it from time to time, on the vaguest of timetables, stopping where anyone wants them to stop. Life is still essentially rural, peaceful and slow.

The only exception, the only real intrusion, is Papeete. One third of the population, about thirty-five thousand people, lives there. On the whole, it is still a pretty place; it could hardly be otherwise in its setting of mountains and sea. It has a blend, unique to itself, of French elegance and Polynesian charm. The road along the waterfront, where the Queen used to promenade of an evening, is still called Boulevade Pomare; parallel to it inland is the Rue du Général de Gaulle, and among the lesser streets are the Avenue Dupetit Thouars and the Rue Cook. But it has the blemishes of any modern seaport – noise, a proportion of hideous concrete buildings, traffic problems, brothels, bars and nightclubs, and the ostentatious hotels that tourists are supposed to like: above all, a life of urban competition quite foreign to the South Seas. A traveller with any sense of history longs to get out of it. Luckily, that is simple. The blessing of Papeete is that it is easy to get there, and having got there it is easy to get away. One can go very cheaply, and with some discomfort, in the trucks, or hire a car or a moped or a bicycle, or even walk, and be sure of friendliness everywhere, or one can take the daily boat or even the plane to Eimeo, which is called Moorea now; it was always a refuge, and still is. For that matter, an hour or so by plane will take one to a score of the lesser islands that enter this story, Huahine, Raietea, or the Marquesas.

If anyone goes to Tahiti now in the hope of finding the traditional South Sea life he will be disappointed. He will have to go further to find it, if it can be found at all: to the smallest, remotest islands. Colonization is ebbing, but the tentacles of tourism extend ever further, year after year, all over the world; and if one reaches a place they have not reached, one's very presence there is extending them further still. One may try to escape from the world, but it goes without saying one cannot escape from oneself.

Tahitian society never grew up: it never had a chance. It passed straight from the innocence of youth – 'the real youth of the world', as Rousseau had called it – to the distresses of terminal sickness, and by the time the French arrived in the 1840s it was dying. Tahiti is not the place to look for it now. Most modern Tahitians, living as ever in the present, have no recollection of it, and an official French document dismisses it as a legend. This book will be accused of reviving a legend.

But it is not a legend. The doctrine of the Noble Savage was legendary; the quality of Tahitian society is not. Like all historical fact, it only exists in documents of the time, which can only be found in the largest libraries – in this case, the journals of the scores of people, up to the early years of the nineteenth century, who saw the Tahitians in their primal state.

In retrospect, the destruction of their culture seems a cruel tragedy; yet the tragedy was seldom deliberate, and nobody was to blame. All these people, sailors, sea captains, and missionaries, British, Spanish, American, and French, were men of their time, not ours; and one cannot blame them for being what their time had made them. There was no room for innocence in the nineteenth-century world.

Nor was the tragedy purely black in Tahitian philosophy. Tahitians, with no sense of history, could never have felt nostalgia. Happiness, they knew, was transient; life was ephemeral. All men had to go into night, and they would have said, when they thought about it, that all human institutions also had to go into night. Tahitian society was good, and it was good that it had existed; it mattered less that it could not exist for ever.   .

Yet it would be a pity, towards the end of the twentieth century, to forget entirely what the Tahitians achieved. They did make a society which, in a simple way, came near perfection: nearer perhaps than any other that has been recorded. They were able to do it because they were left alone, and because the place where they lived provided plenty of all the needs of human life: enough food, enough warmth, enough beauty and leisure and fun; and because they had no ambition to struggle for anything more, and were generous and unselfish people, happy to see that everyone else, not only themselves, had enough.

In the near future, for the first time in our history, we also seem to be promised enough of these needs for everyone, through technological revolution. Shall we make good use of it, like the Tahitians, or did they have innate qualities we have lost and can never retrieve? It is at least an arguable question, without a simple answer. Even Rousseau admitted that people can never go back. Neither he nor anyone else until the last few years thought civilization itself might offer enough for all. It has always offered too much for a few and too little for most, dividing people into rich and poor, and creating envy and strife.

Technology can only cure the second part of that inequality – too little for most. The first part, too much for a few, needs a more difficult change. It is a deep-rooted feeling that special skills, long training or hard work should have extra material rewards – and that unskilled, untrained, or lazy people scarcely deserve to have enough and would not know what to do with wealth or leisure. In the civilized world it has always been so, but it was not so in Tahiti. Clever Tahitians – canoe-builders or navigators, say – used their skill for no reward except the pleasure of using it and knowing other people would be grateful for it, not envious. They did not grow rich, and no Tahitians were poor. Perhaps we shall find a reward for skill which is immaterial, yet as acceptable as wealth. The change would need the virtue Christianity enjoins and Tahitians had by instinct: kindness.

It is not the job of a simple history book to stray into sociology. All it can do is offer the example of Tahitian history, in the distant hope that wiser people may think about it, for the benefit of all.